BATMAN BEYOND
HUSH BEYOND

ADAM BEECHEN WRITER
RYAN BENJAMIN PENCILLER
JOHN STANISCI INKER
DAVID BARON COLORIST
TRAVIS LANHAM LETTERER
DUSTIN NGUYEN COVERS

BATMAN CREATED BY BOB KANE
HUSH CREATED BY JEPH LOEB AND JIM LEE

Chris Conroy Michael Siglain Editors-original series
Harvey Richards Assistant Editor-original series
Bob Harras Group Editor-Collected Editions
Robbin Brosterman Design Director-Books

DC COMICS

Diane Nelson President
Dan DiDio and **Jim Lee** Co-Publishers
Geoff Johns Chief Creative Officer
Patrick Caldon EVP-Finance and Administration
John Rood EVP-Sales, Marketing and Business Development
Amy Genkins SVP-Business and Legal Affairs
Steve Rotterdam SVP-Sales and Marketing
John Cunningham VP-Marketing
Terri Cunningham VP-Managing Editor
Alison Gill VP-Manufacturing
David Hyde VP-Publicity
Sue Pohja VP-Book Trade Sales
Alysse Soll VP-Advertising and Custom Publishing
Bob Wayne VP-Sales
Mark Chiarello Art Director

BATMAN BEYOND: HUSH BEYOND

Published by DC Comics. Cover and compilation Copyright © 2011 DC Comics. All Rights Reserved.

Originally published in single magazine form in BATMAN BEYOND 1-6. Copyright © 2010, 2011
DC Comics. All Rights Reserved. All characters, their distinctive likenesses and related elements
featured in this publication are trademarks of DC Comics. The stories, characters and incidents
featured in this publication are entirely fictional. DC Comics does not read or accept unsolicited
submissions of ideas, stories or artwork.

DC Comics, 1700 Broadway, New York, NY 10019
A Warner Bros. Entertainment Company
Printed by Quad/Graphics, Dubuque, IA, USA. 1/28/11. First printing.
ISBN: 978-1-4012-2988-7

PART 1: HISTORY REPEATS

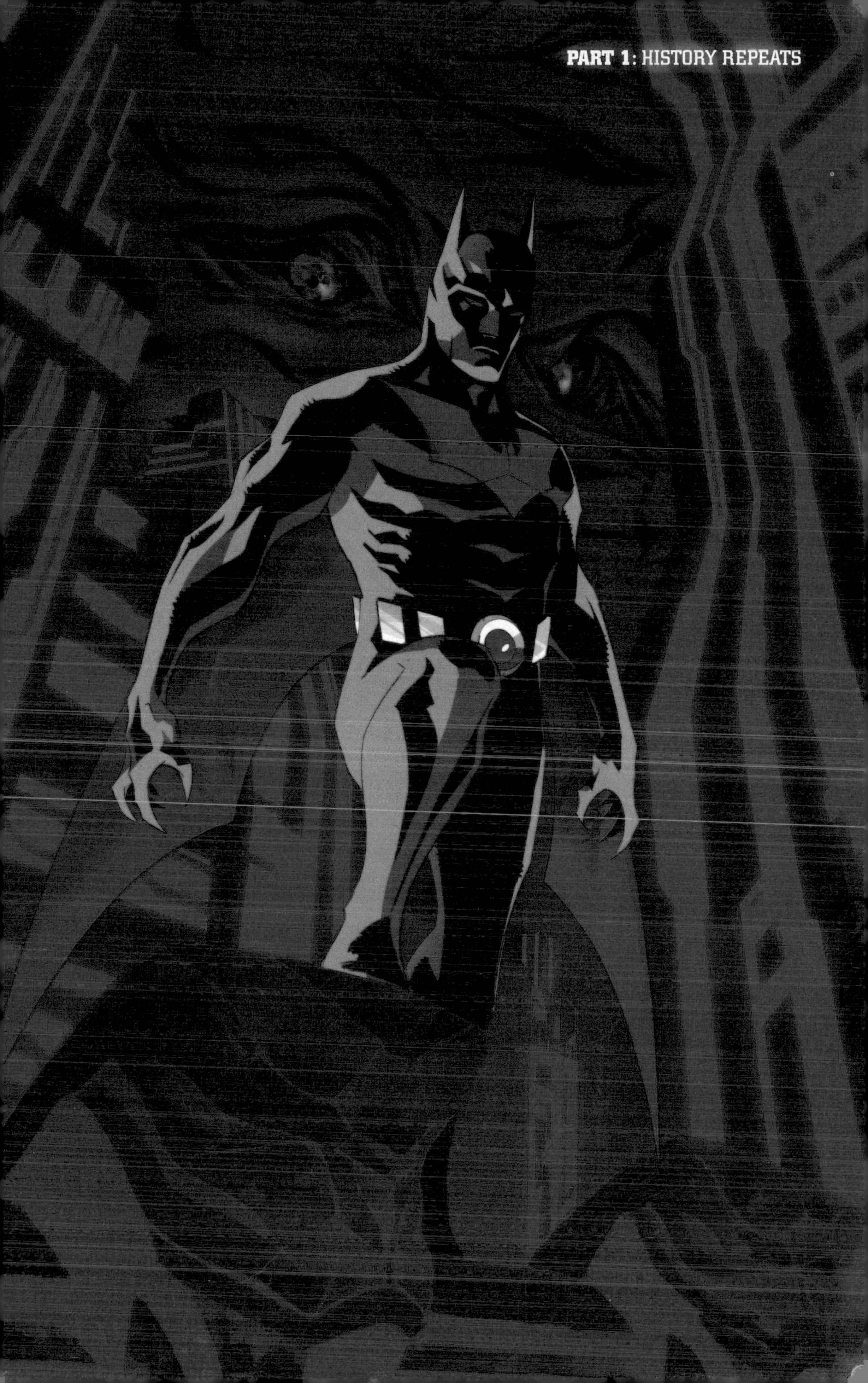

BATMAN BEYOND #1 Variant cover by J.H. Williams III

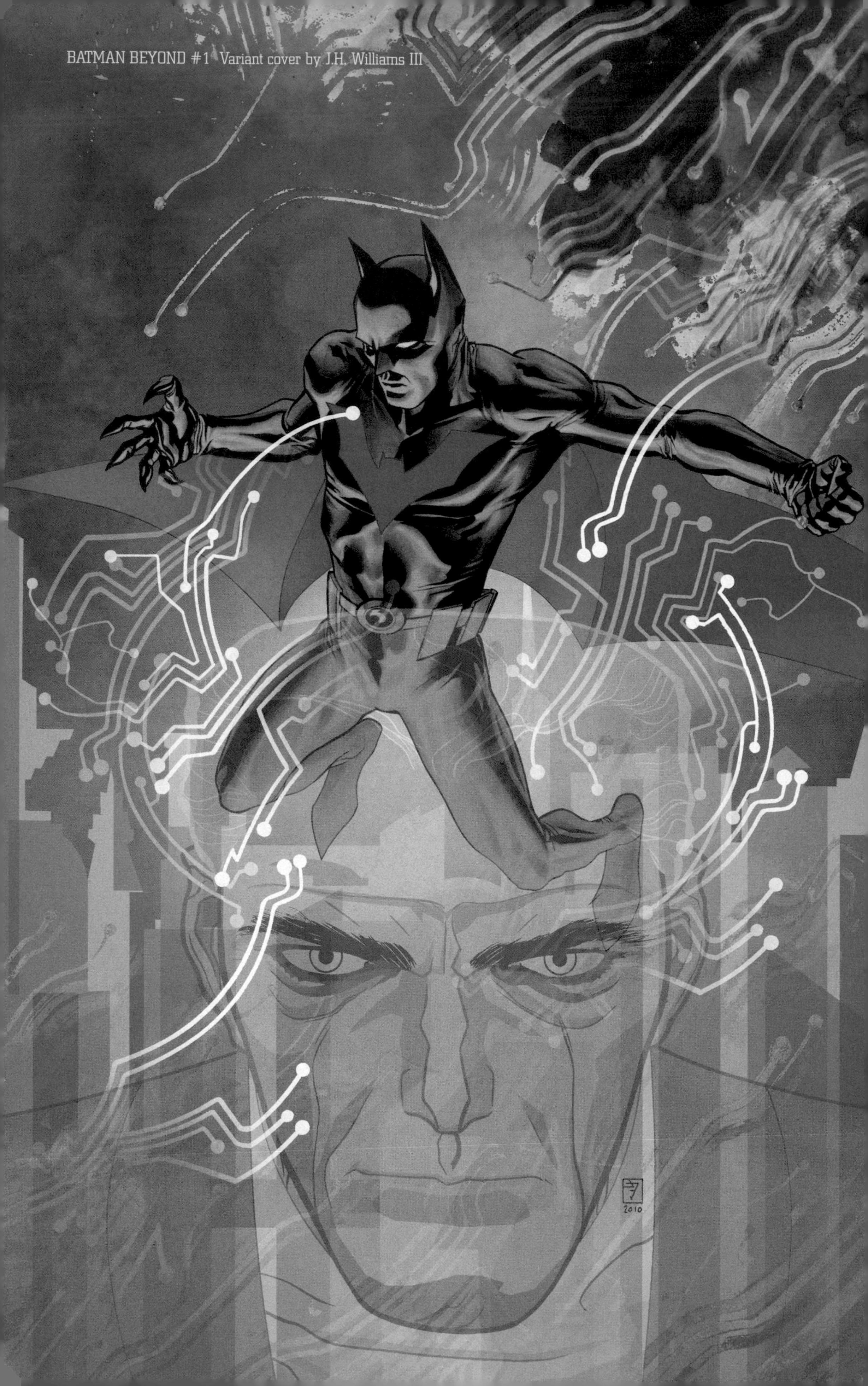
2010

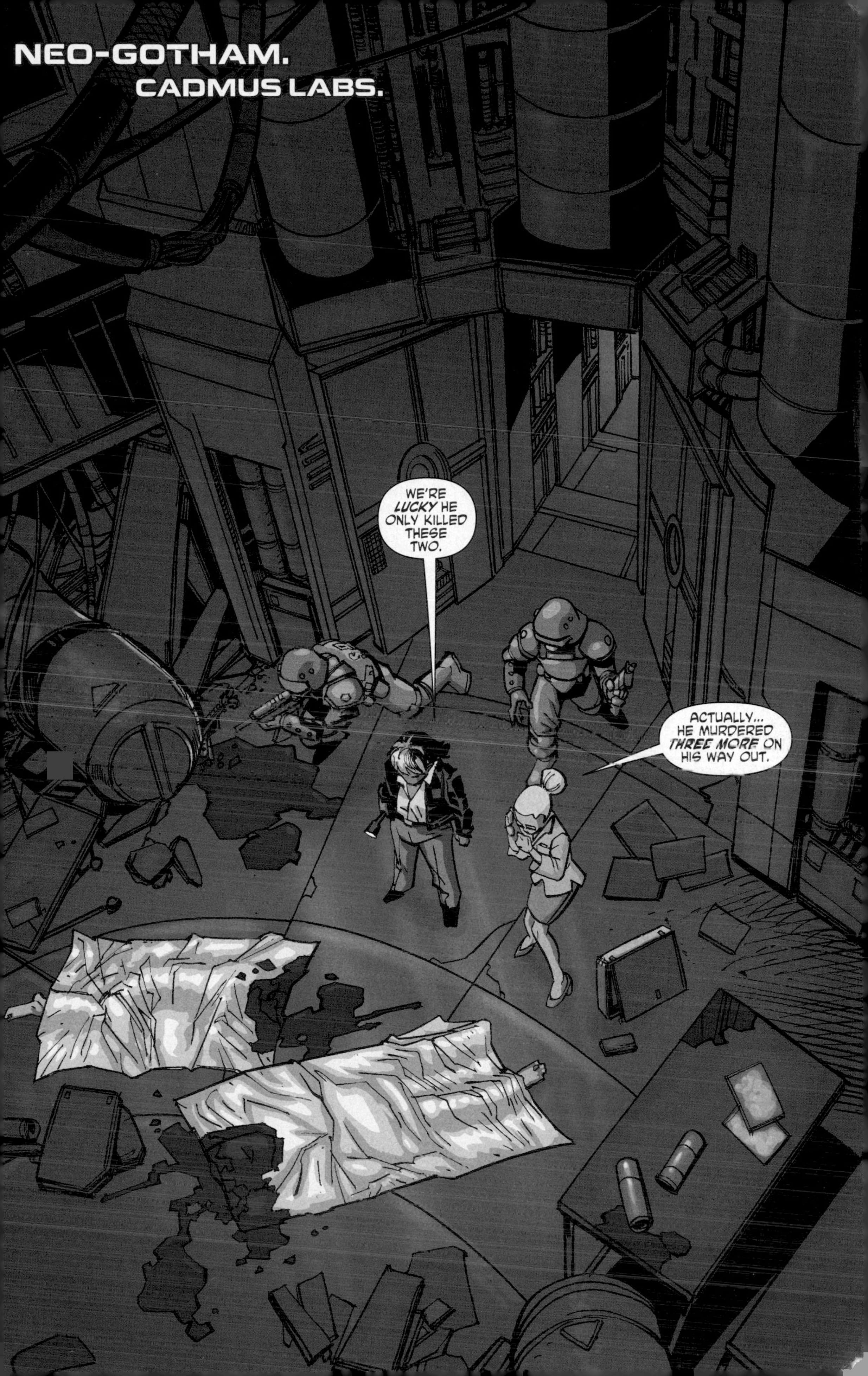
NEO-GOTHAM.
CADMUS LABS.
WE'RE LUCKY HE ONLY KILLED THESE TWO.
ACTUALLY... HE MURDERED THREE MORE ON HIS WAY OUT.

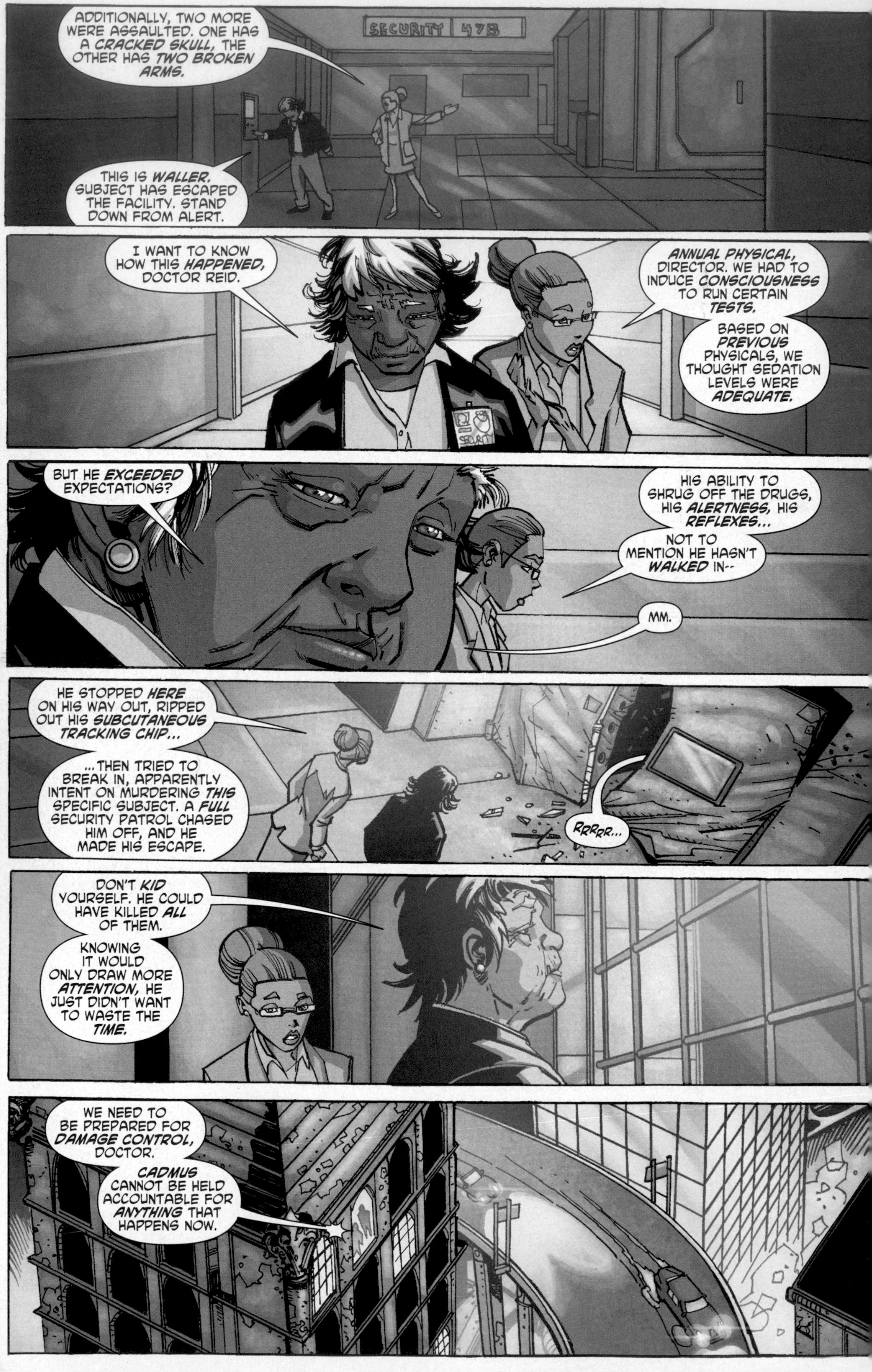
ADDITIONALLY, TWO MORE WERE ASSAULTED. ONE HAS A CRACKED SKULL, THE OTHER HAS TWO BROKEN ARMS.
SECURITY 478
THIS IS WALLER. SUBJECT HAS ESCAPED THE FACILITY. STAND DOWN FROM ALERT.
I WANT TO KNOW HOW THIS HAPPENED, DOCTOR REID.
ANNUAL PHYSICAL, DIRECTOR. WE HAD TO INDUCE CONSCIOUSNESS TO RUN CERTAIN TESTS.
BASED ON PREVIOUS PHYSICALS, WE THOUGHT SEDATION LEVELS WERE ADEQUATE.
BUT HE EXCEEDED EXPECTATIONS?
HIS ABILITY TO SHRUG OFF THE DRUGS, HIS ALERTNESS, HIS REFLEXES...
NOT TO MENTION HE HASN'T WALKED IN--
MM.
HE STOPPED HERE ON HIS WAY OUT, RIPPED OUT HIS SUBCUTANEOUS TRACKING CHIP...
...THEN TRIED TO BREAK IN, APPARENTLY INTENT ON MURDERING THIS SPECIFIC SUBJECT. A FULL SECURITY PATROL CHASED HIM OFF, AND HE MADE HIS ESCAPE.
RRRRR...
DON'T KID YOURSELF. HE COULD HAVE KILLED ALL OF THEM.
KNOWING IT WOULD ONLY DRAW MORE ATTENTION, HE JUST DIDN'T WANT TO WASTE THE TIME.
WE NEED TO BE PREPARED FOR DAMAGE CONTROL, DOCTOR.
CADMUS CANNOT BE HELD ACCOUNTABLE FOR ANYTHING THAT HAPPENS NOW.

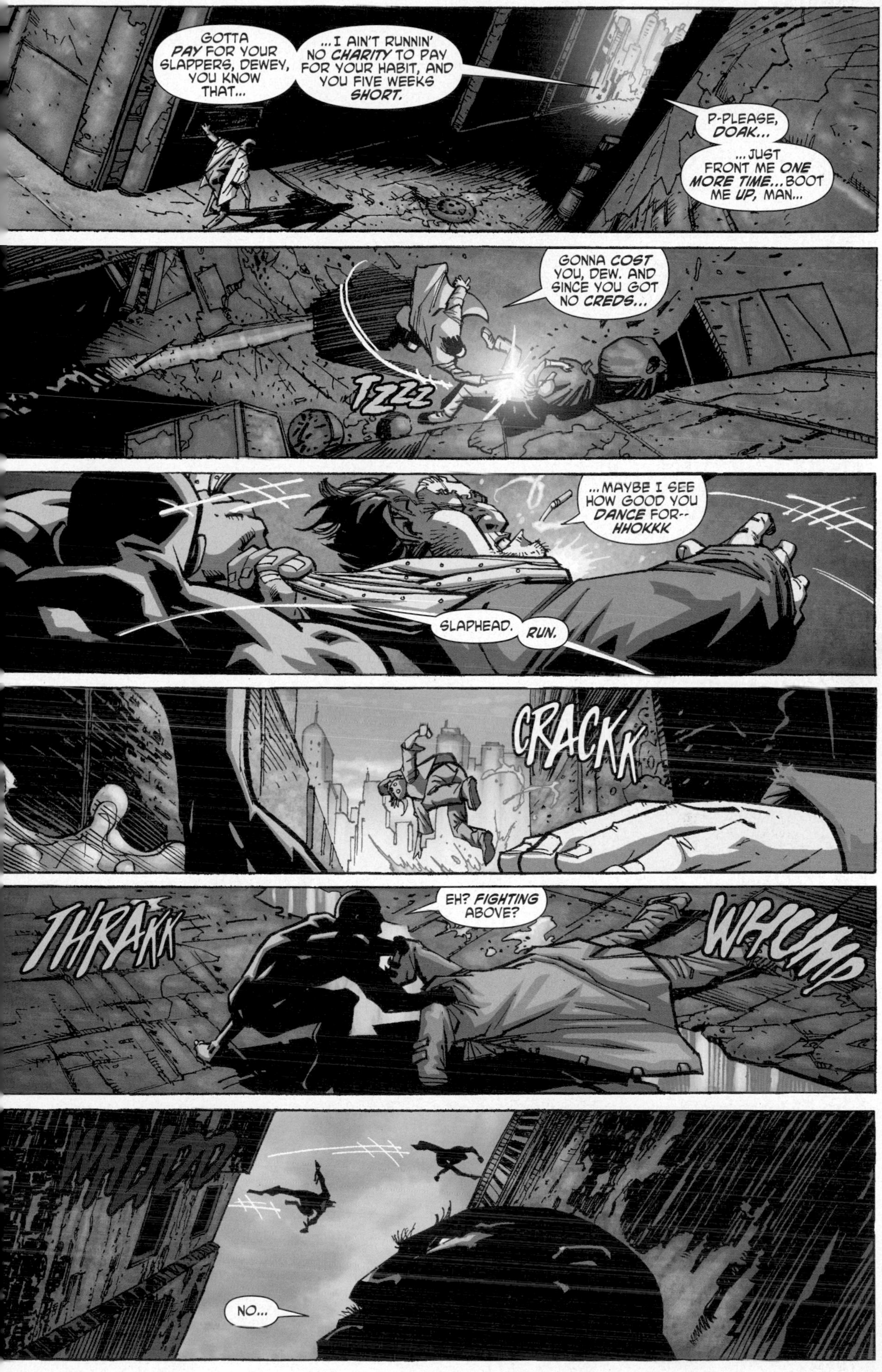

GOTTA PAY FOR YOUR SLAPPERS, DEWEY, YOU KNOW THAT...
...I AIN'T RUNNIN' NO CHARITY TO PAY FOR YOUR HABIT, AND YOU FIVE WEEKS SHORT.
P-PLEASE, DOAK...
...JUST FRONT ME ONE MORE TIME... BOOT ME UP, MAN...
GONNA COST YOU, DEW. AND SINCE YOU GOT NO CREDS...
TZZZ
...MAYBE I SEE HOW GOOD YOU DANCE FOR-- HHOKKK
SLAPHEAD.
RUN.
CRACKK
THRAKK
EH? FIGHTING ABOVE?
WHUMP
NO...

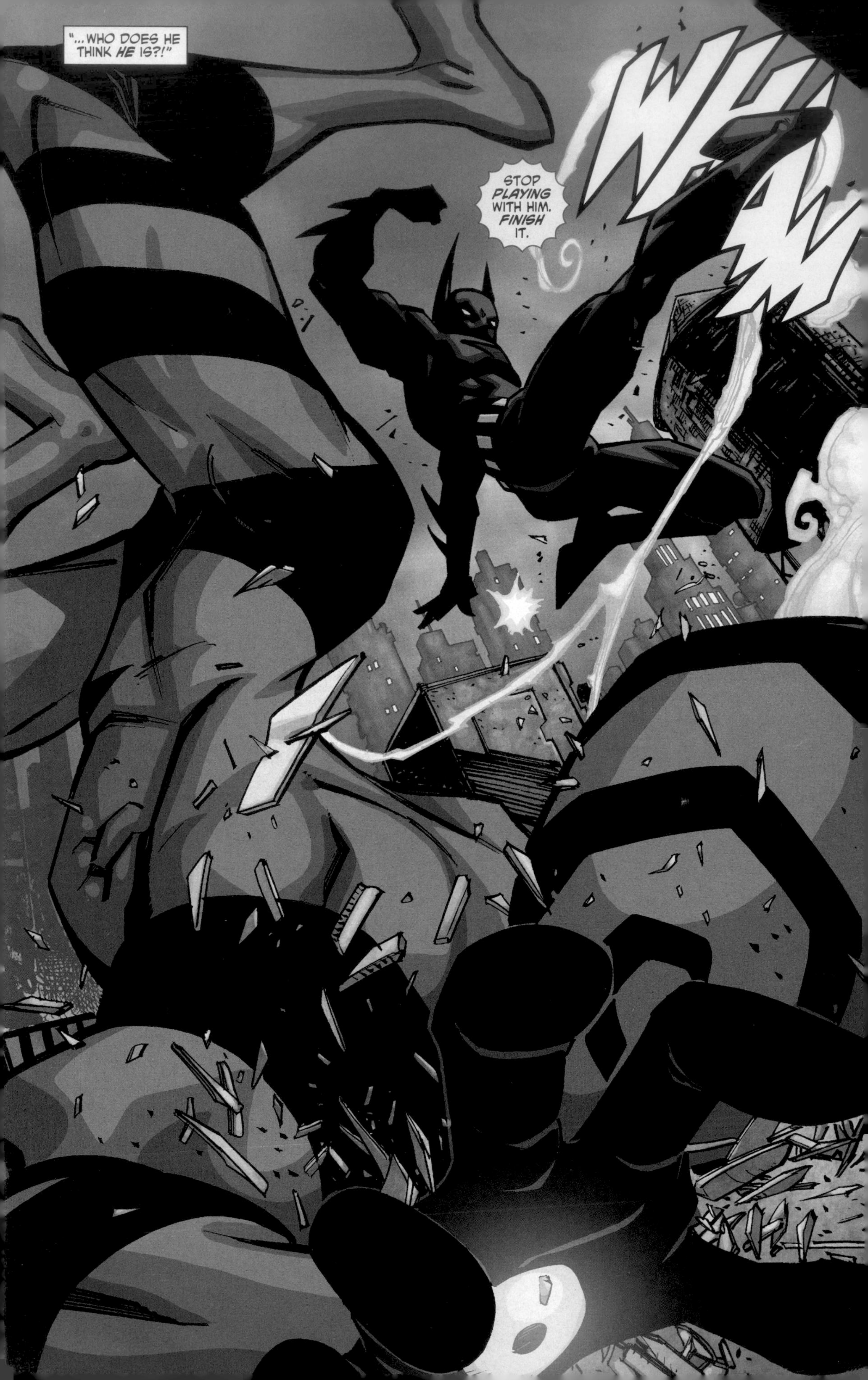
"...WHO DOES HE THINK HE IS?!"
STOP PLAYING WITH HIM. FINISH IT.
WHAM

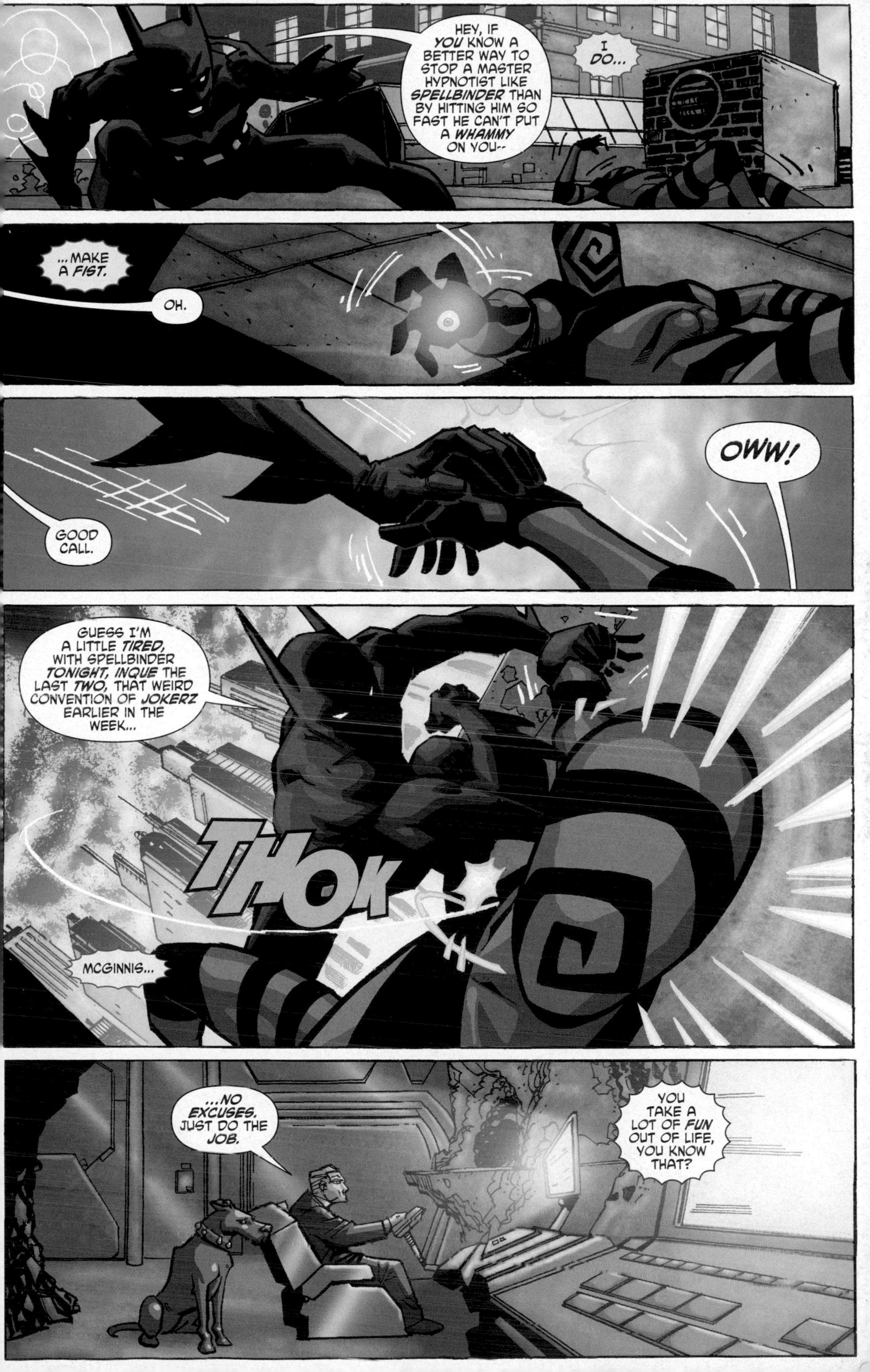
HEY, IF YOU KNOW A BETTER WAY TO STOP A MASTER HYPNOTIST LIKE SPELLBINDER THAN BY HITTING HIM SO FAST HE CAN'T PUT A WHAMMY ON YOU--
I DO...
...MAKE A FIST.
OH.
OWW!
GOOD CALL.
GUESS I'M A LITTLE TIRED, WITH SPELLBINDER TONIGHT, INQUE THE LAST TWO, THAT WEIRD CONVENTION OF JOKERZ EARLIER IN THE WEEK...
THOK
MCGINNIS...
...NO EXCUSES. JUST DO THE JOB.
YOU TAKE A LOT OF FUN OUT OF LIFE, YOU KNOW THAT?

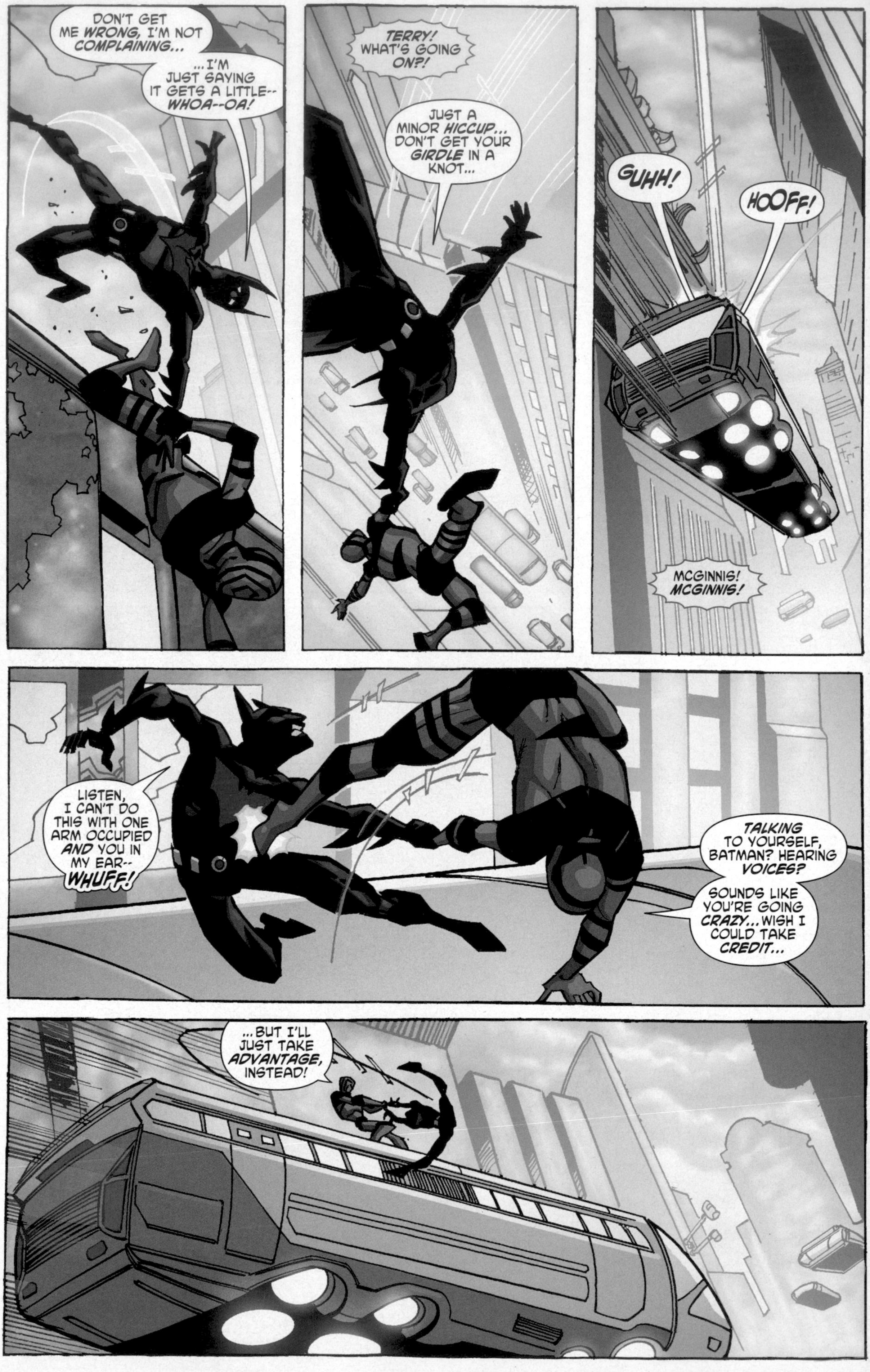
DON'T GET ME WRONG, I'M NOT COMPLAINING...
...I'M JUST SAYING IT GETS A LITTLE-- WHOA--OA!
TERRY! WHAT'S GOING ON?!
JUST A MINOR HICCUP... DON'T GET YOUR GIRDLE IN A KNOT...
GUHH!
HOOFF!
MCGINNIS! MCGINNIS!
LISTEN, I CAN'T DO THIS WITH ONE ARM OCCUPIED AND YOU IN MY EAR-- WHUFF!
TALKING TO YOURSELF, BATMAN? HEARING VOICES?
SOUNDS LIKE YOU'RE GOING CRAZY... WISH I COULD TAKE CREDIT...
...BUT I'LL JUST TAKE ADVANTAGE, INSTEAD!

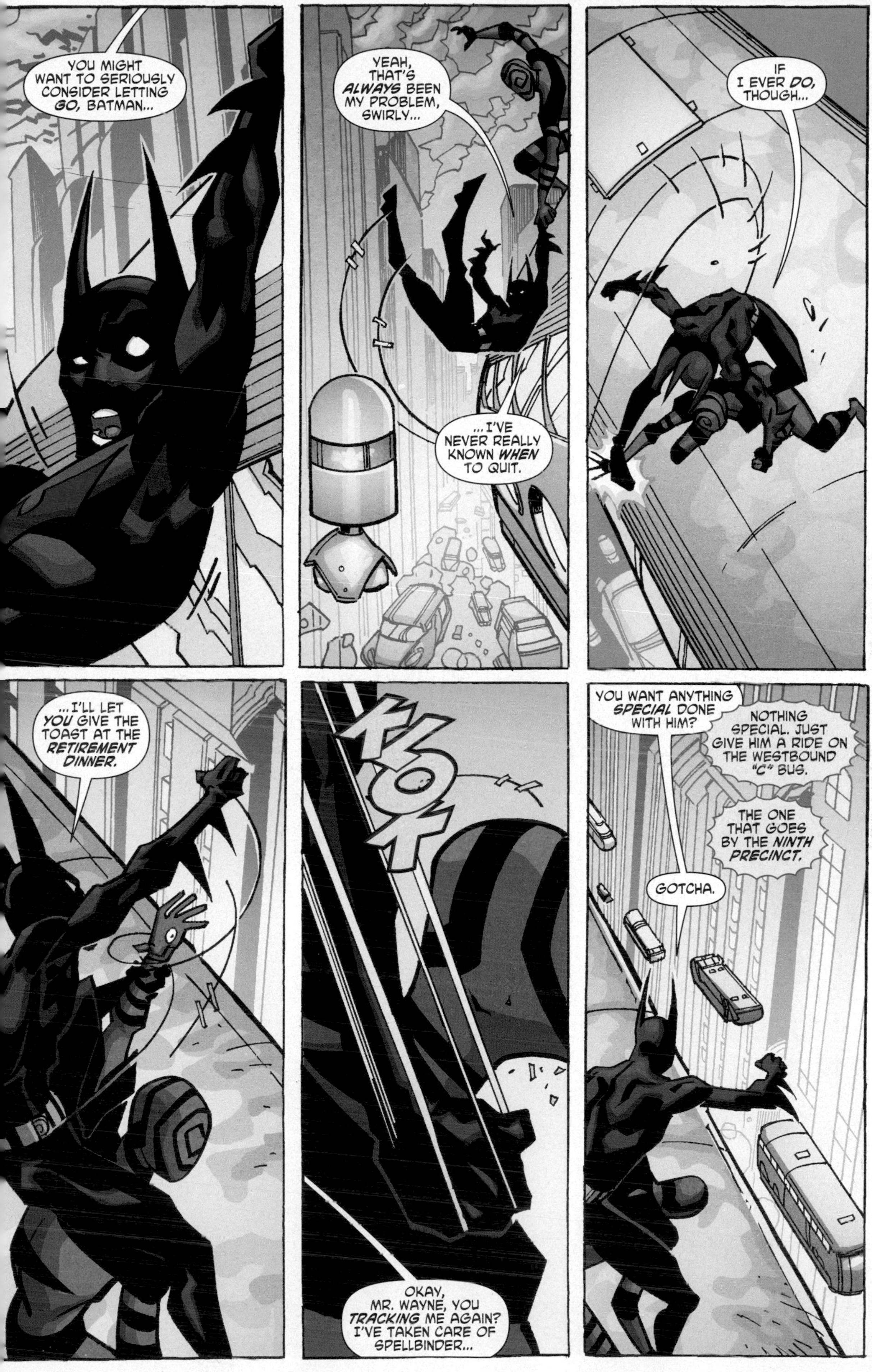
YOU MIGHT WANT TO SERIOUSLY CONSIDER LETTING GO, BATMAN...
YEAH, THAT'S ALWAYS BEEN MY PROBLEM, SWIRLY...
...I'VE NEVER REALLY KNOWN WHEN TO QUIT.
IF I EVER DO, THOUGH...
...I'LL LET YOU GIVE THE TOAST AT THE RETIREMENT DINNER.
KLOK
OKAY, MR. WAYNE, YOU TRACKING ME AGAIN? I'VE TAKEN CARE OF SPELLBINDER...
YOU WANT ANYTHING SPECIAL DONE WITH HIM?
NOTHING SPECIAL. JUST GIVE HIM A RIDE ON THE WESTBOUND "C" BUS.
THE ONE THAT GOES BY THE NINTH PRECINCT.
GOTCHA.

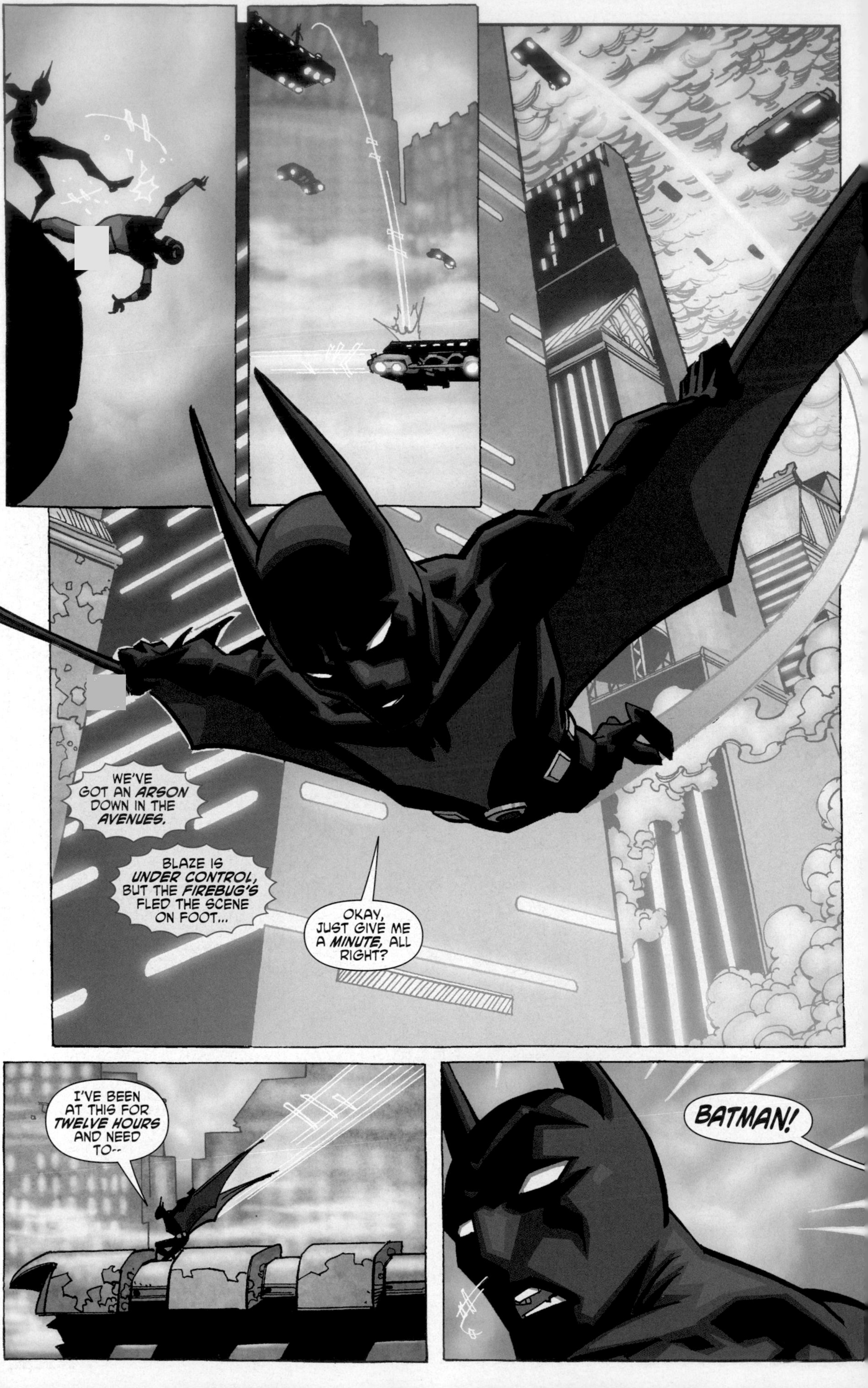

WE'VE GOT AN ARSON DOWN IN THE AVENUES.
BLAZE IS UNDER CONTROL, BUT THE FIREBUG'S FLED THE SCENE ON FOOT...
OKAY, JUST GIVE ME A MINUTE, ALL RIGHT?
I'VE BEEN AT THIS FOR TWELVE HOURS AND NEED TO--
BATMAN!

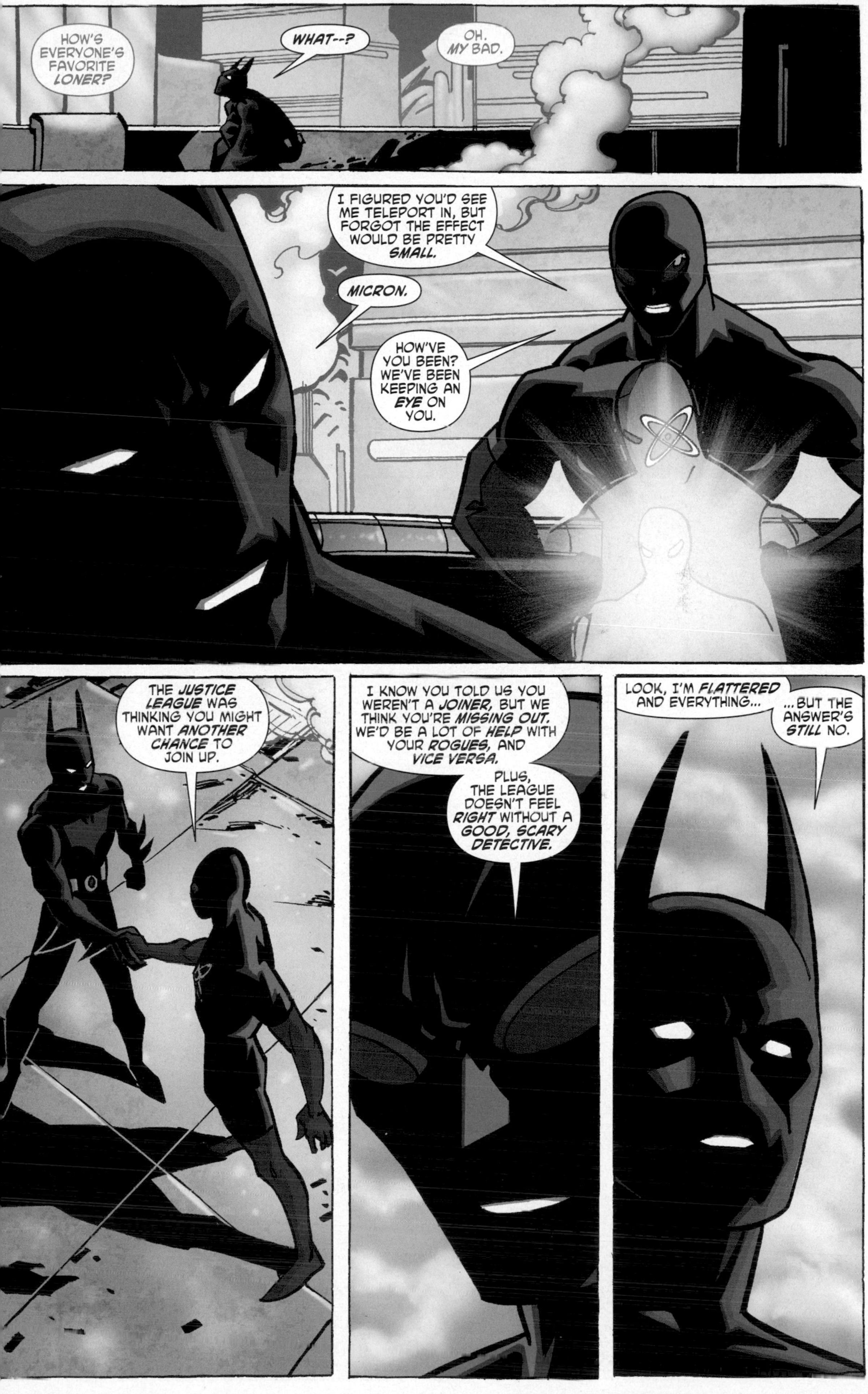
HOW'S EVERYONE'S FAVORITE LONER?
WHAT--?
OH. MY BAD.
I FIGURED YOU'D SEE ME TELEPORT IN, BUT FORGOT THE EFFECT WOULD BE PRETTY SMALL.
MICRON.
HOW'VE YOU BEEN? WE'VE BEEN KEEPING AN EYE ON YOU.
THE JUSTICE LEAGUE WAS THINKING YOU MIGHT WANT ANOTHER CHANCE TO JOIN UP.
I KNOW YOU TOLD US YOU WEREN'T A JOINER, BUT WE THINK YOU'RE MISSING OUT. WE'D BE A LOT OF HELP WITH YOUR ROGUES, AND VICE VERSA.
PLUS, THE LEAGUE DOESN'T FEEL RIGHT WITHOUT A GOOD, SCARY DETECTIVE.
LOOK, I'M FLATTERED AND EVERYTHING...
...BUT THE ANSWER'S STILL NO.

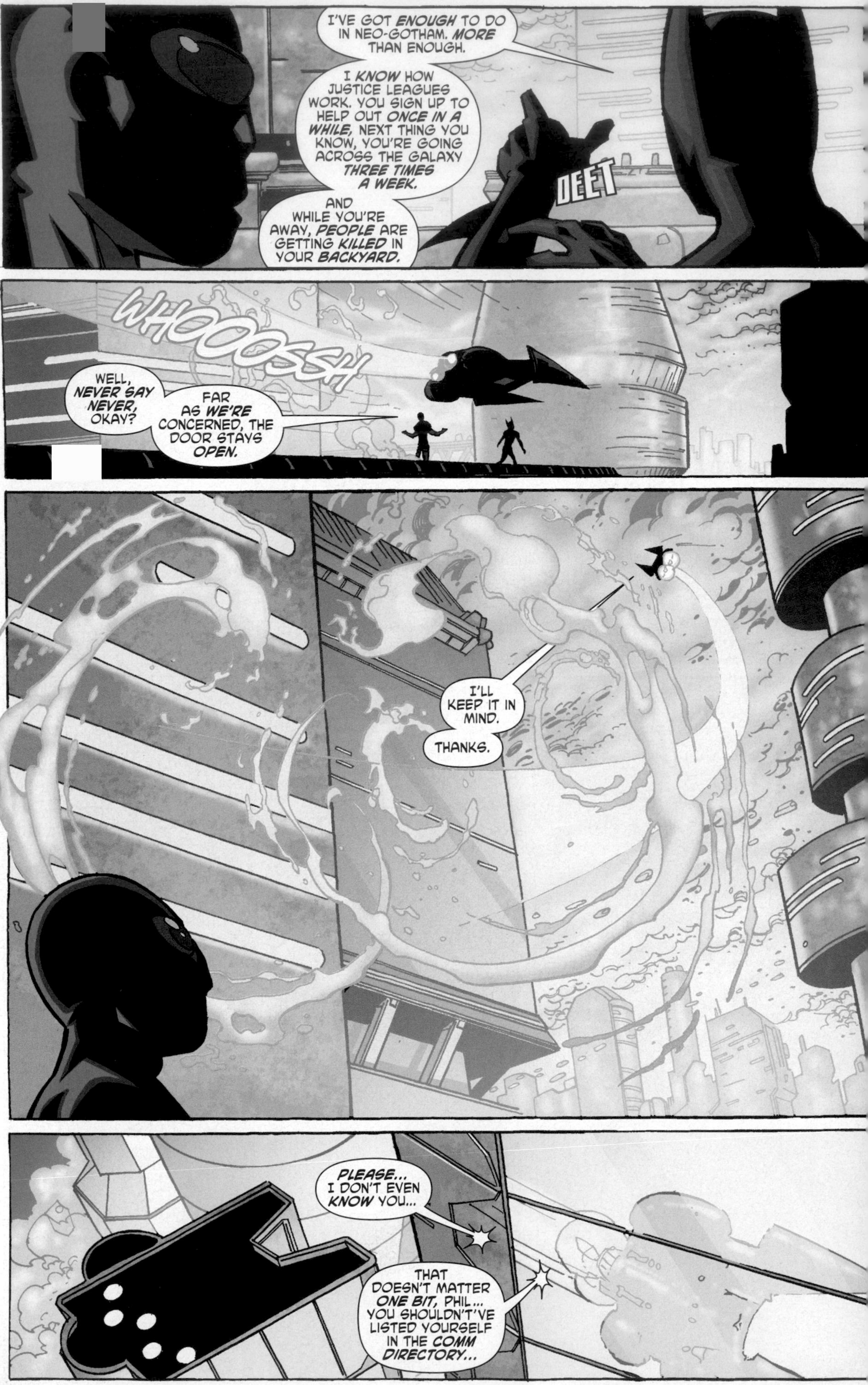
I'VE GOT ENOUGH TO DO IN NEO-GOTHAM. MORE THAN ENOUGH.
I KNOW HOW JUSTICE LEAGUES WORK. YOU SIGN UP TO HELP OUT ONCE IN A WHILE, NEXT THING YOU KNOW, YOU'RE GOING ACROSS THE GALAXY THREE TIMES A WEEK.
AND WHILE YOU'RE AWAY, PEOPLE ARE GETTING KILLED IN YOUR BACKYARD.
DEET
WHOOOOSSH
WELL, NEVER SAY NEVER, OKAY?
FAR AS WE'RE CONCERNED, THE DOOR STAYS OPEN.
I'LL KEEP IT IN MIND.
THANKS.
PLEASE... I DON'T EVEN KNOW YOU...
THAT DOESN'T MATTER ONE BIT, PHIL... YOU SHOULDN'T'VE LISTED YOURSELF IN THE COMM DIRECTORY...

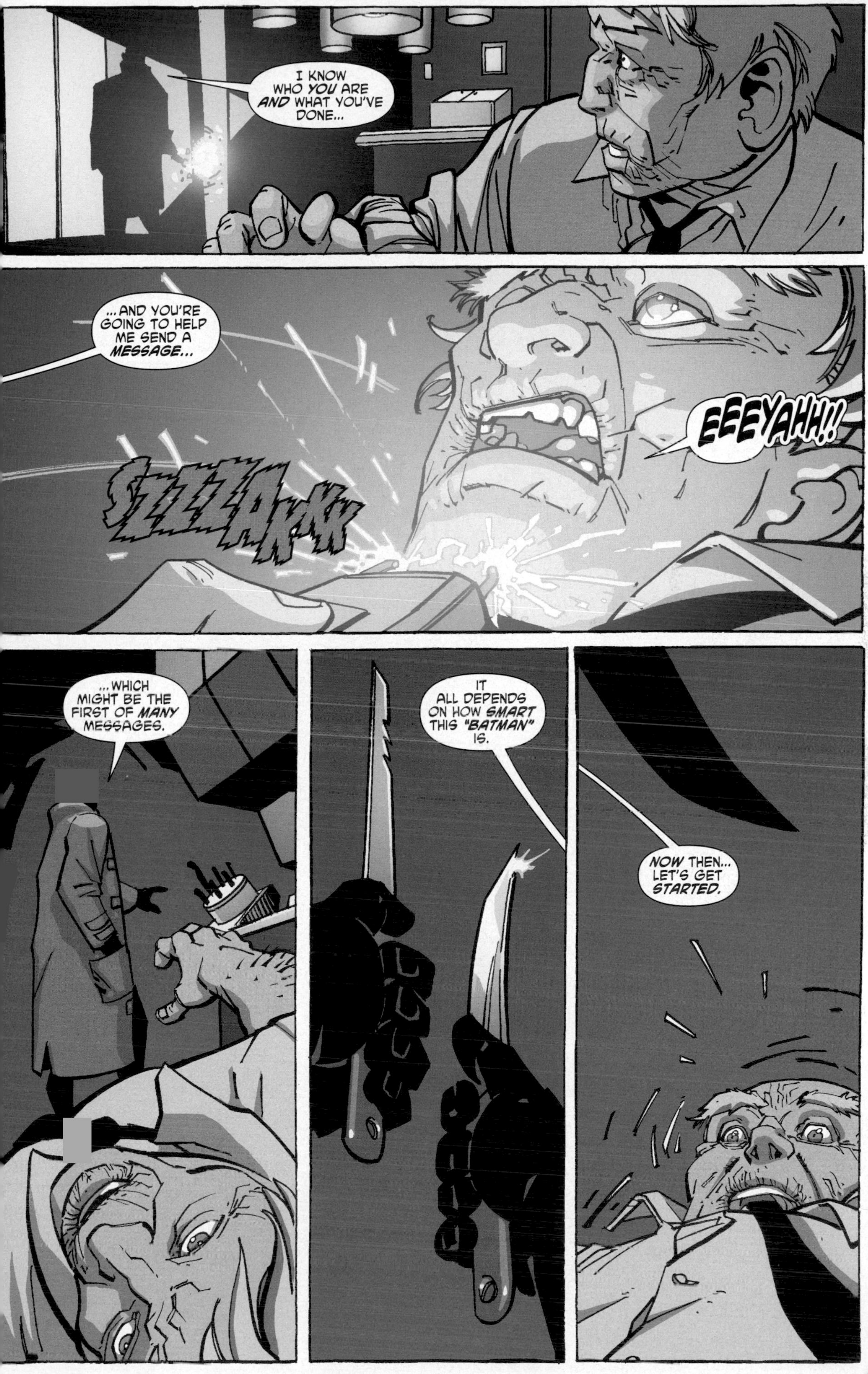
I KNOW WHO YOU ARE AND WHAT YOU'VE DONE...
...AND YOU'RE GOING TO HELP ME SEND A MESSAGE...
SZZZZAKKK
EEEYAHH!!
...WHICH MIGHT BE THE FIRST OF MANY MESSAGES.
IT ALL DEPENDS ON HOW SMART THIS "BATMAN" IS.
NOW THEN... LET'S GET STARTED.

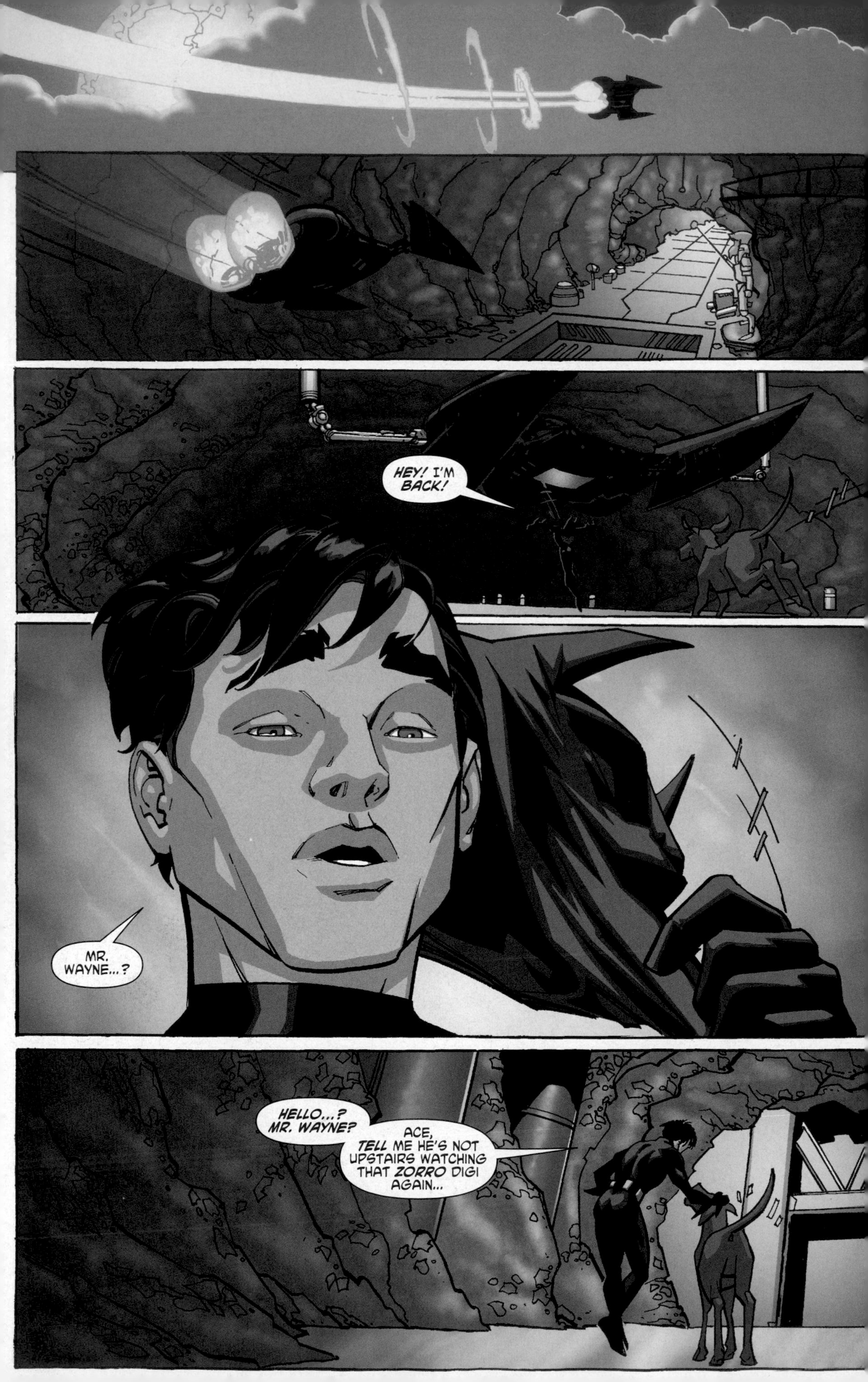
HEY! I'M BACK!
MR. WAYNE...?
HELLO...? MR. WAYNE?
ACE, TELL ME HE'S NOT UPSTAIRS WATCHING THAT ZORRO DIGI AGAIN...

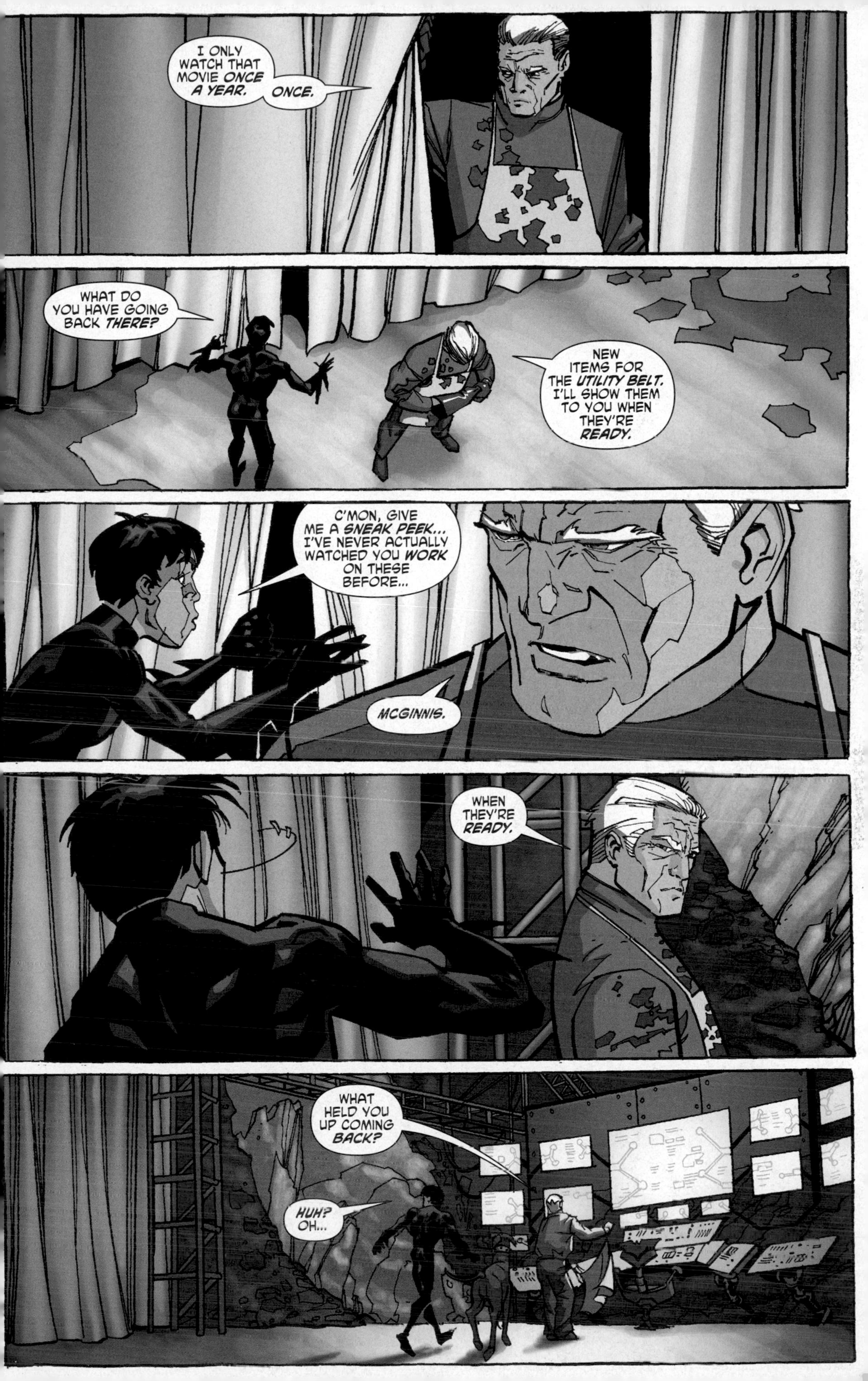
I ONLY WATCH THAT MOVIE ONCE A YEAR.
ONCE.
WHAT DO YOU HAVE GOING BACK THERE?
NEW ITEMS FOR THE UTILITY BELT. I'LL SHOW THEM TO YOU WHEN THEY'RE READY.
C'MON, GIVE ME A SNEAK PEEK... I'VE NEVER ACTUALLY WATCHED YOU WORK ON THESE BEFORE...
MCGINNIS.
WHEN THEY'RE READY.
WHAT HELD YOU UP COMING BACK?
HUH? OH...

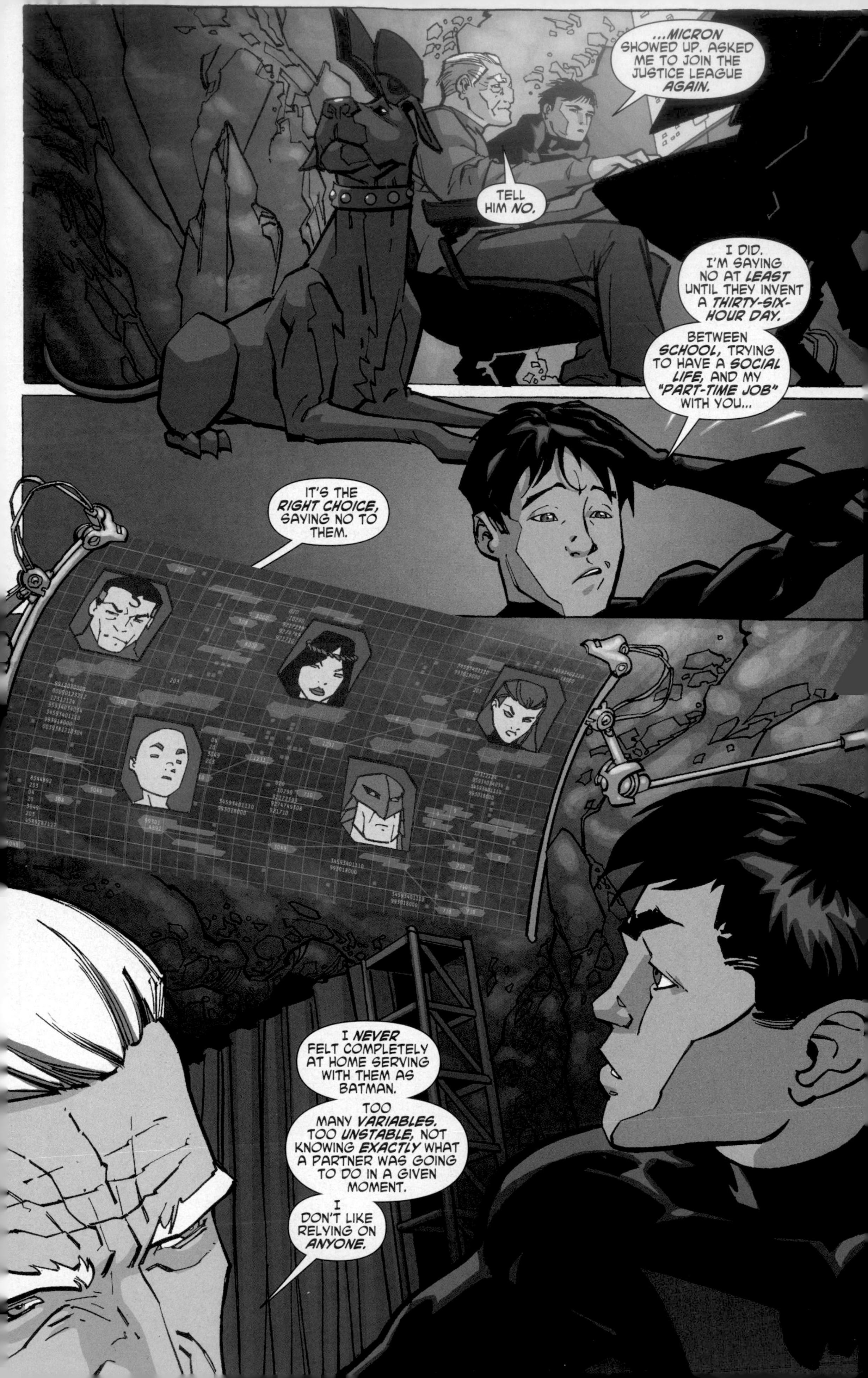
...MICRON SHOWED UP. ASKED ME TO JOIN THE JUSTICE LEAGUE AGAIN.
TELL HIM NO.
I DID. I'M SAYING NO AT LEAST UNTIL THEY INVENT A THIRTY-SIX-HOUR DAY.
BETWEEN SCHOOL, TRYING TO HAVE A SOCIAL LIFE, AND MY "PART-TIME JOB" WITH YOU...
IT'S THE RIGHT CHOICE, SAYING NO TO THEM.
I NEVER FELT COMPLETELY AT HOME SERVING WITH THEM AS BATMAN.
TOO MANY VARIABLES. TOO UNSTABLE, NOT KNOWING EXACTLY WHAT A PARTNER WAS GOING TO DO IN A GIVEN MOMENT.
I DON'T LIKE RELYING ON ANYONE.

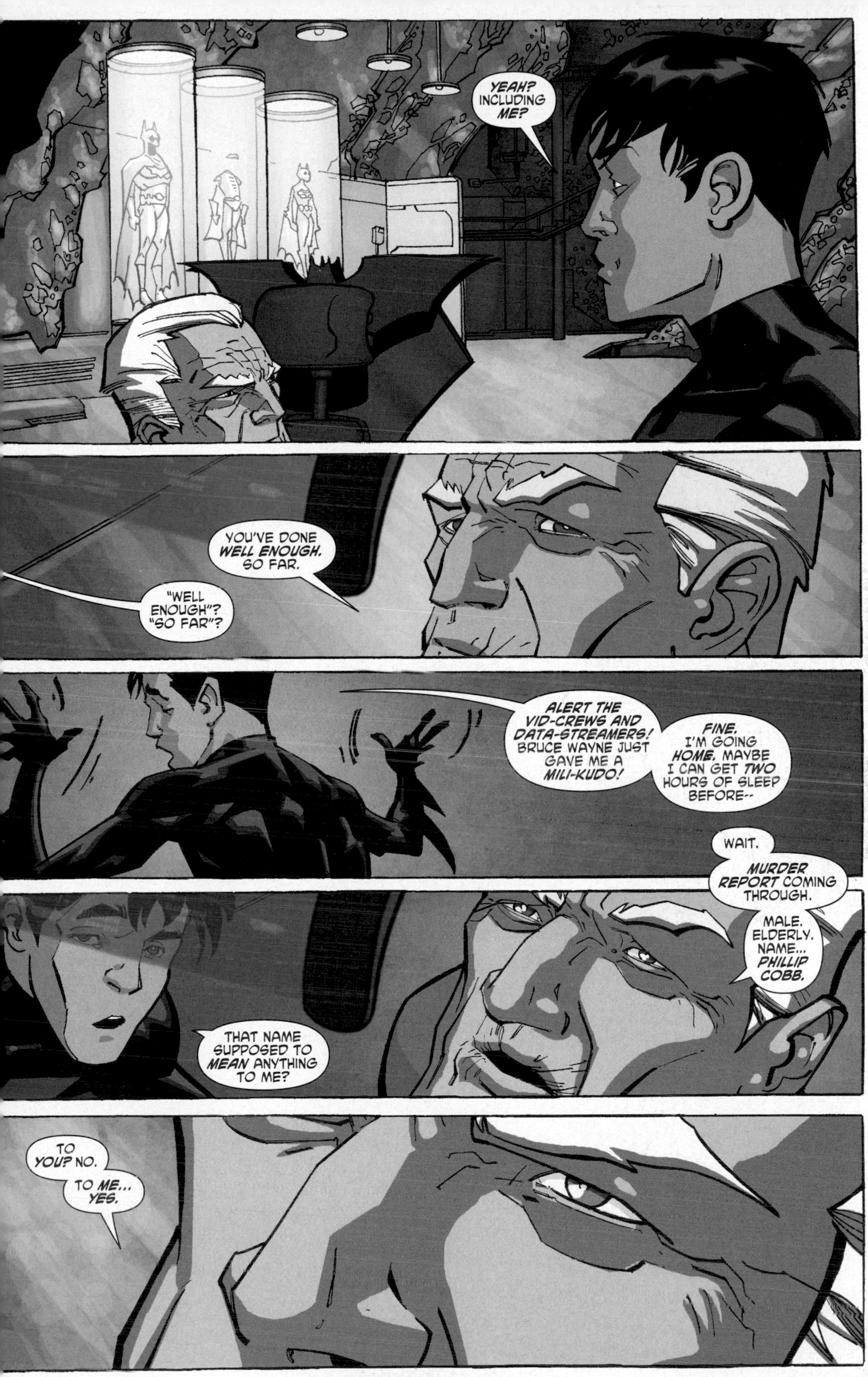
YEAH? INCLUDING ME?
YOU'VE DONE WELL ENOUGH. SO FAR.
"WELL ENOUGH"? "SO FAR"?
ALERT THE VID-CREWS AND DATA-STREAMERS! BRUCE WAYNE JUST GAVE ME A MILI-KUDO!
FINE. I'M GOING HOME. MAYBE I CAN GET TWO HOURS OF SLEEP BEFORE--
WAIT.
MURDER REPORT COMING THROUGH.
MALE. ELDERLY. NAME... PHILLIP COBB.
THAT NAME SUPPOSED TO MEAN ANYTHING TO ME?
TO YOU? NO.
TO ME... YES.

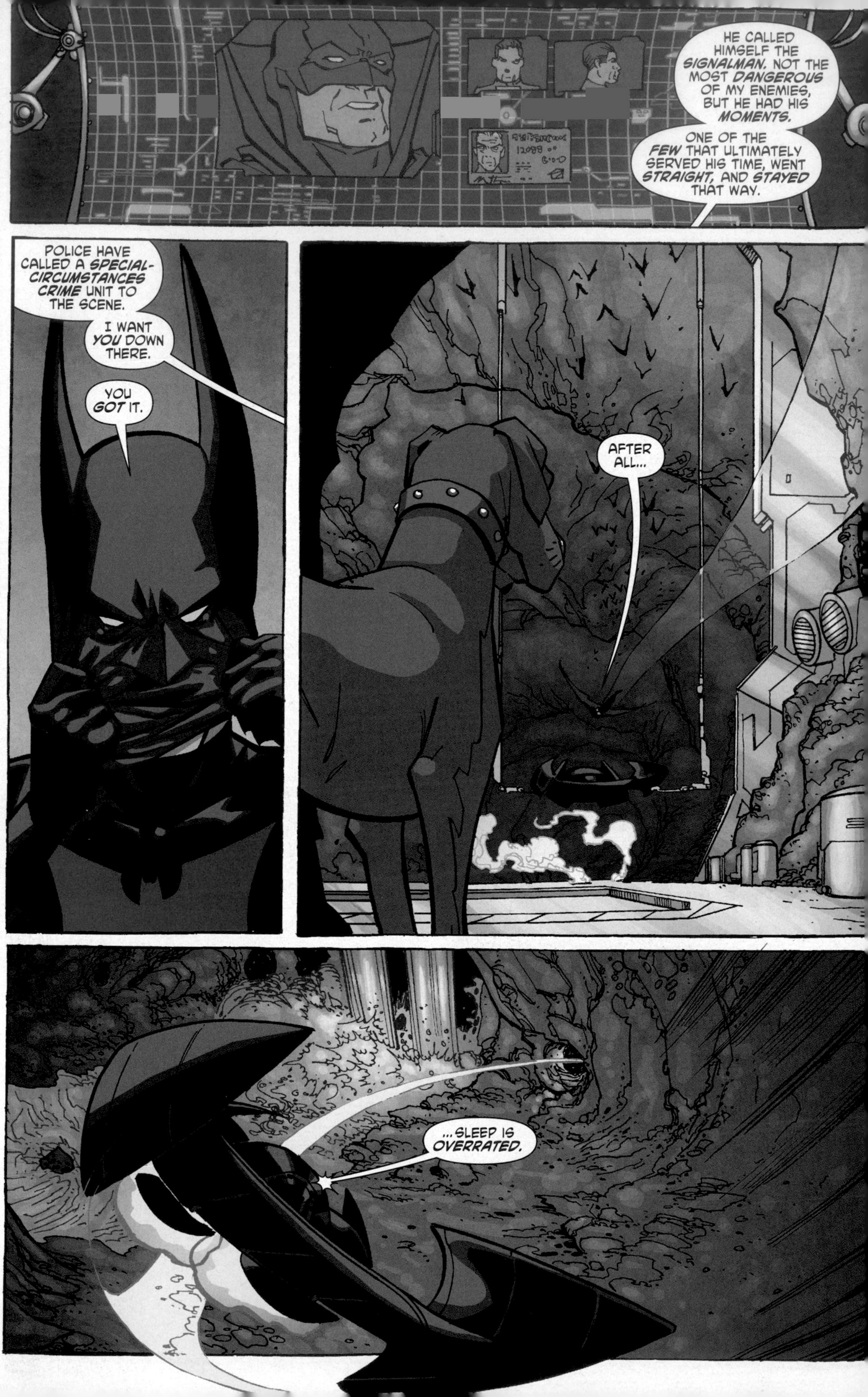
HE CALLED HIMSELF THE SIGNALMAN. NOT THE MOST DANGEROUS OF MY ENEMIES, BUT HE HAD HIS MOMENTS.
ONE OF THE FEW THAT ULTIMATELY SERVED HIS TIME, WENT STRAIGHT, AND STAYED THAT WAY.
POLICE HAVE CALLED A SPECIAL-CIRCUMSTANCES CRIME UNIT TO THE SCENE.
I WANT YOU DOWN THERE.
YOU GOT IT.
AFTER ALL...
...SLEEP IS OVERRATED.

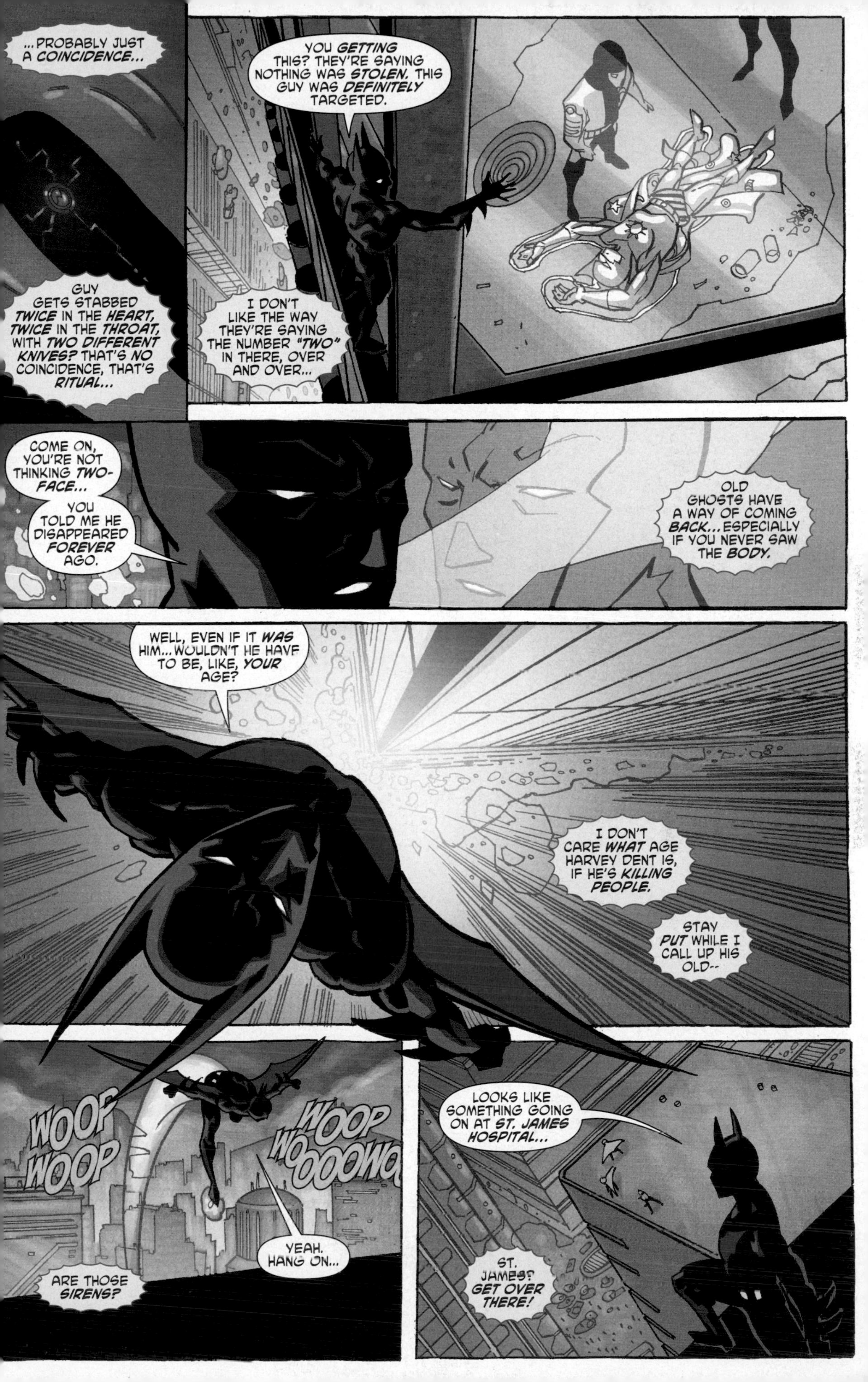
...PROBABLY JUST A COINCIDENCE...
GUY GETS STABBED TWICE IN THE HEART, TWICE IN THE THROAT, WITH TWO DIFFERENT KNIVES? THAT'S NO COINCIDENCE, THAT'S RITUAL...
YOU GETTING THIS? THEY'RE SAYING NOTHING WAS STOLEN. THIS GUY WAS DEFINITELY TARGETED.
I DON'T LIKE THE WAY THEY'RE SAYING THE NUMBER "TWO" IN THERE, OVER AND OVER...
COME ON, YOU'RE NOT THINKING TWO-FACE...
YOU TOLD ME HE DISAPPEARED FOREVER AGO.
OLD GHOSTS HAVE A WAY OF COMING BACK... ESPECIALLY IF YOU NEVER SAW THE BODY.
WELL, EVEN IF IT WAS HIM... WOULDN'T HE HAVE TO BE, LIKE, YOUR AGE?
I DON'T CARE WHAT AGE HARVEY DENT IS, IF HE'S KILLING PEOPLE.
STAY PUT WHILE I CALL UP HIS OLD--
WOOP WOOP
WOOP WOOOOWO
ARE THOSE SIRENS?
YEAH. HANG ON...
LOOKS LIKE SOMETHING GOING ON AT ST. JAMES HOSPITAL...
ST. JAMES? GET OVER THERE!

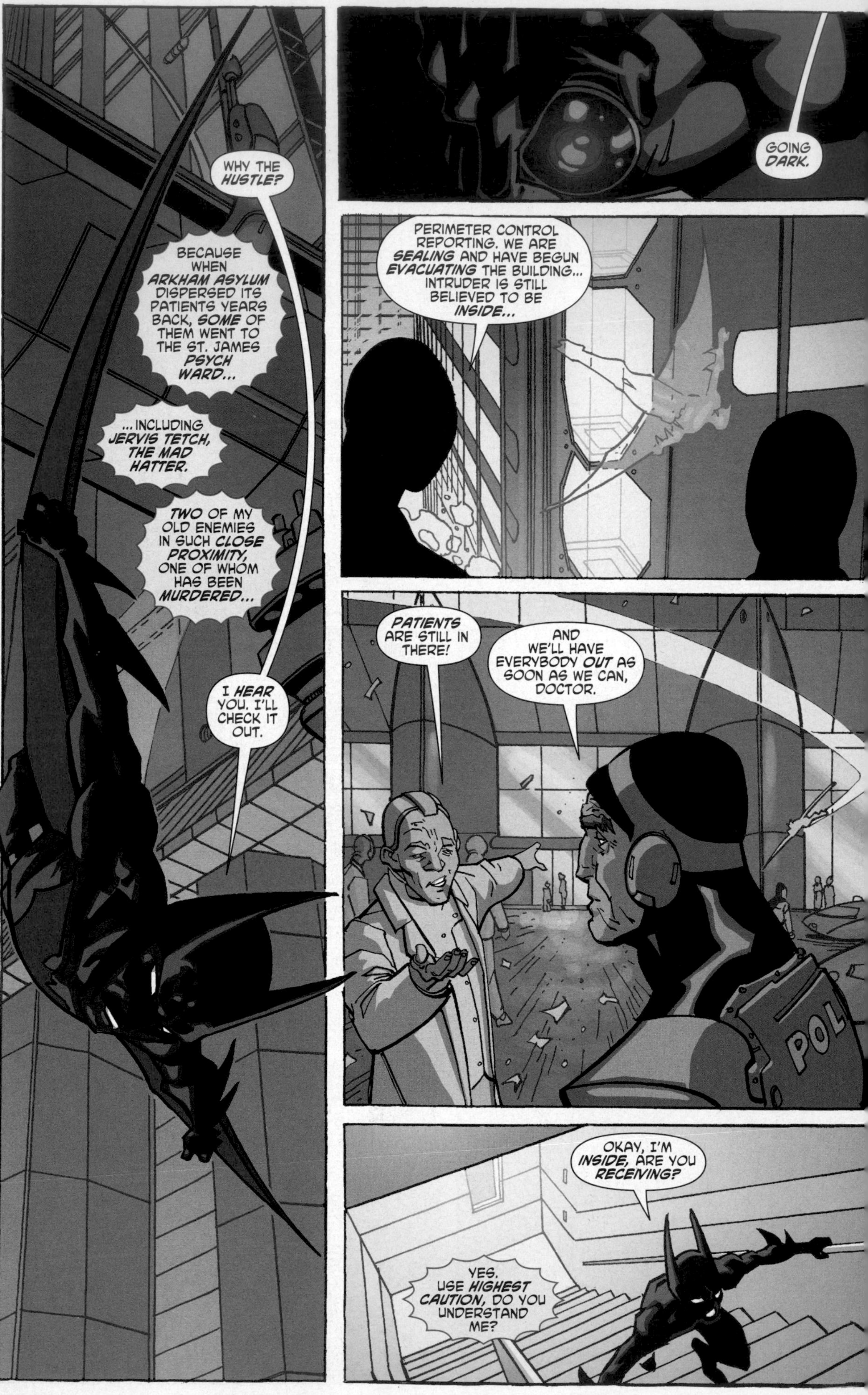
WHY THE HUSTLE?
BECAUSE WHEN ARKHAM ASYLUM DISPERSED ITS PATIENTS YEARS BACK, SOME OF THEM WENT TO THE ST. JAMES PSYCH WARD...
...INCLUDING JERVIS TETCH, THE MAD HATTER.
TWO OF MY OLD ENEMIES IN SUCH CLOSE PROXIMITY, ONE OF WHOM HAS BEEN MURDERED...
I HEAR YOU. I'LL CHECK IT OUT.
GOING DARK.
PERIMETER CONTROL REPORTING. WE ARE SEALING AND HAVE BEGUN EVACUATING THE BUILDING... INTRUDER IS STILL BELIEVED TO BE INSIDE...
PATIENTS ARE STILL IN THERE!
AND WE'LL HAVE EVERYBODY OUT AS SOON AS WE CAN, DOCTOR.
POL
OKAY, I'M INSIDE, ARE YOU RECEIVING?
YES. USE HIGHEST CAUTION, DO YOU UNDERSTAND ME?

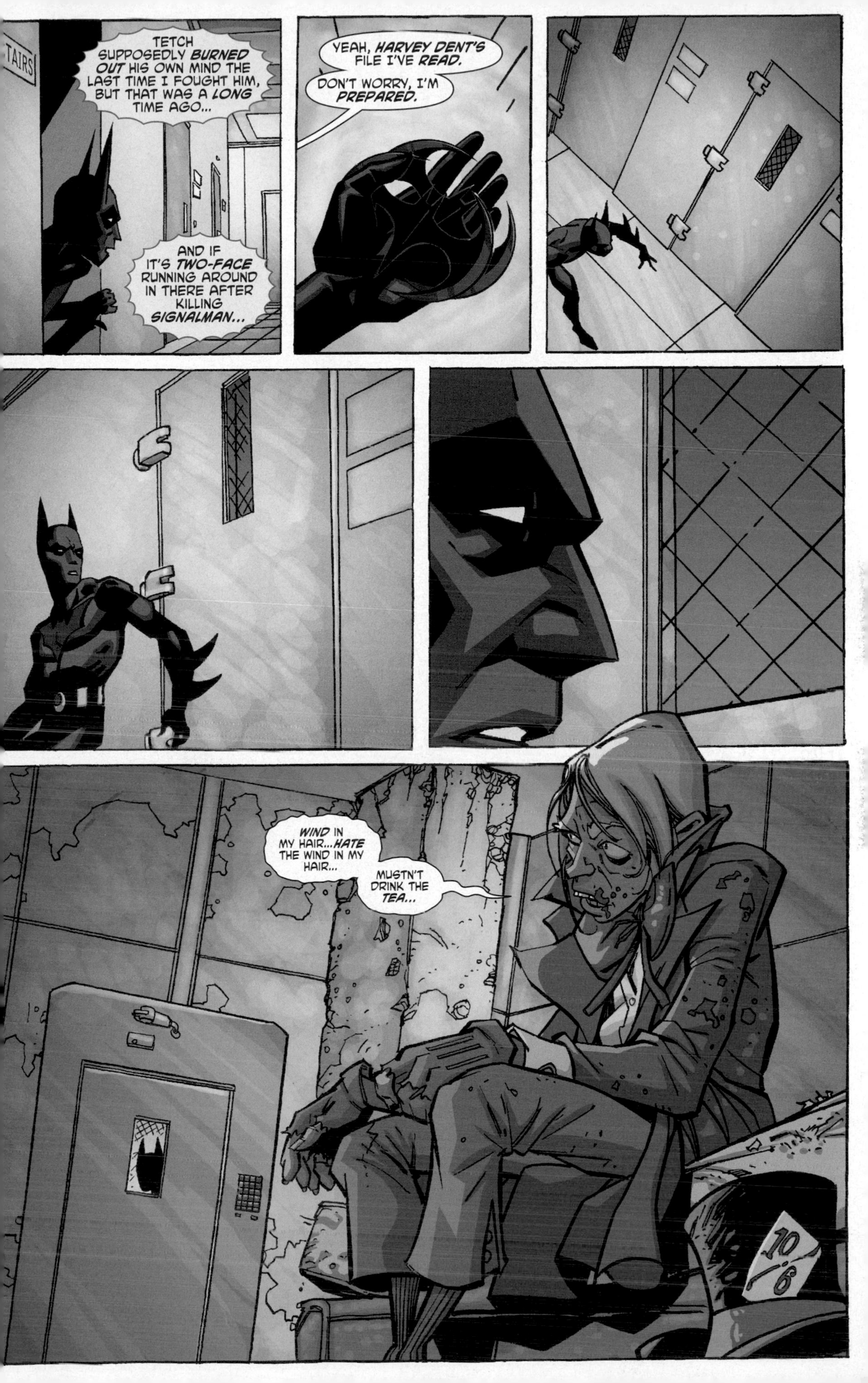
TAIRS
TETCH SUPPOSEDLY BURNED OUT HIS OWN MIND THE LAST TIME I FOUGHT HIM, BUT THAT WAS A LONG TIME AGO...
AND IF IT'S TWO-FACE RUNNING AROUND IN THERE AFTER KILLING SIGNALMAN...
YEAH, HARVEY DENT'S FILE I'VE READ.
DON'T WORRY, I'M PREPARED.
WIND IN MY HAIR...HATE THE WIND IN MY HAIR...
MUSTN'T DRINK THE TEA...
10/6

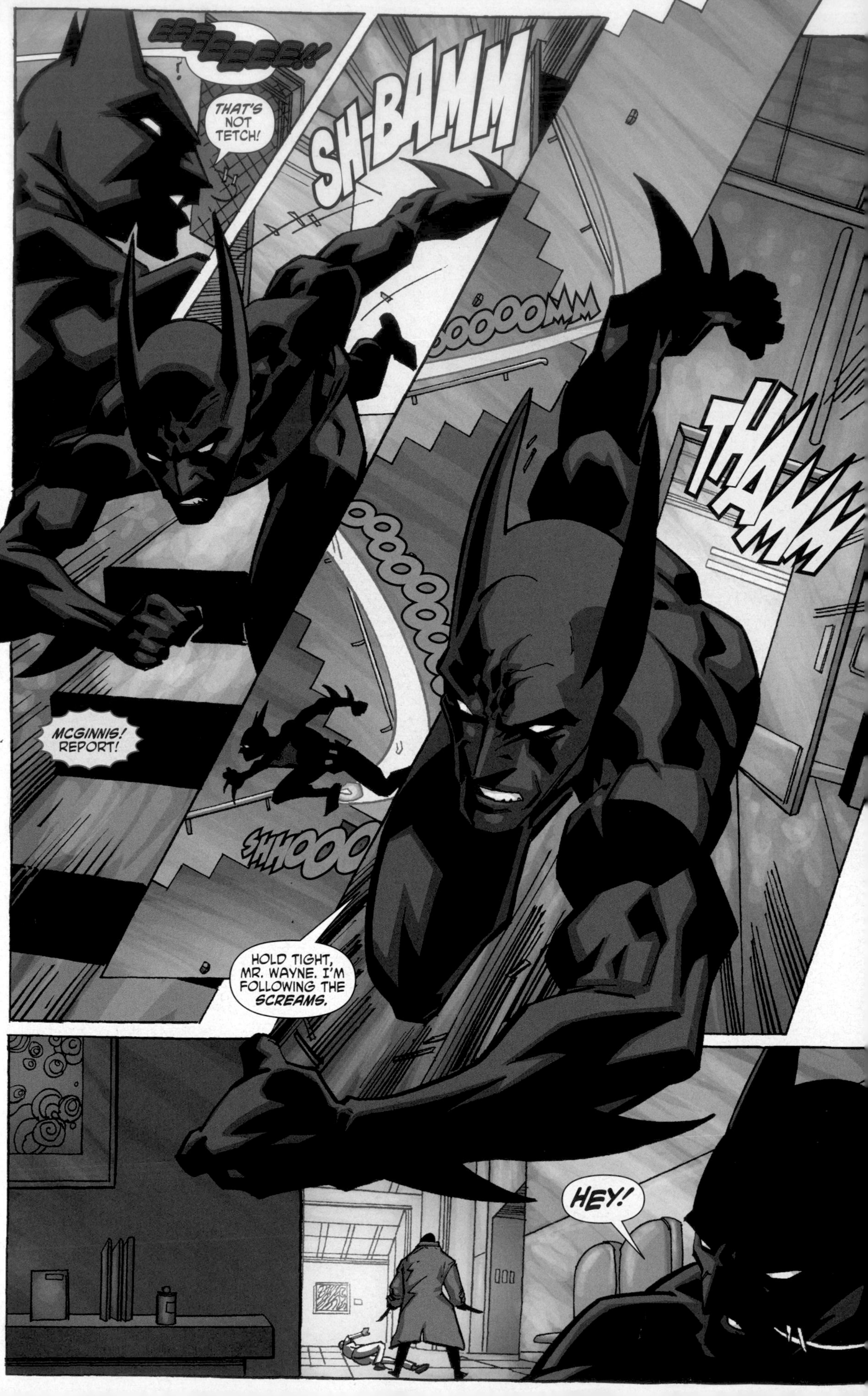
EEEEEEEEE!!
THAT'S NOT TETCH!
SH-BAMM
OOOOOMM
THAMM
MCGINNIS! REPORT!
SHHOOO
HOLD TIGHT, MR. WAYNE. I'M FOLLOWING THE SCREAMS.
HEY!

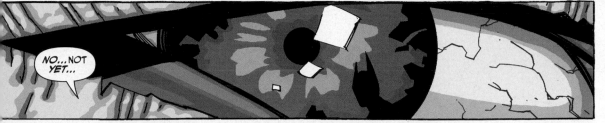

NO...NOT YET...

NURSE... ARE YOU ALL RIGHT?

HE...HE WAS GOING TO *KILL* ME!

IT'S *OKAY*... HE'S *GONE* NOW...

HE WANTED ME TO TELL HIM WHERE *MISTER TETCH* WAS, AND WHEN I SAID I *DIDN'T KNOW*, HE WASN'T ON MY *FLOOR*, HE STARTED *CUTTING* ME, JUST *LITTLE* ONES!

HE SAID THEY'D GET *WORSE* IF I DIDN'T *TELL* HIM!

I *SWORE!* I *SWORE* I DIDN'T *KNOW!*

I *KNOW,* I *KNOW...* LISTEN, DID HE SAY ANYTHING *ELSE?*

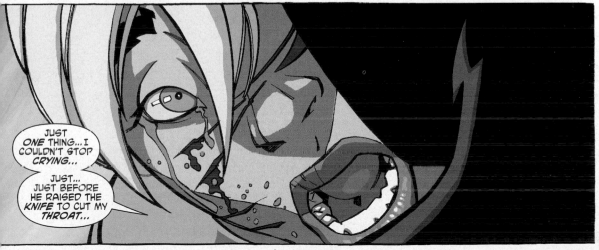

JUST *ONE* THING... I COULDN'T STOP CRYING...

JUST... JUST BEFORE HE RAISED THE *KNIFE* TO CUT MY *THROAT*...

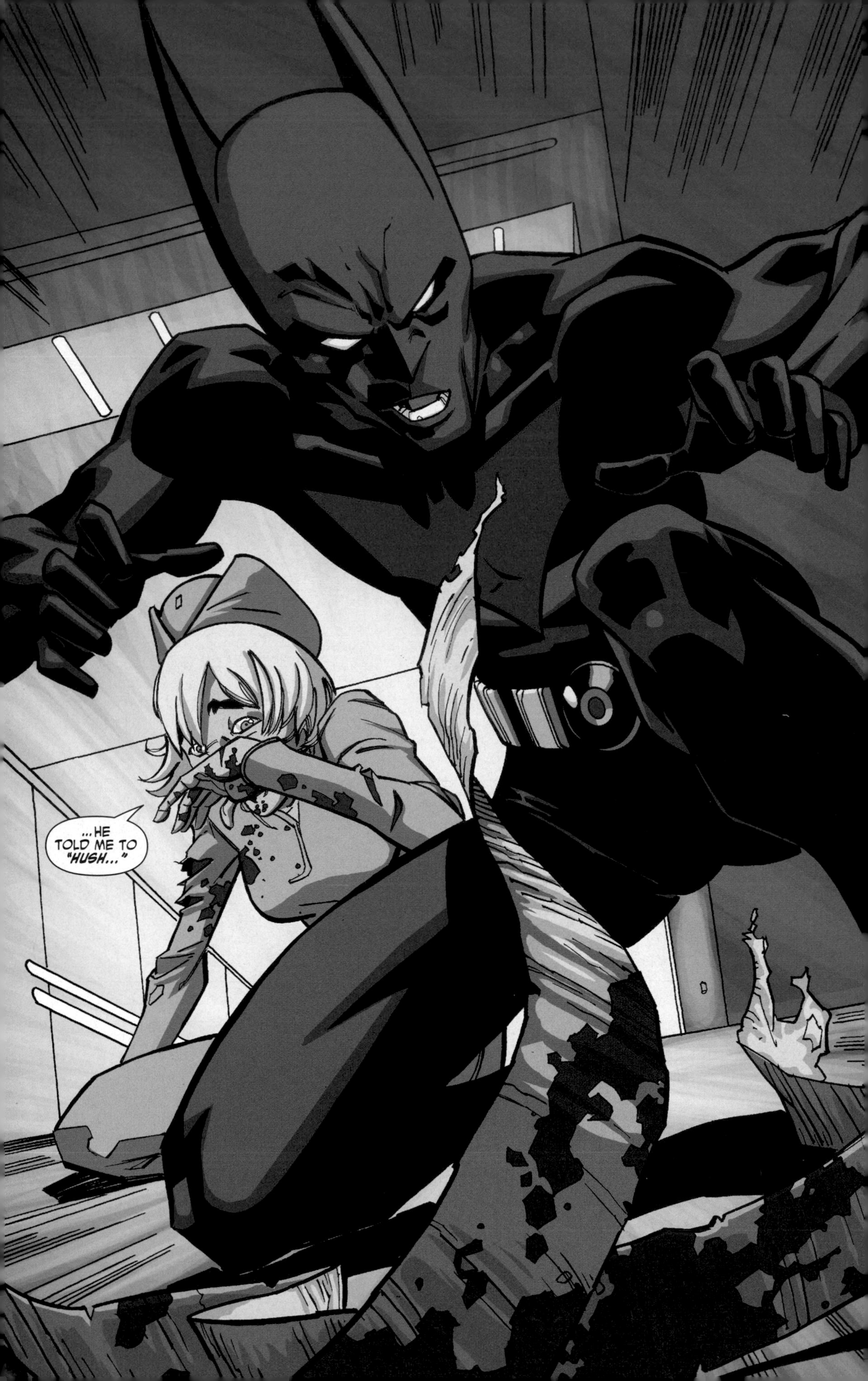
...HE TOLD ME TO "HUSH..."

PART 2: PAST CRIMES

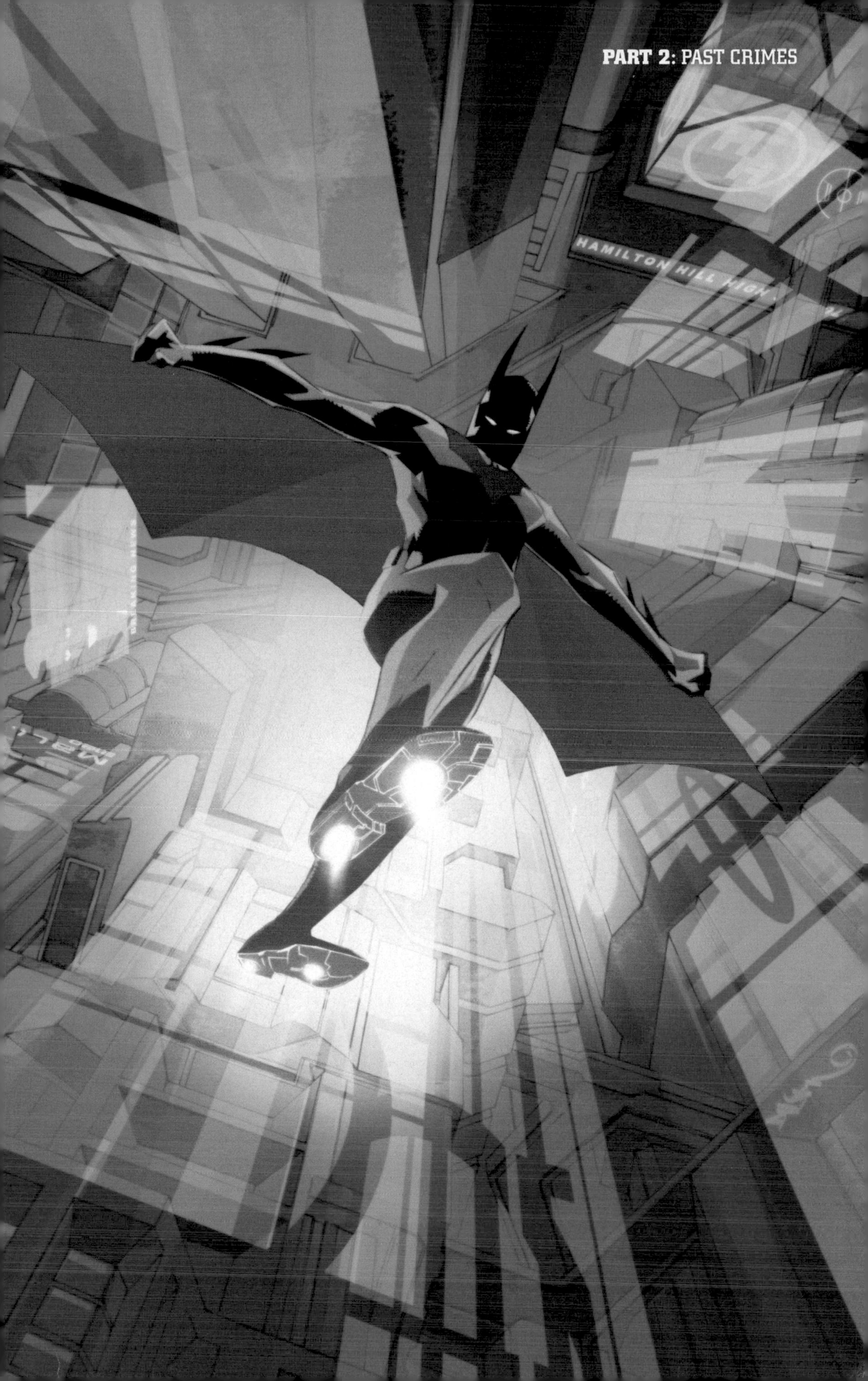
HAMILTON HILL HIGH

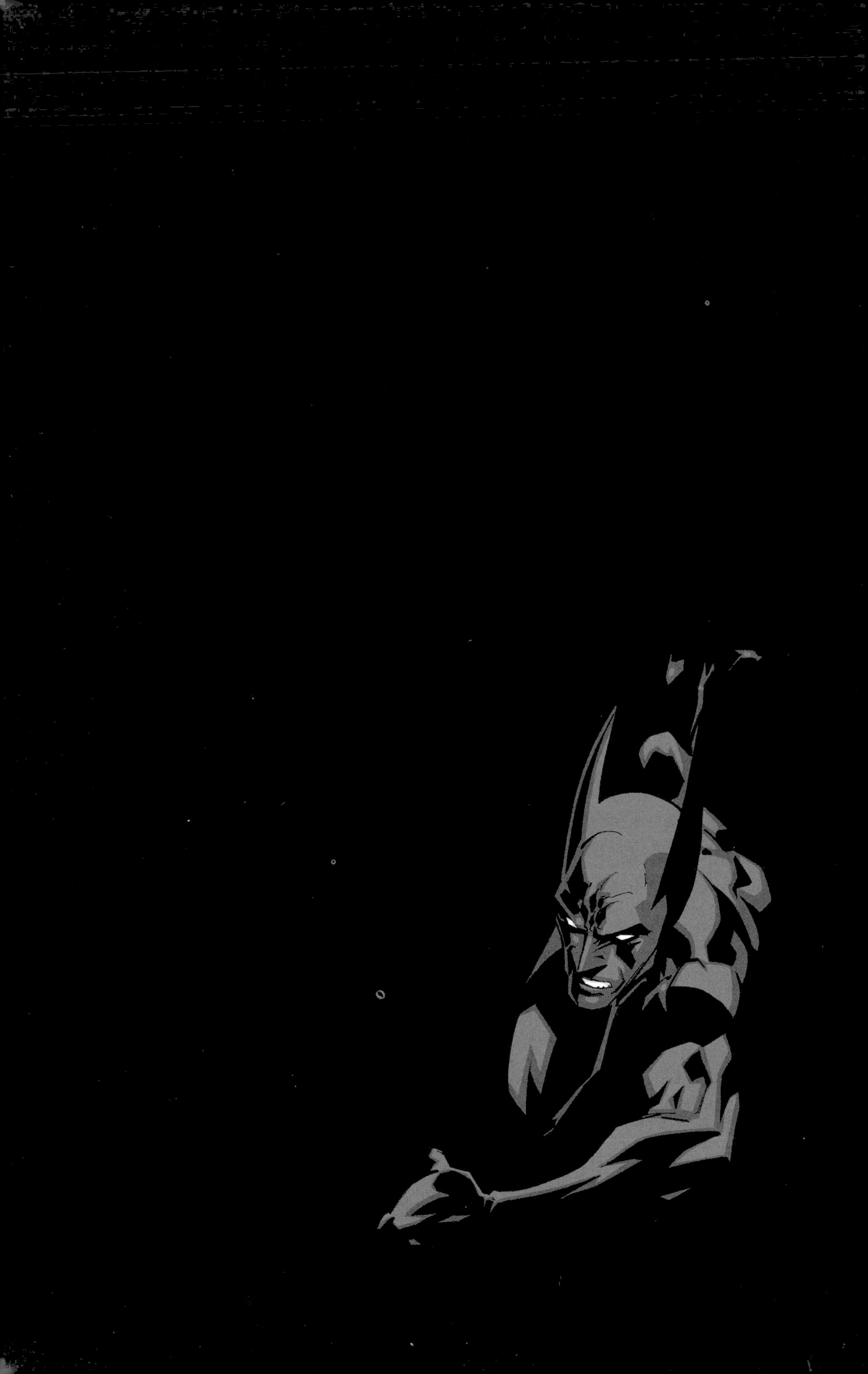

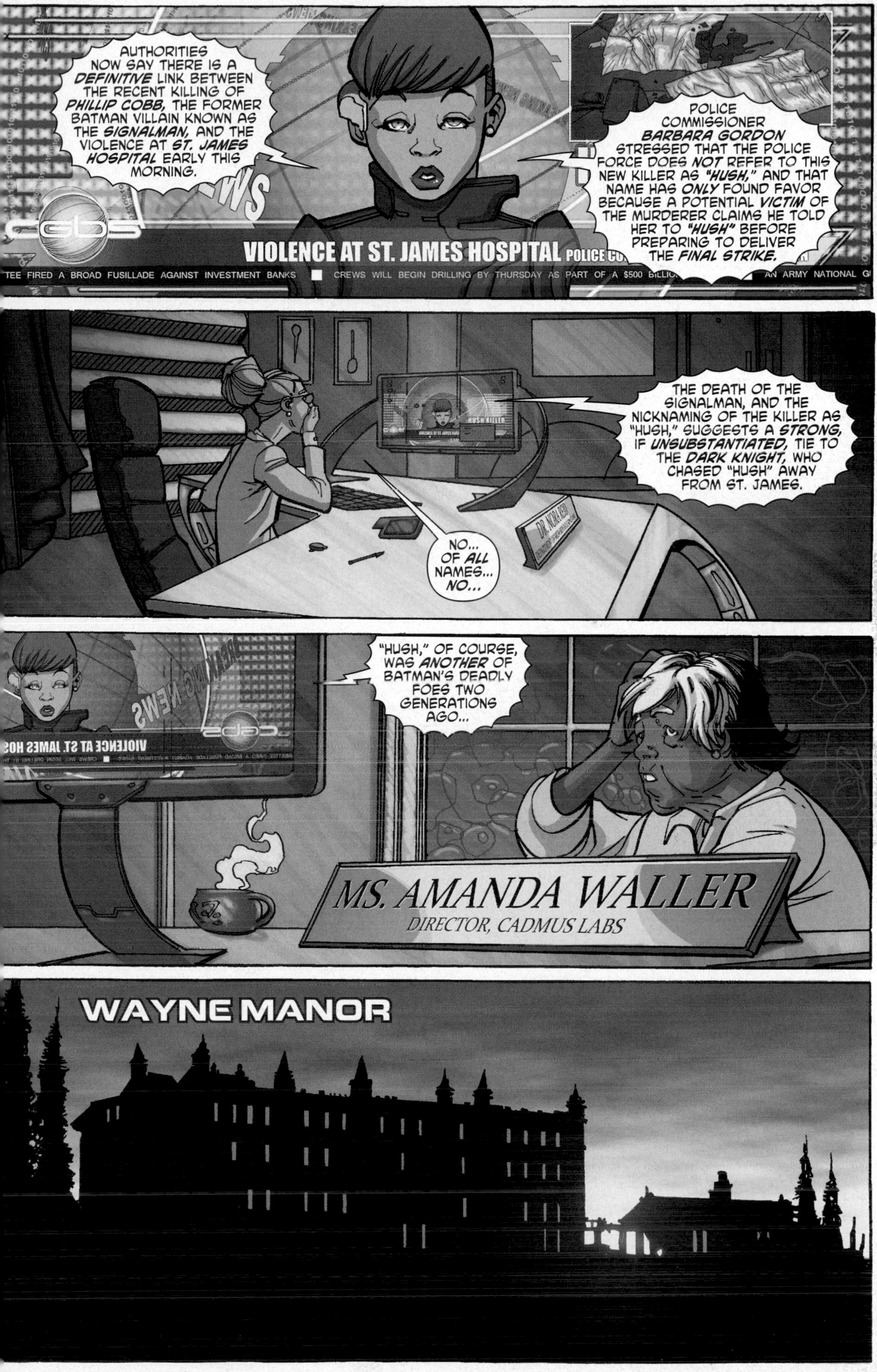
AUTHORITIES NOW SAY THERE IS A DEFINITIVE LINK BETWEEN THE RECENT KILLING OF PHILLIP COBB, THE FORMER BATMAN VILLAIN KNOWN AS THE SIGNALMAN, AND THE VIOLENCE AT ST. JAMES HOSPITAL EARLY THIS MORNING.
POLICE COMMISSIONER BARBARA GORDON STRESSED THAT THE POLICE FORCE DOES NOT REFER TO THIS NEW KILLER AS "HUSH," AND THAT NAME HAS ONLY FOUND FAVOR BECAUSE A POTENTIAL VICTIM OF THE MURDERER CLAIMS HE TOLD HER TO "HUSH" BEFORE PREPARING TO DELIVER THE FINAL STRIKE.
VIOLENCE AT ST. JAMES HOSPITAL
TEE FIRED A BROAD FUSILLADE AGAINST INVESTMENT BANKS
CREWS WILL BEGIN DRILLING BY THURSDAY AS PART OF A $500
AN ARMY NATIONAL
THE DEATH OF THE SIGNALMAN, AND THE NICKNAMING OF THE KILLER AS "HUSH," SUGGESTS A STRONG, IF UNSUBSTANTIATED, TIE TO THE DARK KNIGHT, WHO CHASED "HUSH" AWAY FROM ST. JAMES.
HUSH KILLER
NO... OF ALL NAMES... NO...
"HUSH," OF COURSE, WAS ANOTHER OF BATMAN'S DEADLY FOES TWO GENERATIONS AGO...
MS. AMANDA WALLER
DIRECTOR, CADMUS LABS
WAYNE MANOR

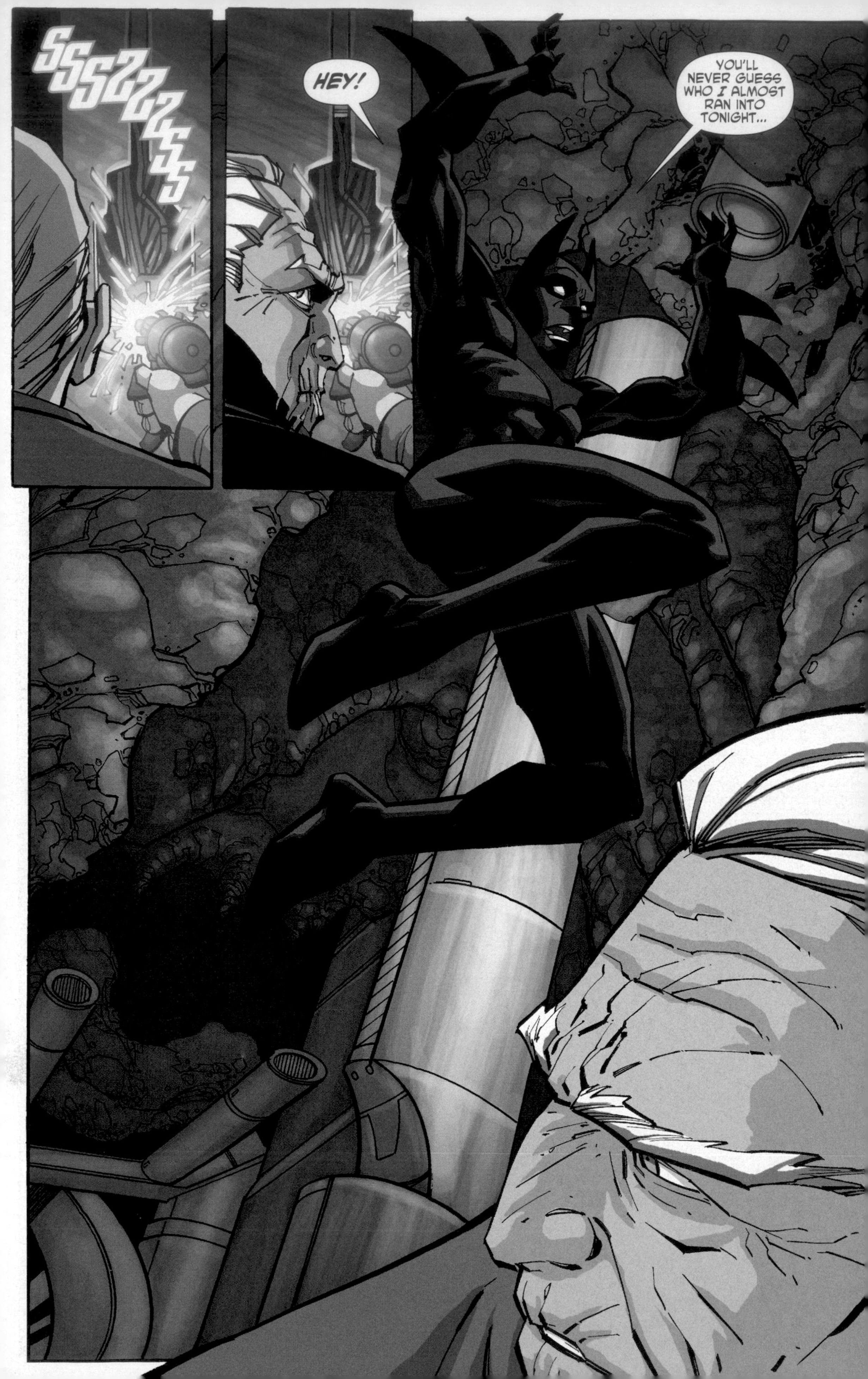
SSSZZZZSSS
HEY!
YOU'LL NEVER GUESS WHO I ALMOST RAN INTO TONIGHT...

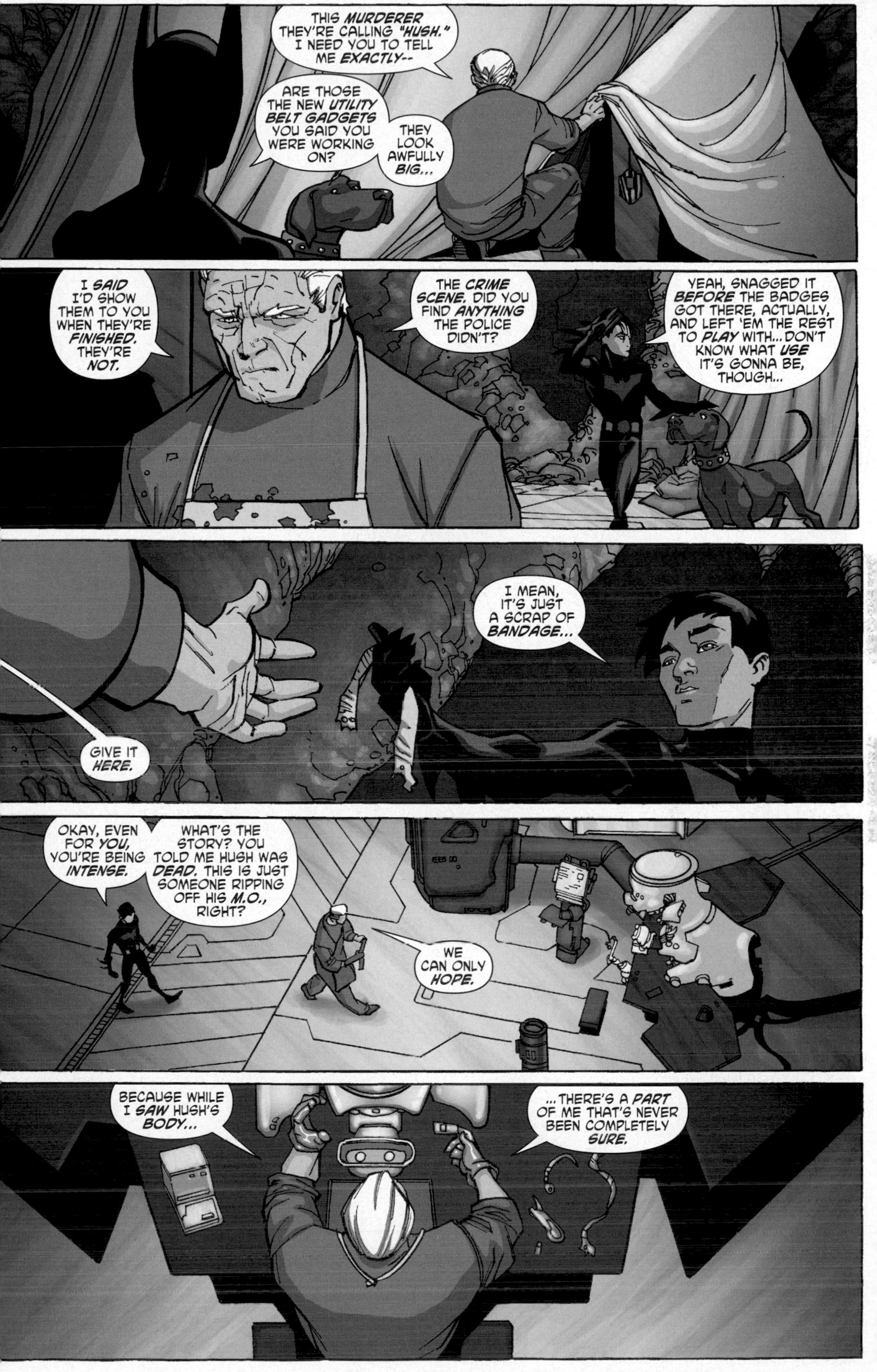
THIS MURDERER THEY'RE CALLING "HUSH." I NEED YOU TO TELL ME EXACTLY--
ARE THOSE THE NEW UTILITY BELT GADGETS YOU SAID YOU WERE WORKING ON?
THEY LOOK AWFULLY BIG...
I SAID I'D SHOW THEM TO YOU WHEN THEY'RE FINISHED. THEY'RE NOT.
THE CRIME SCENE. DID YOU FIND ANYTHING THE POLICE DIDN'T?
YEAH, SNAGGED IT BEFORE THE BADGES GOT THERE, ACTUALLY, AND LEFT 'EM THE REST TO PLAY WITH... DON'T KNOW WHAT USE IT'S GONNA BE, THOUGH...
I MEAN, IT'S JUST A SCRAP OF BANDAGE...
GIVE IT HERE.
OKAY, EVEN FOR YOU, YOU'RE BEING INTENSE.
WHAT'S THE STORY? YOU TOLD ME HUSH WAS DEAD. THIS IS JUST SOMEONE RIPPING OFF HIS M.O., RIGHT?
WE CAN ONLY HOPE.
BECAUSE WHILE I SAW HUSH'S BODY...
...THERE'S A PART OF ME THAT'S NEVER BEEN COMPLETELY SURE.

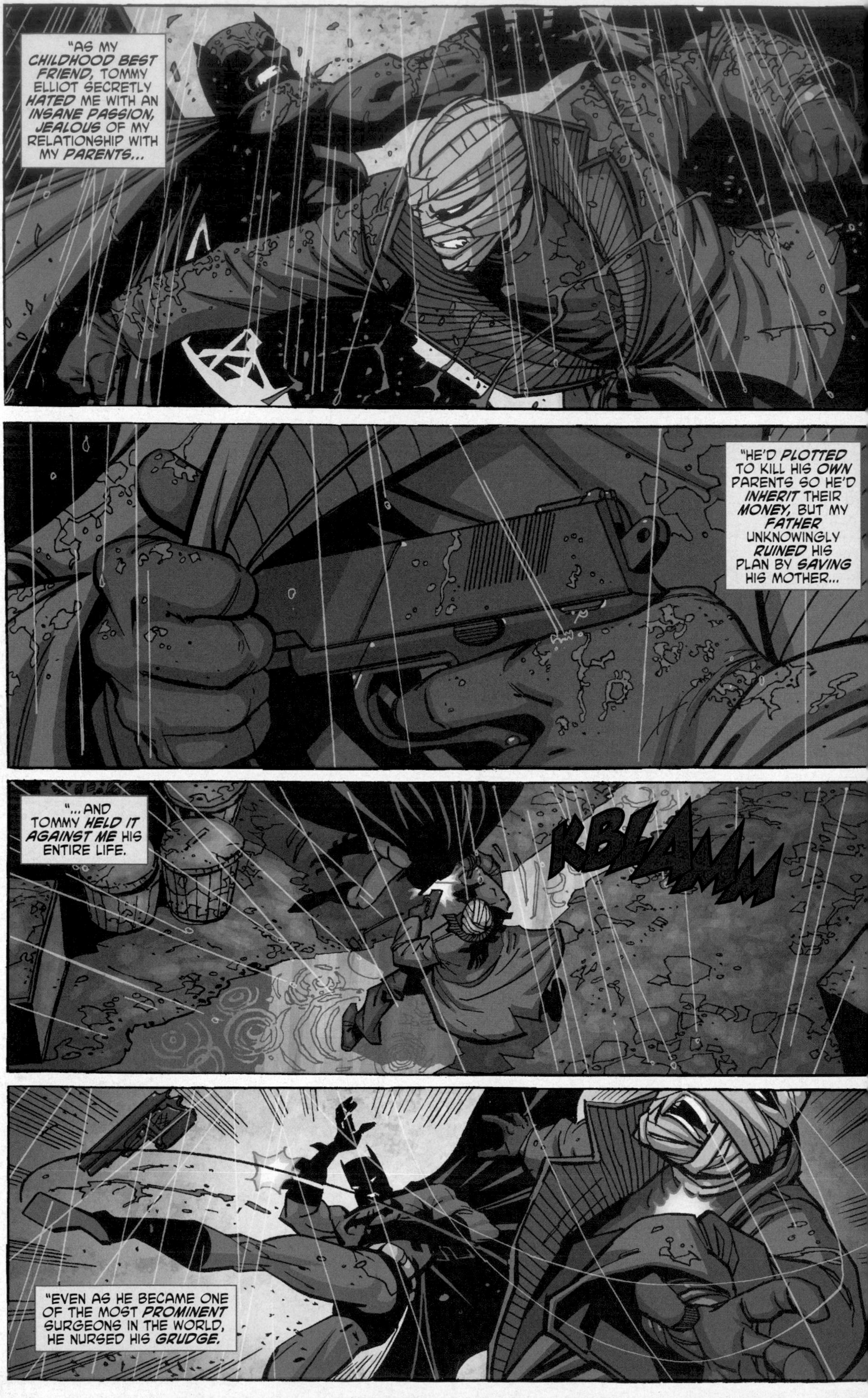
"AS MY CHILDHOOD BEST FRIEND, TOMMY ELLIOT SECRETLY HATED ME WITH AN INSANE PASSION, JEALOUS OF MY RELATIONSHIP WITH MY PARENTS...
"HE'D PLOTTED TO KILL HIS OWN PARENTS SO HE'D INHERIT THEIR MONEY, BUT MY FATHER UNKNOWINGLY RUINED HIS PLAN BY SAVING HIS MOTHER...
"...AND TOMMY HELD IT AGAINST ME HIS ENTIRE LIFE.
KBLAMM
"EVEN AS HE BECAME ONE OF THE MOST PROMINENT SURGEONS IN THE WORLD, HE NURSED HIS GRUDGE.

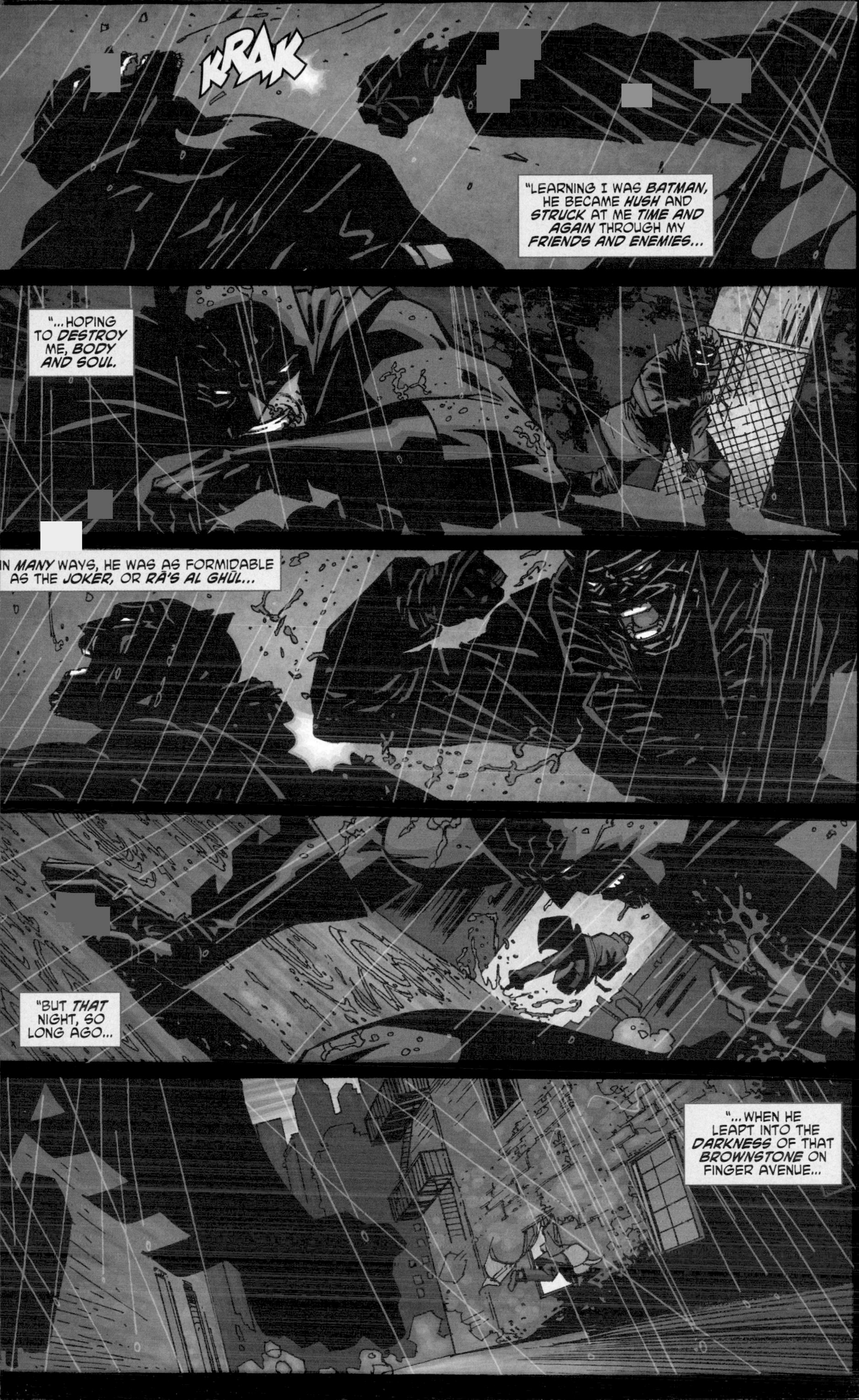
KRAK
"LEARNING I WAS BATMAN, HE BECAME HUSH AND STRUCK AT ME TIME AND AGAIN THROUGH MY FRIENDS AND ENEMIES...
"...HOPING TO DESTROY ME, BODY AND SOUL.
IN MANY WAYS, HE WAS AS FORMIDABLE AS THE JOKER, OR RĀ'S AL GHŪL...
"BUT THAT NIGHT, SO LONG AGO...
"...WHEN HE LEAPT INTO THE DARKNESS OF THAT BROWNSTONE ON FINGER AVENUE...

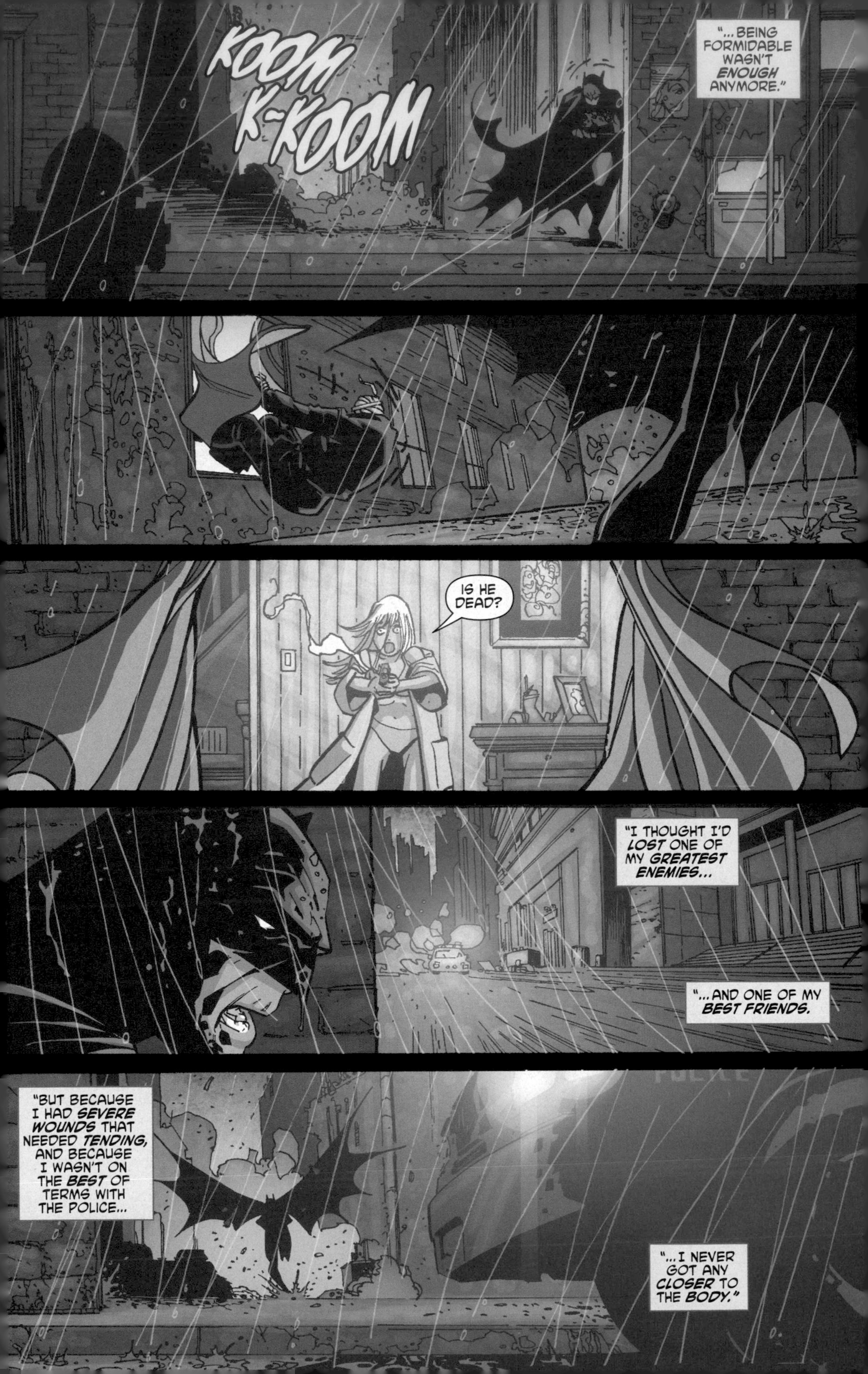
KOOM K-KOOM
"...BEING FORMIDABLE WASN'T ENOUGH ANYMORE."
IS HE DEAD?
"I THOUGHT I'D LOST ONE OF MY GREATEST ENEMIES...
"...AND ONE OF MY BEST FRIENDS.
"BUT BECAUSE I HAD SEVERE WOUNDS THAT NEEDED TENDING, AND BECAUSE I WASN'T ON THE BEST OF TERMS WITH THE POLICE...
"...I NEVER GOT ANY CLOSER TO THE BODY."

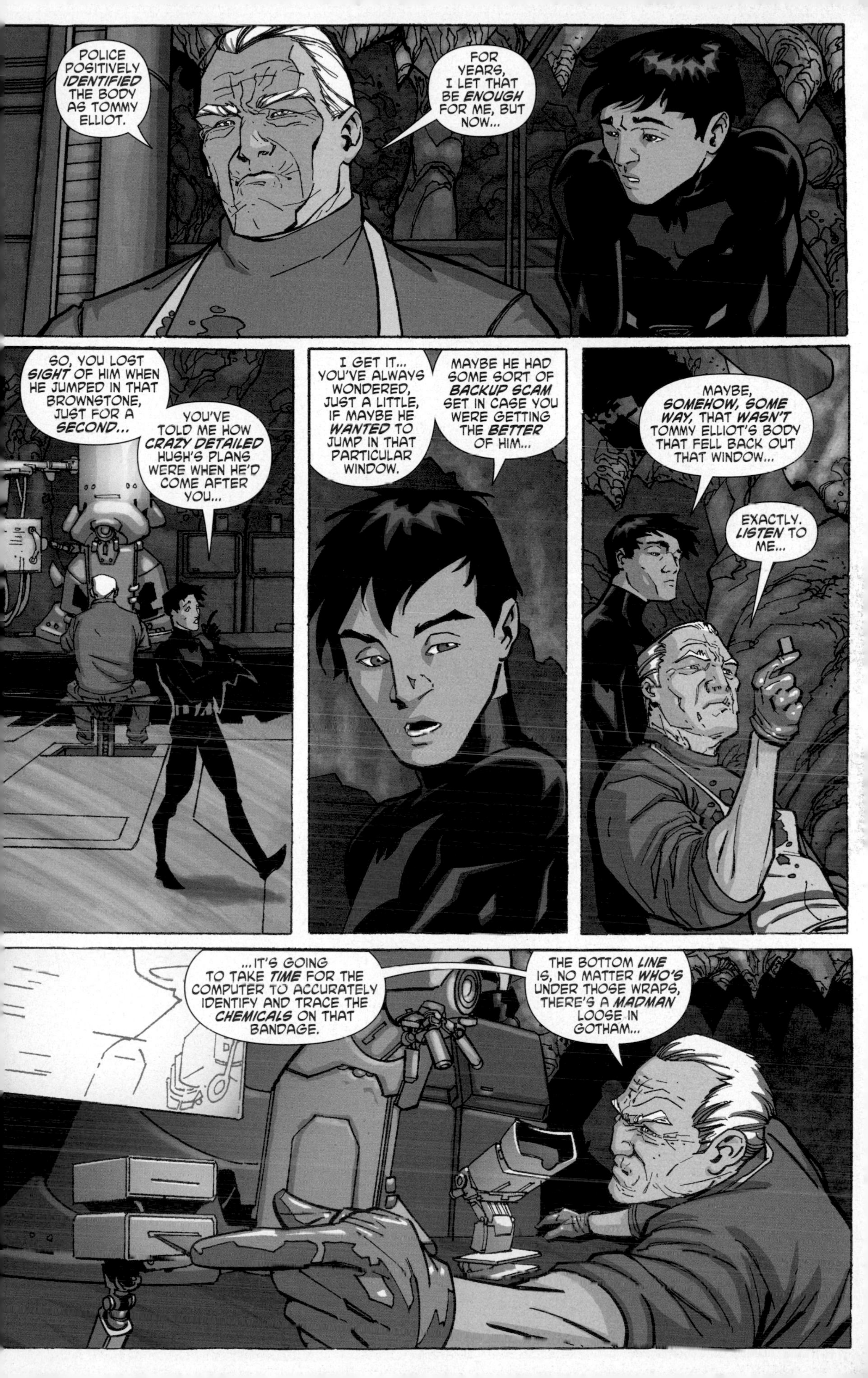
POLICE POSITIVELY IDENTIFIED THE BODY AS TOMMY ELLIOT.
FOR YEARS, I LET THAT BE ENOUGH FOR ME, BUT NOW...
SO, YOU LOST SIGHT OF HIM WHEN HE JUMPED IN THAT BROWNSTONE, JUST FOR A SECOND...
YOU'VE TOLD ME HOW CRAZY DETAILED HUSH'S PLANS WERE WHEN HE'D COME AFTER YOU...
I GET IT... YOU'VE ALWAYS WONDERED, JUST A LITTLE, IF MAYBE HE WANTED TO JUMP IN THAT PARTICULAR WINDOW.
MAYBE HE HAD SOME SORT OF BACKUP SCAM SET IN CASE YOU WERE GETTING THE BETTER OF HIM...
MAYBE, SOMEHOW, SOME WAY, THAT WASN'T TOMMY ELLIOT'S BODY THAT FELL BACK OUT THAT WINDOW...
EXACTLY. LISTEN TO ME...
...IT'S GOING TO TAKE TIME FOR THE COMPUTER TO ACCURATELY IDENTIFY AND TRACE THE CHEMICALS ON THAT BANDAGE.
THE BOTTOM LINE IS, NO MATTER WHO'S UNDER THOSE WRAPS, THERE'S A MADMAN LOOSE IN GOTHAM...

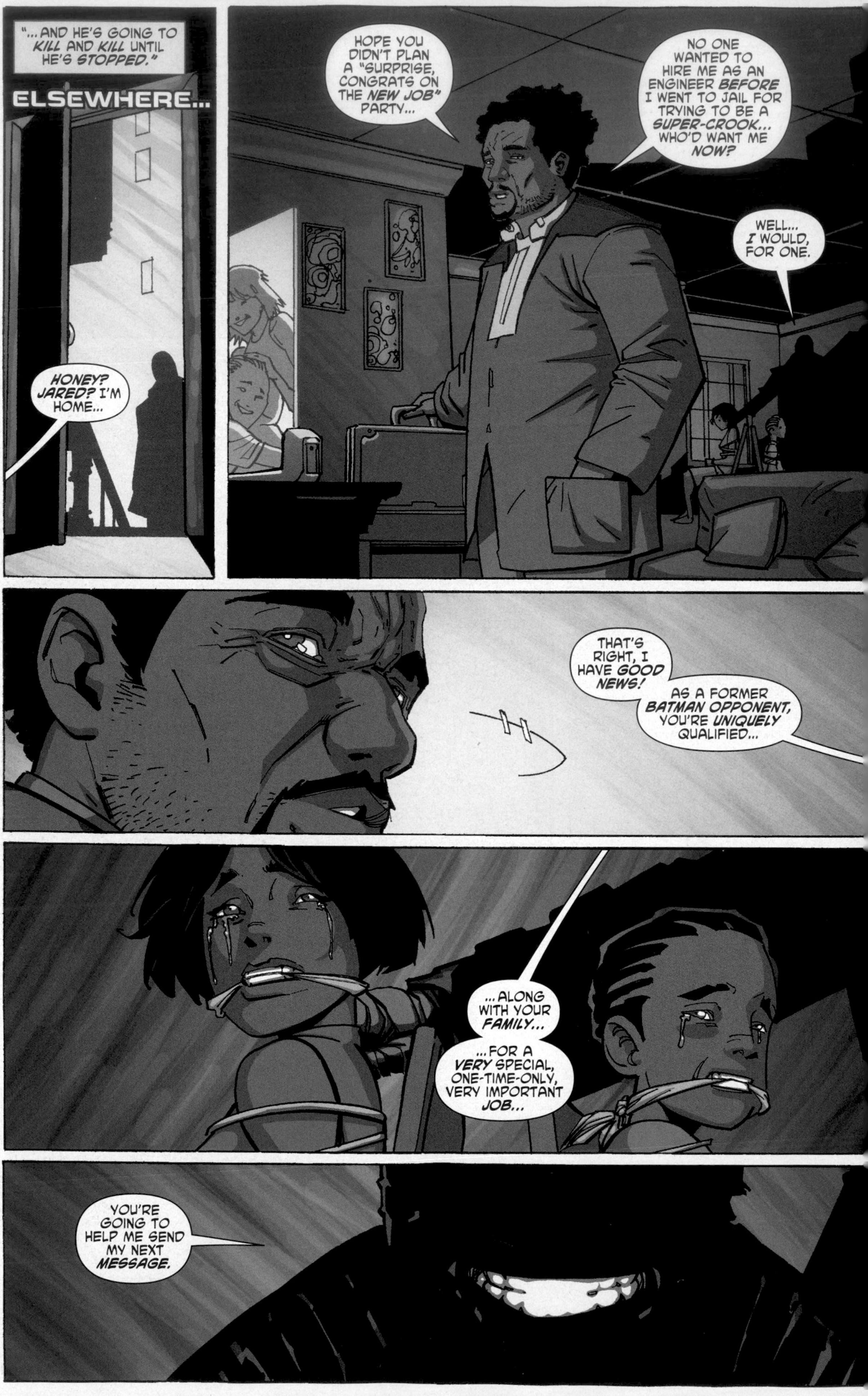
"...AND HE'S GOING TO KILL AND KILL UNTIL HE'S STOPPED."
ELSEWHERE...
HONEY? JARED? I'M HOME...
HOPE YOU DIDN'T PLAN A "SURPRISE, CONGRATS ON THE NEW JOB" PARTY...
NO ONE WANTED TO HIRE ME AS AN ENGINEER BEFORE I WENT TO JAIL FOR TRYING TO BE A SUPER-CROOK... WHO'D WANT ME NOW?
WELL... I WOULD, FOR ONE.
THAT'S RIGHT, I HAVE GOOD NEWS!
AS A FORMER BATMAN OPPONENT, YOU'RE UNIQUELY QUALIFIED...
...ALONG WITH YOUR FAMILY...
...FOR A VERY SPECIAL, ONE-TIME-ONLY, VERY IMPORTANT JOB...
YOU'RE GOING TO HELP ME SEND MY NEXT MESSAGE.

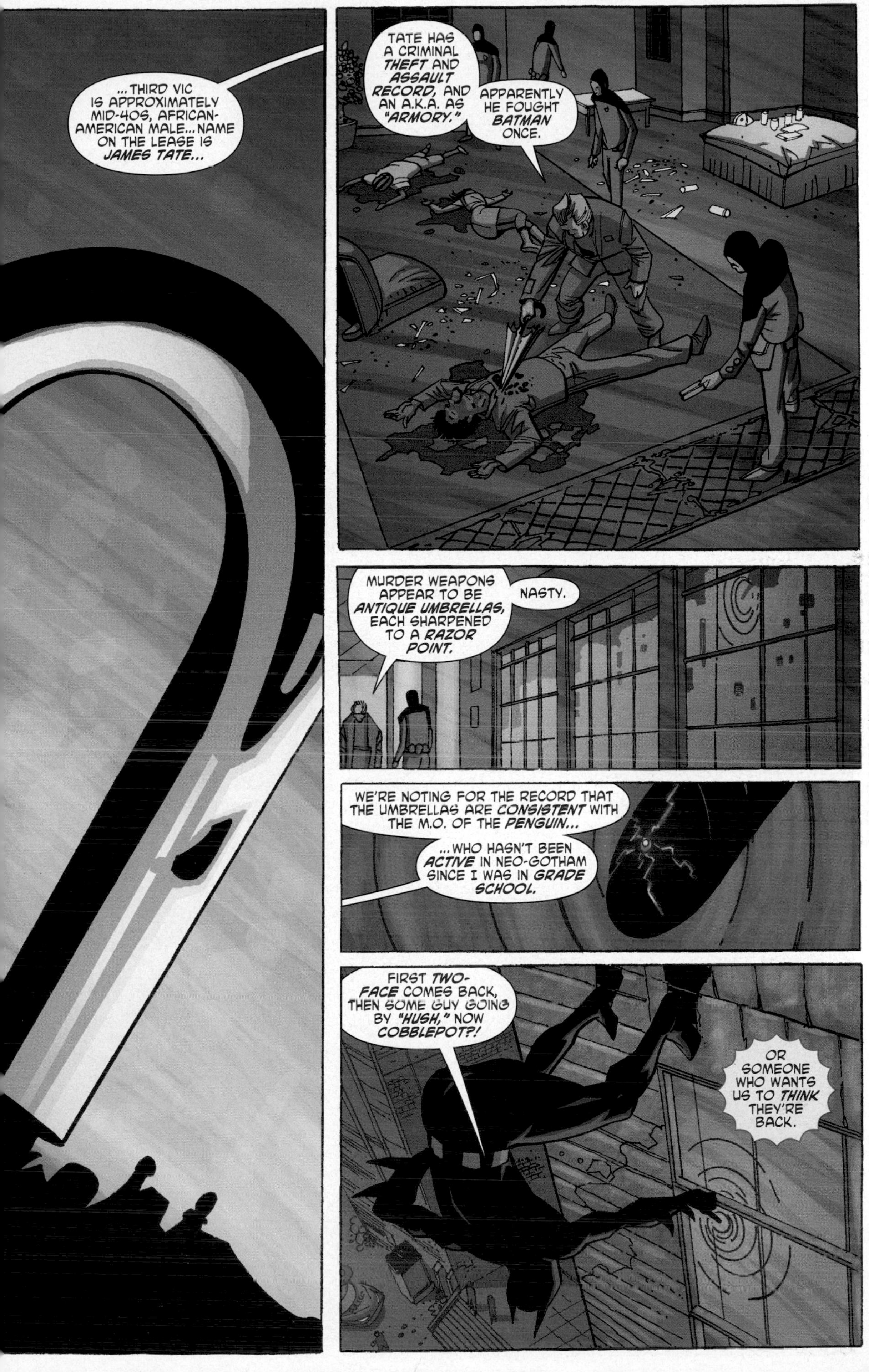
...THIRD VIC IS APPROXIMATELY MID-40S, AFRICAN-AMERICAN MALE...NAME ON THE LEASE IS JAMES TATE...
TATE HAS A CRIMINAL THEFT AND ASSAULT RECORD, AND AN A.K.A. AS "ARMORY."
APPARENTLY HE FOUGHT BATMAN ONCE.
MURDER WEAPONS APPEAR TO BE ANTIQUE UMBRELLAS, EACH SHARPENED TO A RAZOR POINT.
NASTY.
WE'RE NOTING FOR THE RECORD THAT THE UMBRELLAS ARE CONSISTENT WITH THE M.O. OF THE PENGUIN...
...WHO HASN'T BEEN ACTIVE IN NEO-GOTHAM SINCE I WAS IN GRADE SCHOOL.
FIRST TWO-FACE COMES BACK, THEN SOME GUY GOING BY "HUSH," NOW COBBLEPOT?!
OR SOMEONE WHO WANTS US TO THINK THEY'RE BACK.

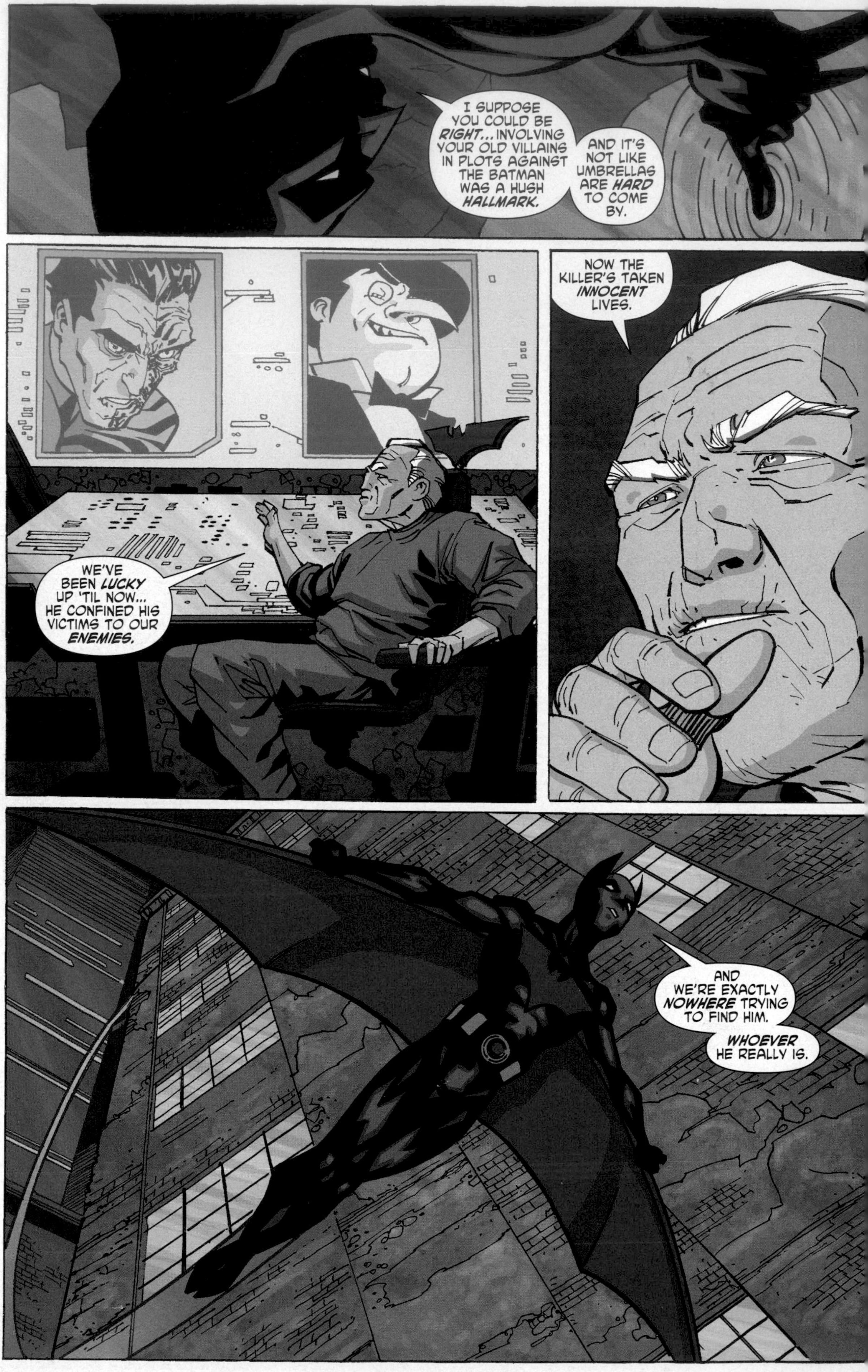
I SUPPOSE YOU COULD BE RIGHT... INVOLVING YOUR OLD VILLAINS IN PLOTS AGAINST THE BATMAN WAS A HUSH HALLMARK.
AND IT'S NOT LIKE UMBRELLAS ARE HARD TO COME BY.
WE'VE BEEN LUCKY UP 'TIL NOW... HE CONFINED HIS VICTIMS TO OUR ENEMIES.
NOW THE KILLER'S TAKEN INNOCENT LIVES.
AND WE'RE EXACTLY NOWHERE TRYING TO FIND HIM.
WHOEVER HE REALLY IS.

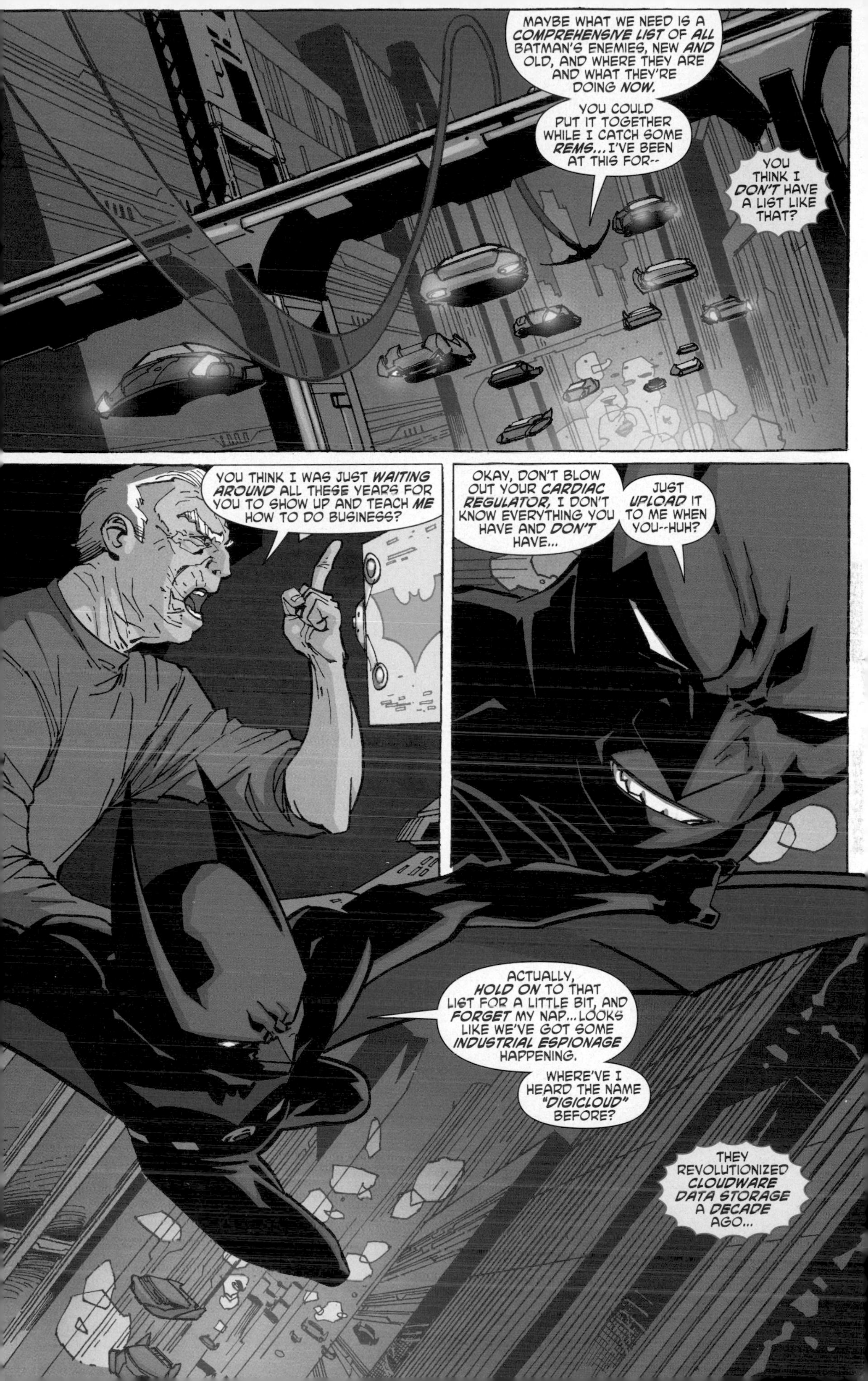
MAYBE WHAT WE NEED IS A COMPREHENSIVE LIST OF ALL BATMAN'S ENEMIES, NEW AND OLD, AND WHERE THEY ARE AND WHAT THEY'RE DOING NOW.
YOU COULD PUT IT TOGETHER WHILE I CATCH SOME REMS... I'VE BEEN AT THIS FOR--
YOU THINK I DON'T HAVE A LIST LIKE THAT?
YOU THINK I WAS JUST WAITING AROUND ALL THESE YEARS FOR YOU TO SHOW UP AND TEACH ME HOW TO DO BUSINESS?
OKAY, DON'T BLOW OUT YOUR CARDIAC REGULATOR, I DON'T KNOW EVERYTHING YOU HAVE AND DON'T HAVE...
JUST UPLOAD IT TO ME WHEN YOU--HUH?
ACTUALLY, HOLD ON TO THAT LIST FOR A LITTLE BIT, AND FORGET MY NAP... LOOKS LIKE WE'VE GOT SOME INDUSTRIAL ESPIONAGE HAPPENING.
WHERE'VE I HEARD THE NAME "DIGICLOUD" BEFORE?
THEY REVOLUTIONIZED CLOUDWARE DATA STORAGE A DECADE AGO...

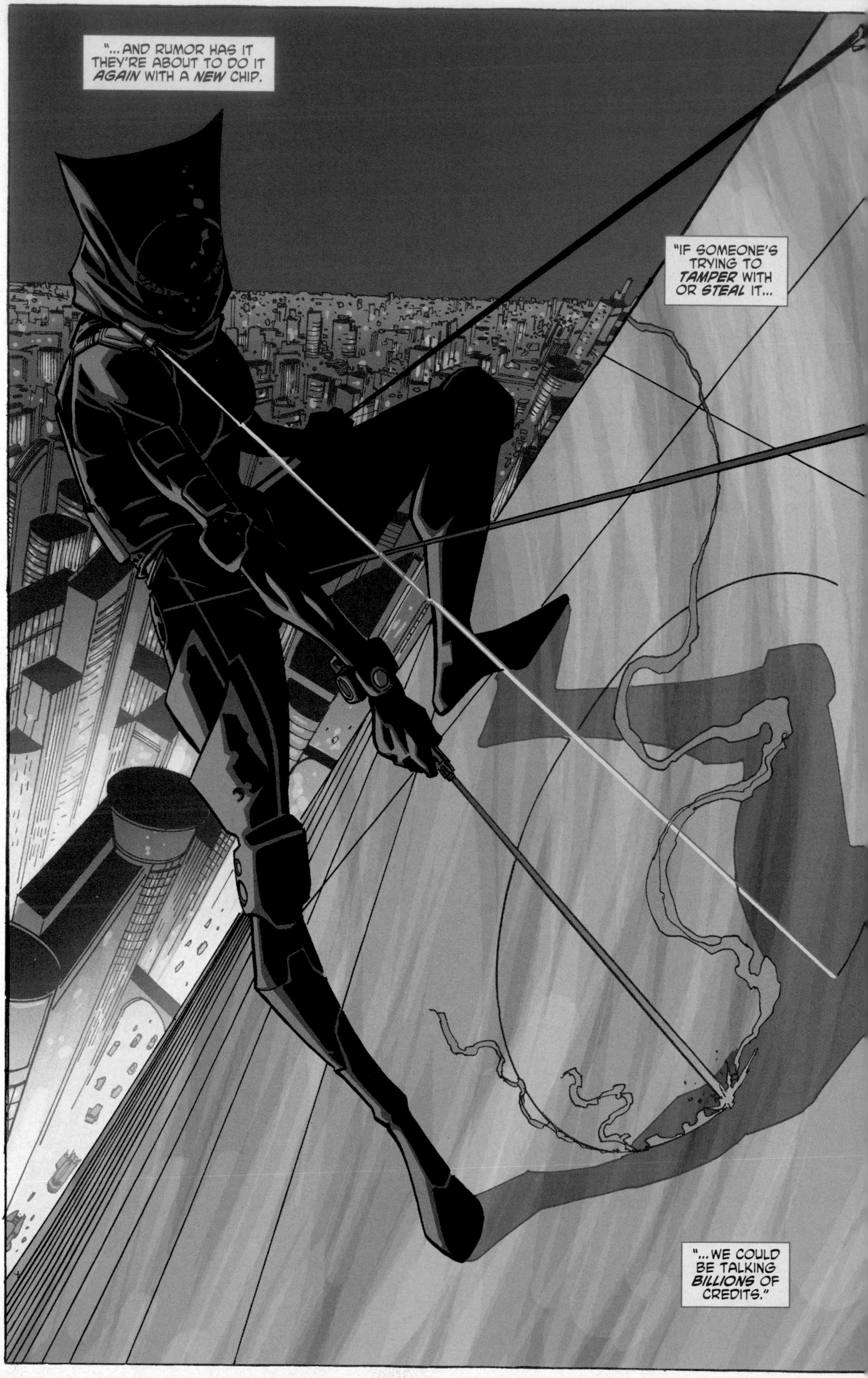
"...AND RUMOR HAS IT THEY'RE ABOUT TO DO IT *AGAIN* WITH A *NEW* CHIP.
"IF SOMEONE'S TRYING TO *TAMPER* WITH OR *STEAL* IT...
"...WE COULD BE TALKING *BILLIONS* OF CREDITS."

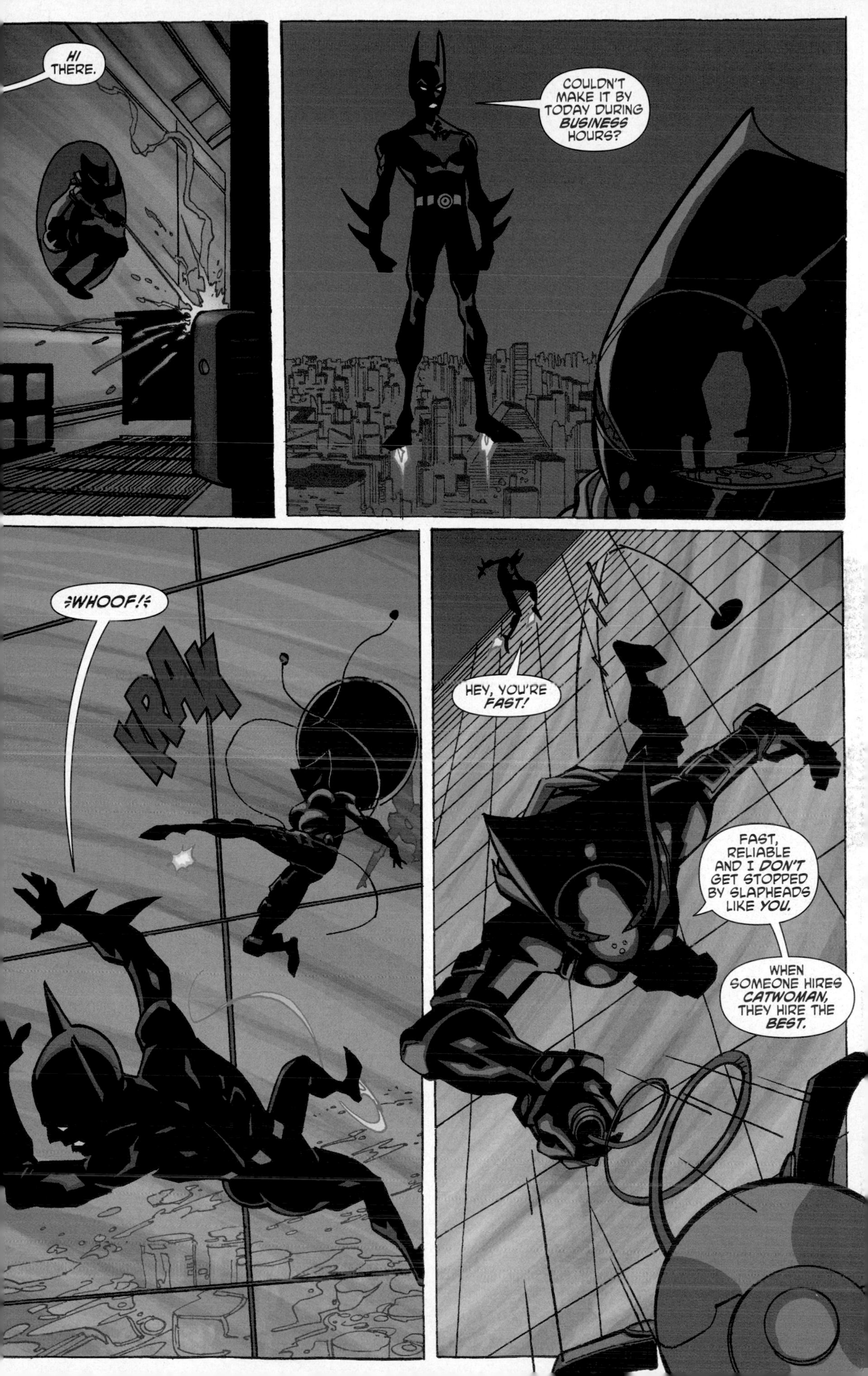
HI THERE.
COULDN'T MAKE IT BY TODAY DURING BUSINESS HOURS?
WHOOF!
KRAK
HEY, YOU'RE FAST!
FAST, RELIABLE AND I DON'T GET STOPPED BY SLAPHEADS LIKE YOU.
WHEN SOMEONE HIRES CATWOMAN, THEY HIRE THE BEST.

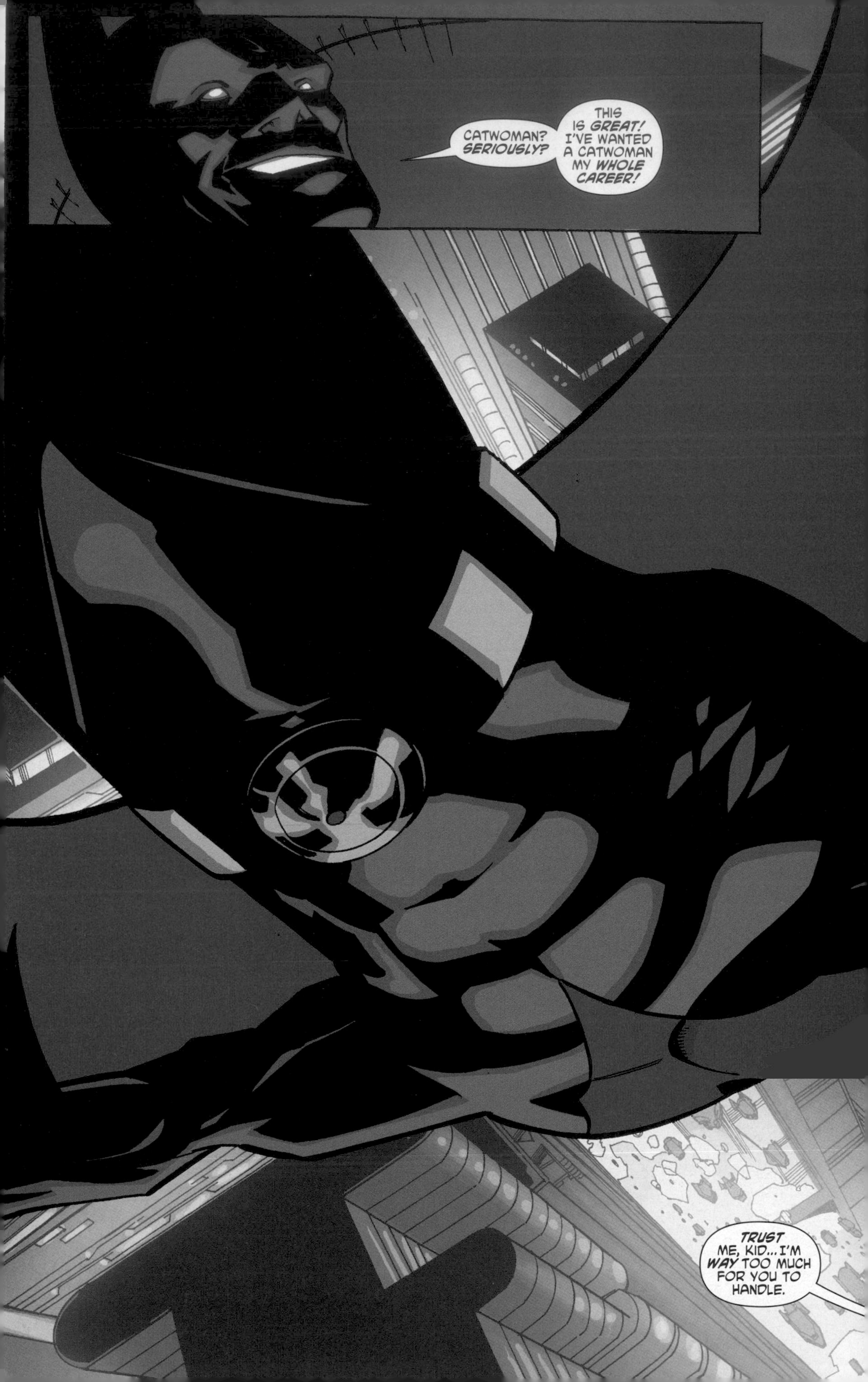
CATWOMAN? SERIOUSLY?
THIS IS GREAT! I'VE WANTED A CATWOMAN MY WHOLE CAREER!
TRUST ME, KID... I'M WAY TOO MUCH FOR YOU TO HANDLE.

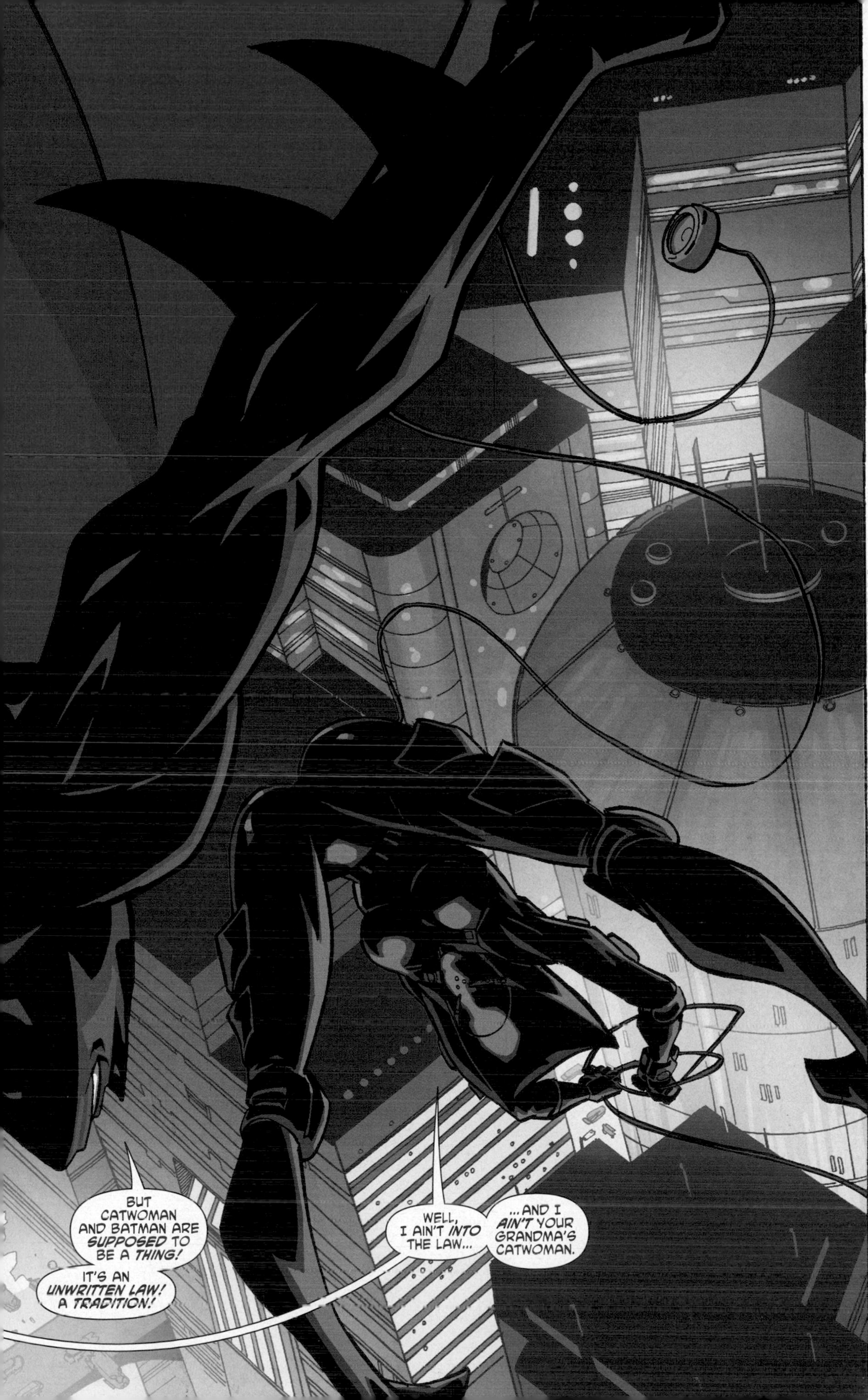
BUT CATWOMAN AND BATMAN ARE SUPPOSED TO BE A THING!
IT'S AN UNWRITTEN LAW! A TRADITION!
WELL, I AIN'T INTO THE LAW...
...AND I AIN'T YOUR GRANDMA'S CATWOMAN.

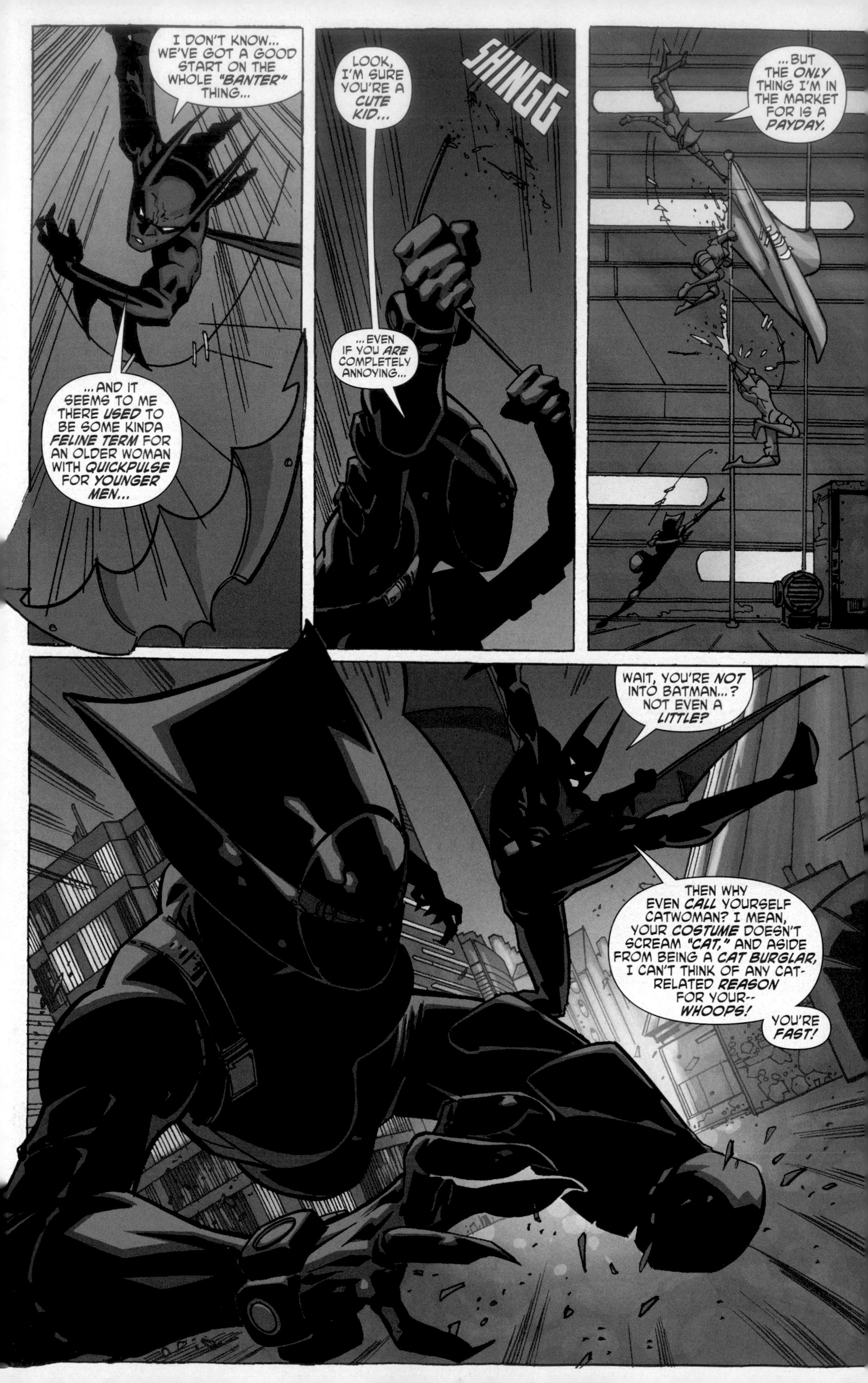
I DON'T KNOW... WE'VE GOT A GOOD START ON THE WHOLE "BANTER" THING...
...AND IT SEEMS TO ME THERE USED TO BE SOME KINDA FELINE TERM FOR AN OLDER WOMAN WITH QUICKPULSE FOR YOUNGER MEN...
LOOK, I'M SURE YOU'RE A CUTE KID...
SHINGG
...EVEN IF YOU ARE COMPLETELY ANNOYING...
...BUT THE ONLY THING I'M IN THE MARKET FOR IS A PAYDAY.
WAIT, YOU'RE NOT INTO BATMAN...? NOT EVEN A LITTLE?
THEN WHY EVEN CALL YOURSELF CATWOMAN? I MEAN, YOUR COSTUME DOESN'T SCREAM "CAT," AND ASIDE FROM BEING A CAT BURGLAR, I CAN'T THINK OF ANY CAT-RELATED REASON FOR YOUR-- WHOOPS!
YOU'RE FAST!

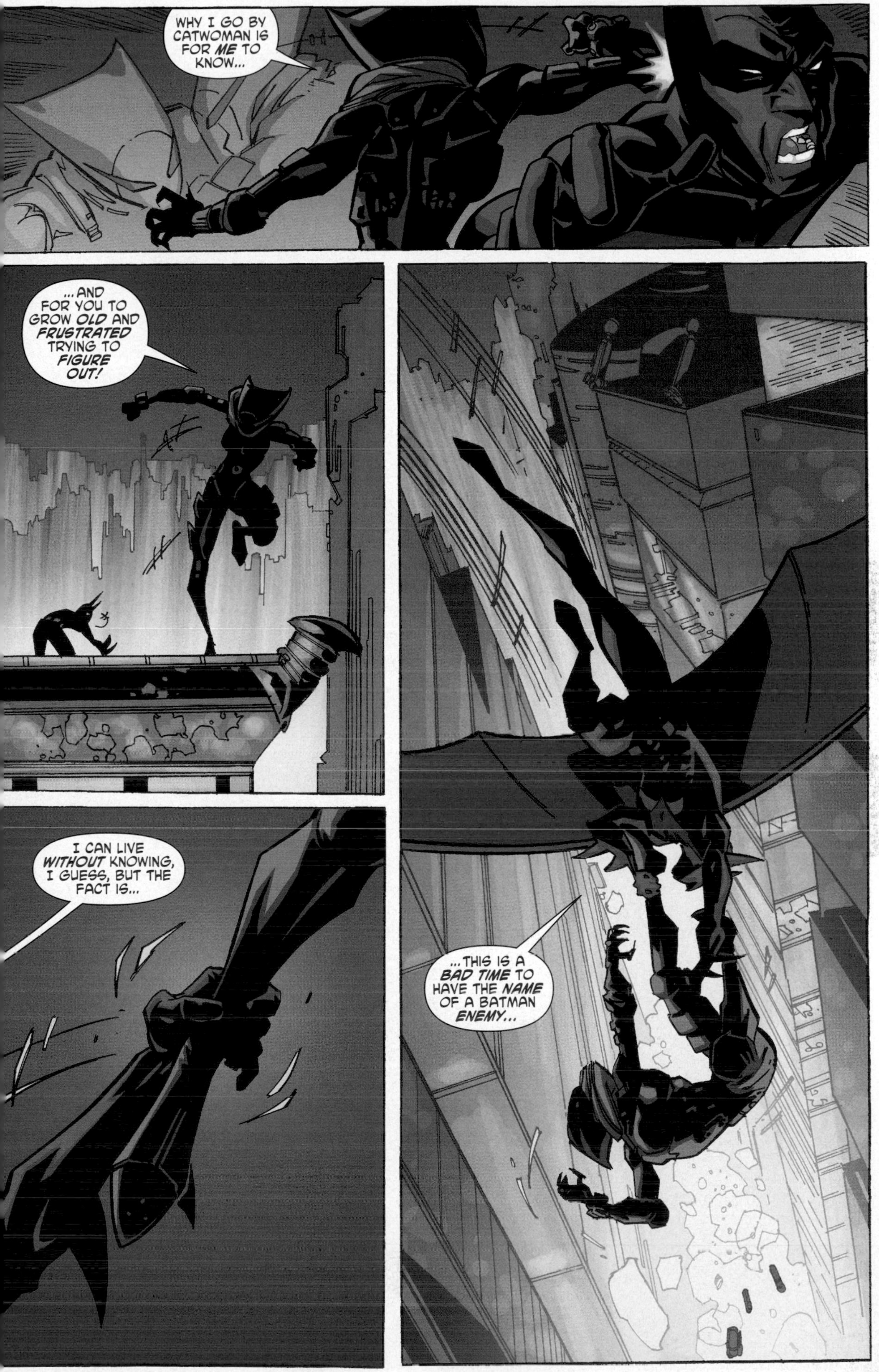
WHY I GO BY CATWOMAN IS FOR ME TO KNOW...
...AND FOR YOU TO GROW OLD AND FRUSTRATED TRYING TO FIGURE OUT!
I CAN LIVE WITHOUT KNOWING, I GUESS, BUT THE FACT IS...
...THIS IS A BAD TIME TO HAVE THE NAME OF A BATMAN ENEMY...

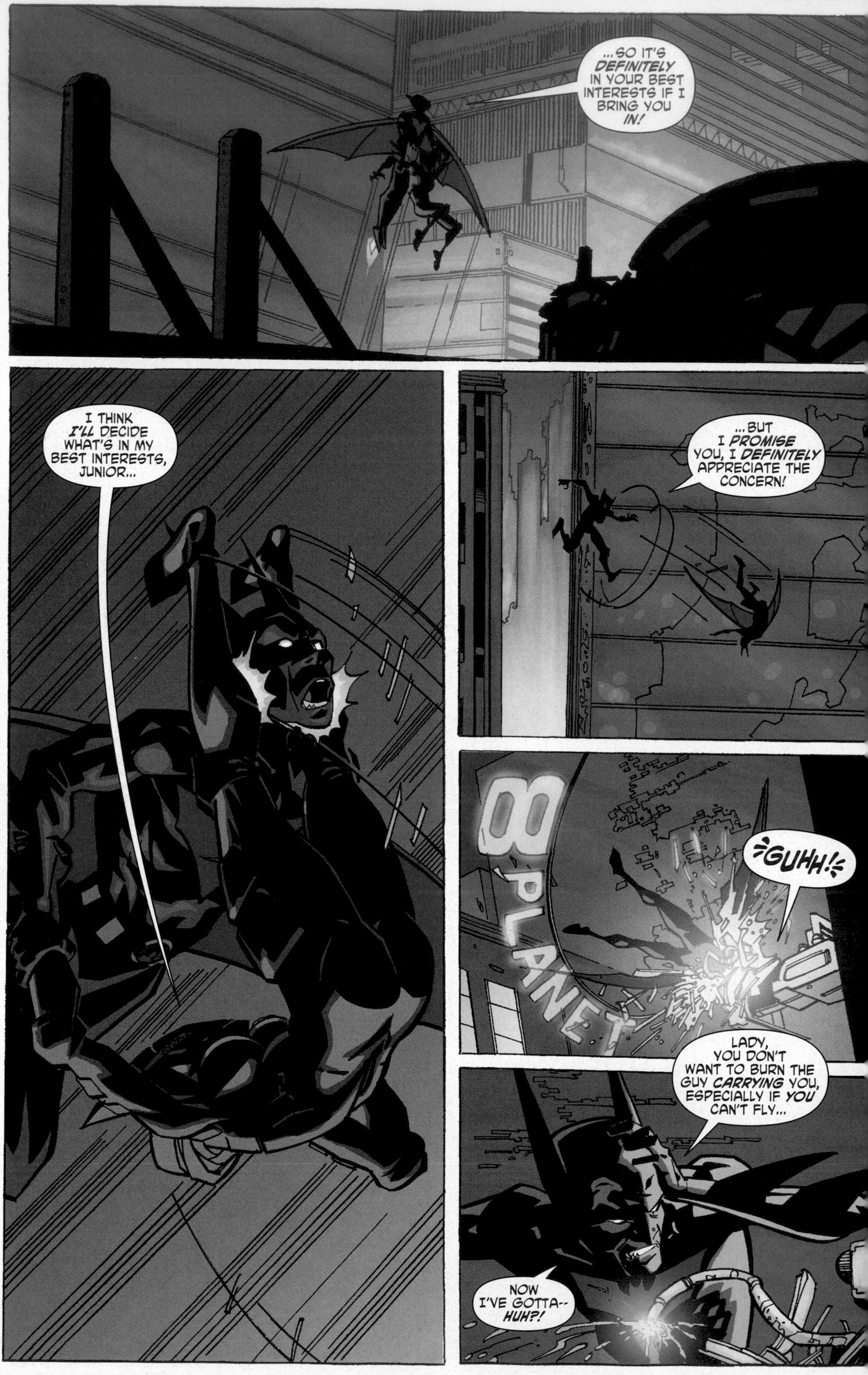
...SO IT'S DEFINITELY IN YOUR BEST INTERESTS IF I BRING YOU IN!
I THINK I'LL DECIDE WHAT'S IN MY BEST INTERESTS, JUNIOR...
...BUT I PROMISE YOU, I DEFINITELY APPRECIATE THE CONCERN!
PLANET
GUHH!
LADY, YOU DON'T WANT TO BURN THE GUY CARRYING YOU, ESPECIALLY IF YOU CAN'T FLY...
NOW I'VE GOTTA-- HUH?!

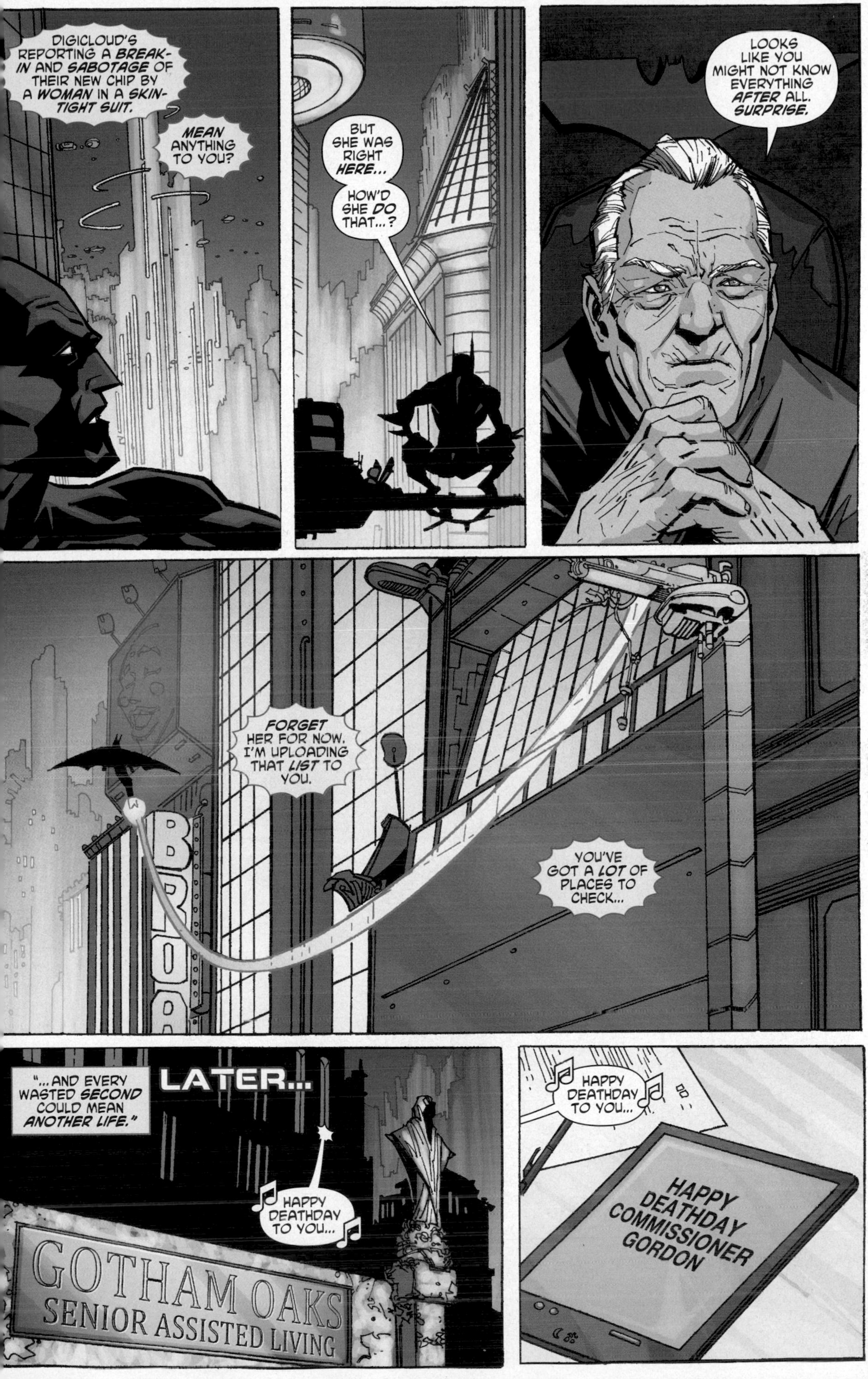
DIGICLOUD'S REPORTING A BREAK-IN AND SABOTAGE OF THEIR NEW CHIP BY A WOMAN IN A SKIN-TIGHT SUIT.
MEAN ANYTHING TO YOU?
BUT SHE WAS RIGHT HERE...
HOW'D SHE DO THAT...?
LOOKS LIKE YOU MIGHT NOT KNOW EVERYTHING AFTER ALL. SURPRISE.
FORGET HER FOR NOW. I'M UPLOADING THAT LIST TO YOU.
YOU'VE GOT A LOT OF PLACES TO CHECK...
"...AND EVERY WASTED SECOND COULD MEAN ANOTHER LIFE."
LATER...
HAPPY DEATHDAY TO YOU...
GOTHAM OAKS
SENIOR ASSISTED LIVING
HAPPY DEATHDAY TO YOU...
HAPPY DEATHDAY COMMISSIONER GORDON

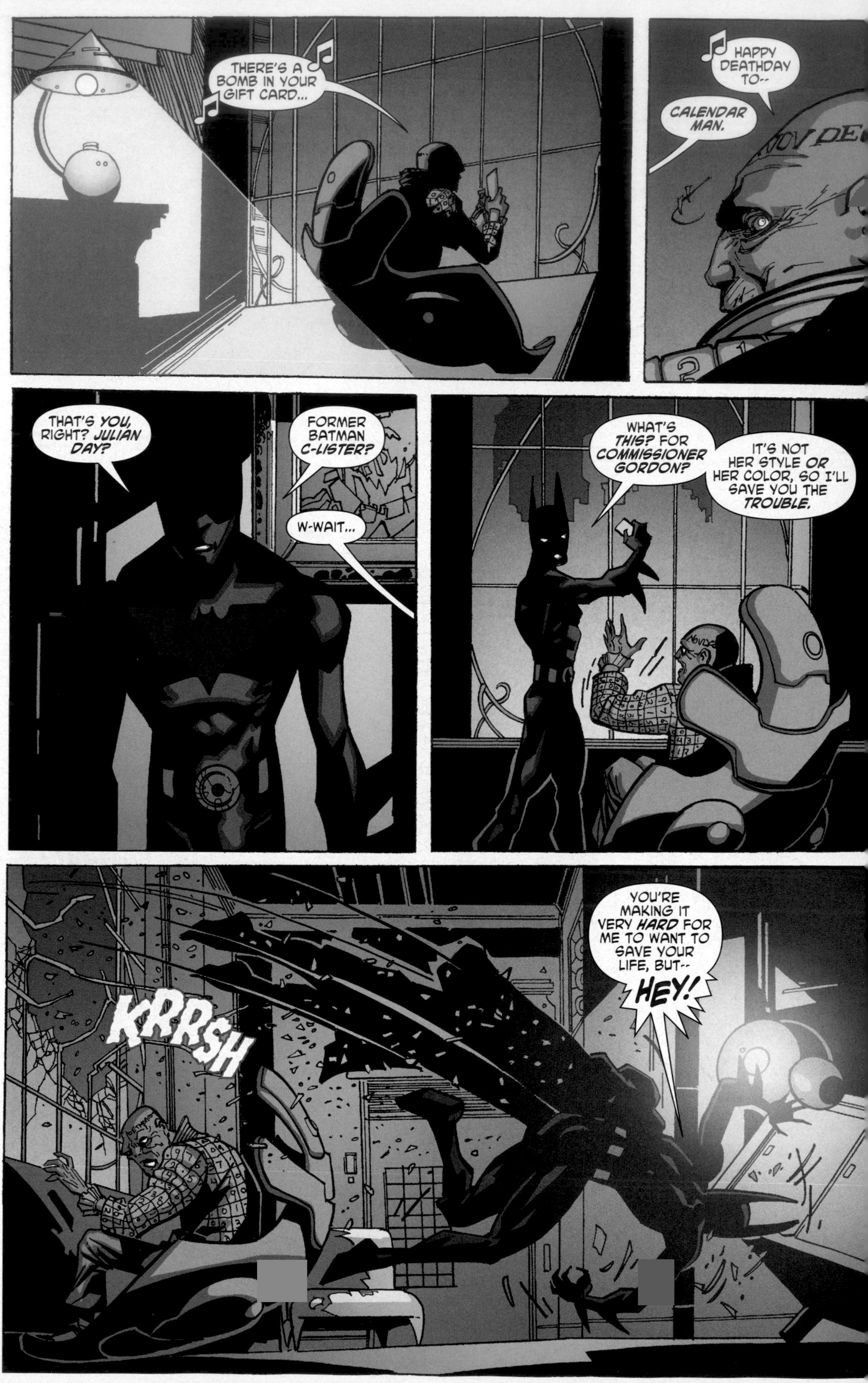
THERE'S A BOMB IN YOUR GIFT CARD...
HAPPY DEATHDAY TO--
CALENDAR MAN.
THAT'S YOU, RIGHT? JULIAN DAY?
FORMER BATMAN C-LISTER?
W-WAIT...
WHAT'S THIS? FOR COMMISSIONER GORDON?
IT'S NOT HER STYLE OR HER COLOR, SO I'LL SAVE YOU THE TROUBLE.
KRRSH
YOU'RE MAKING IT VERY HARD FOR ME TO WANT TO SAVE YOUR LIFE, BUT--
HEY!

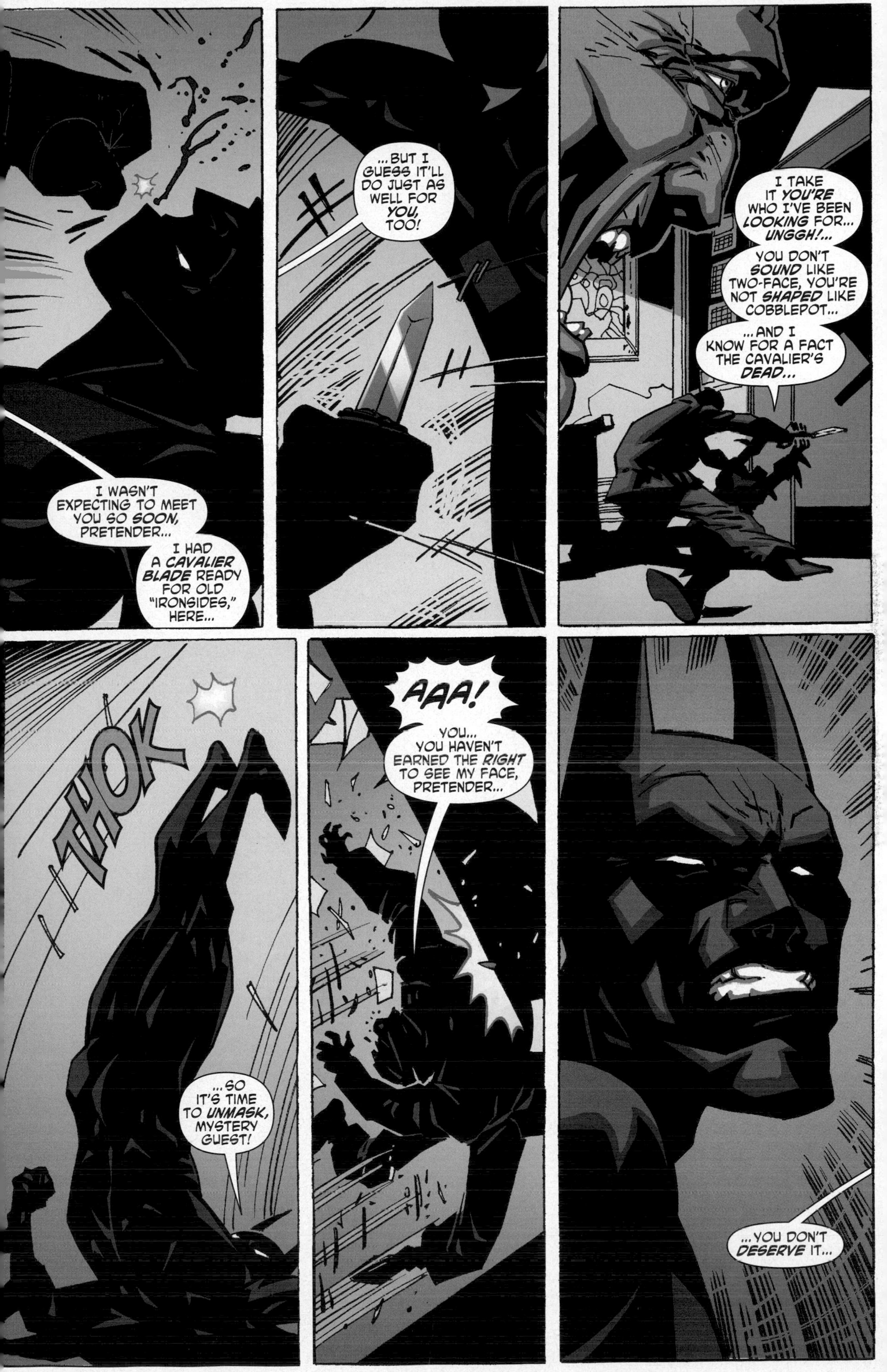
I WASN'T EXPECTING TO MEET YOU SO SOON, PRETENDER...
I HAD A CAVALIER BLADE READY FOR OLD "IRONSIDES," HERE...
...BUT I GUESS IT'LL DO JUST AS WELL FOR YOU, TOO!
I TAKE IT YOU'RE WHO I'VE BEEN LOOKING FOR... UNGGH!...
YOU DON'T SOUND LIKE TWO-FACE, YOU'RE NOT SHAPED LIKE COBBLEPOT...
...AND I KNOW FOR A FACT THE CAVALIER'S DEAD...
THOK
...SO IT'S TIME TO UNMASK, MYSTERY GUEST!
AAA!
YOU... YOU HAVEN'T EARNED THE RIGHT TO SEE MY FACE, PRETENDER...
...YOU DON'T DESERVE IT...

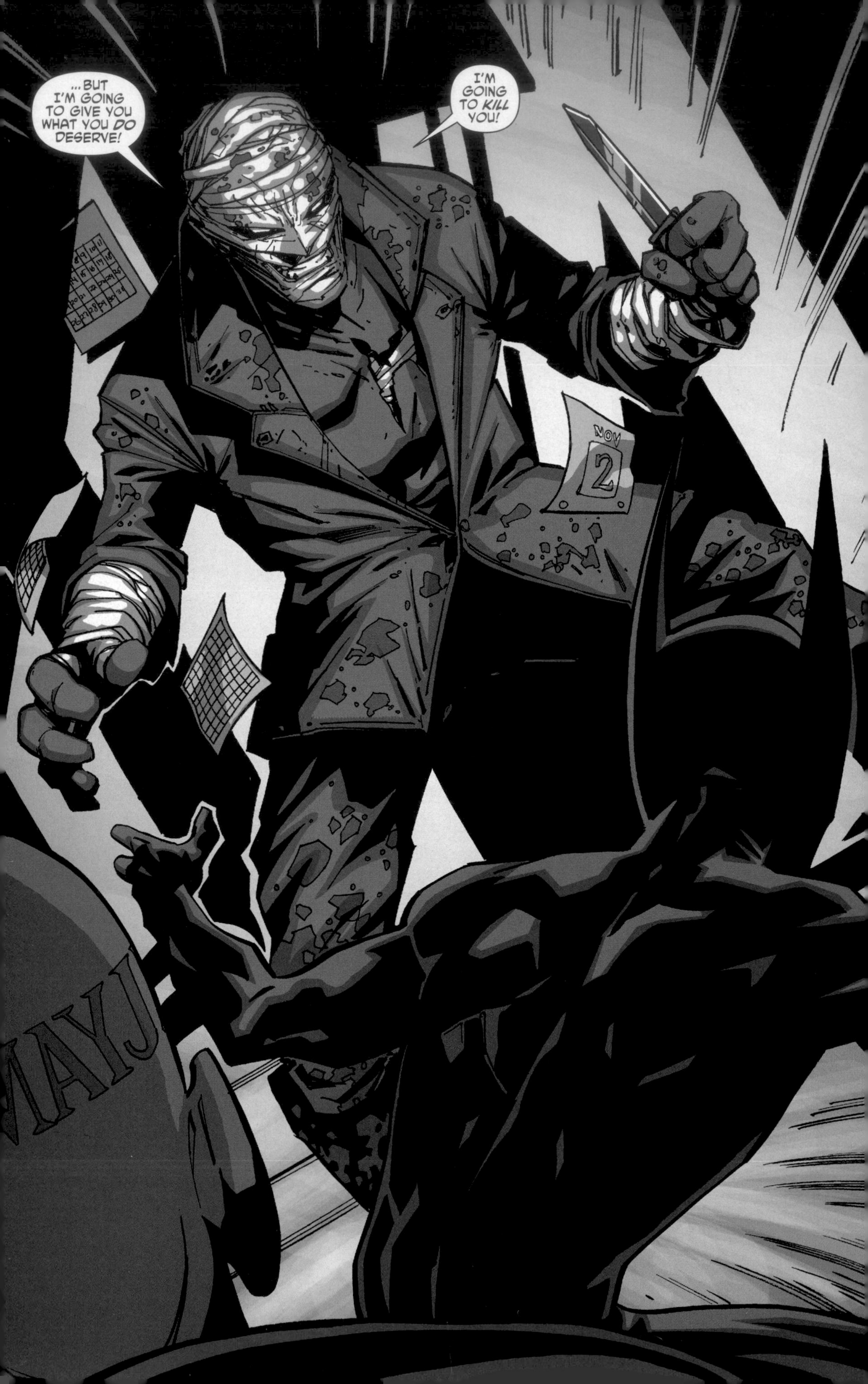
...BUT I'M GOING TO GIVE YOU WHAT YOU DO DESERVE!
I'M GOING TO KILL YOU!
NOV
2
MAY

PART 3: CLOSE ENCOUNTERS

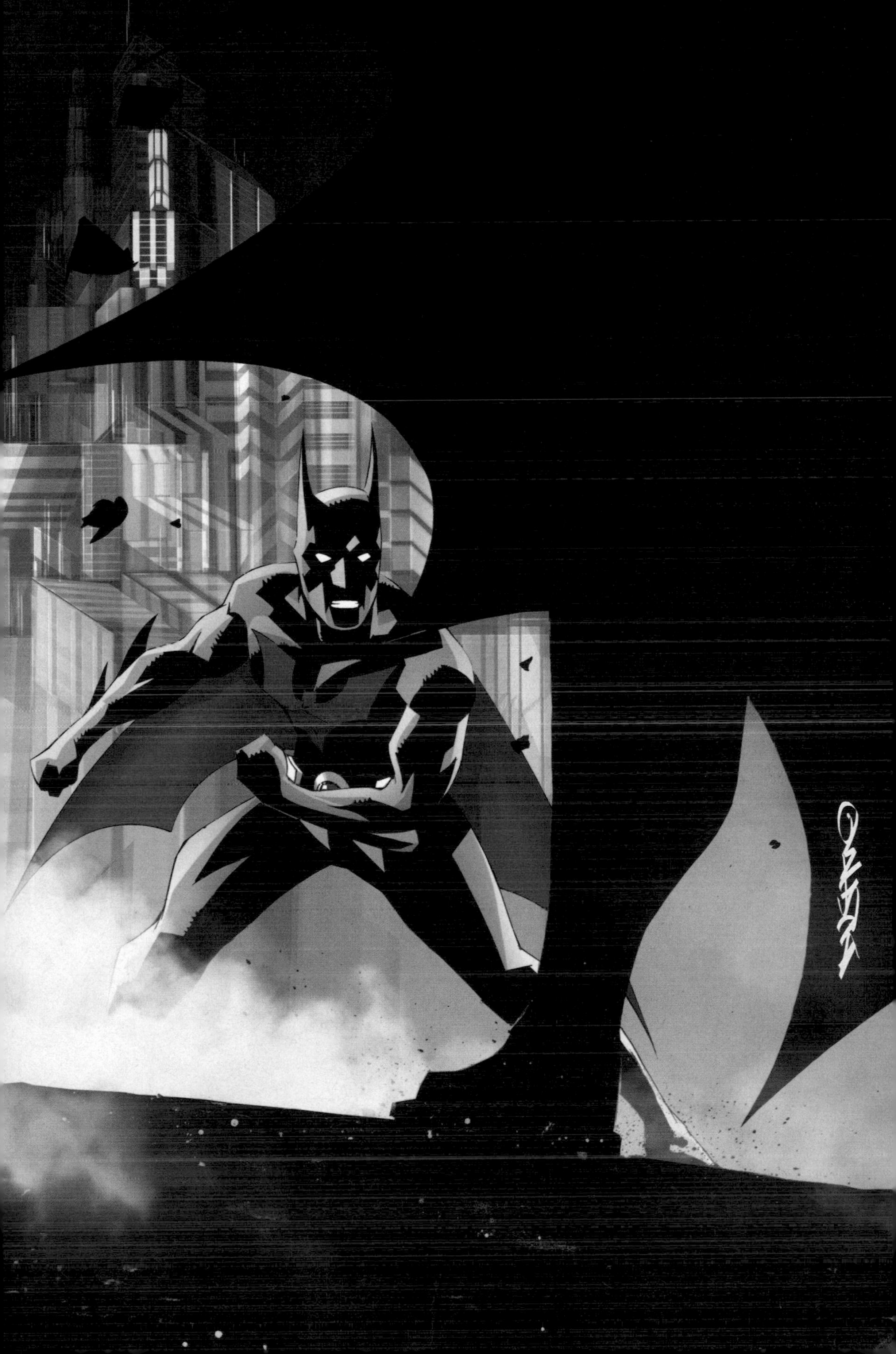

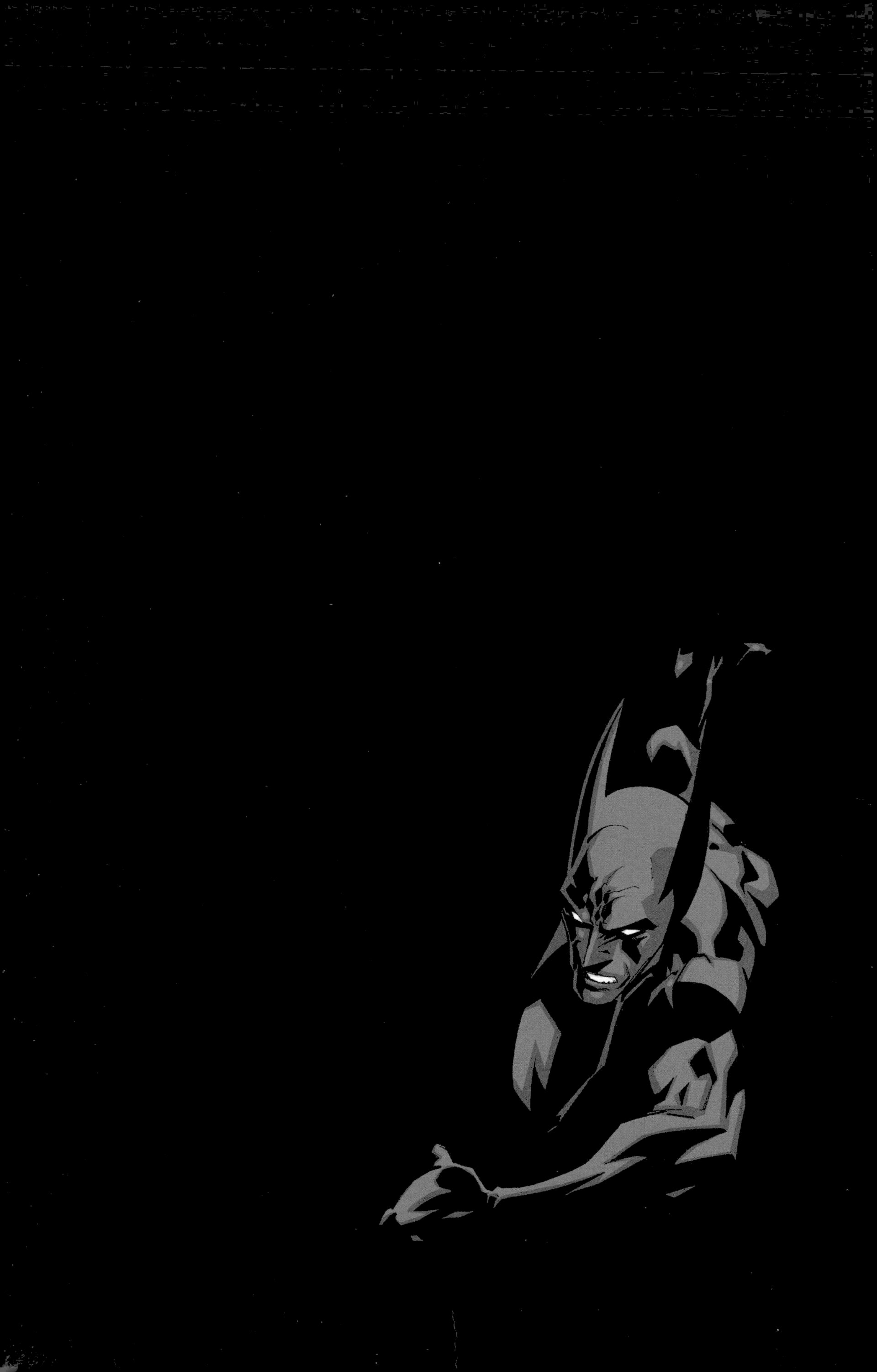

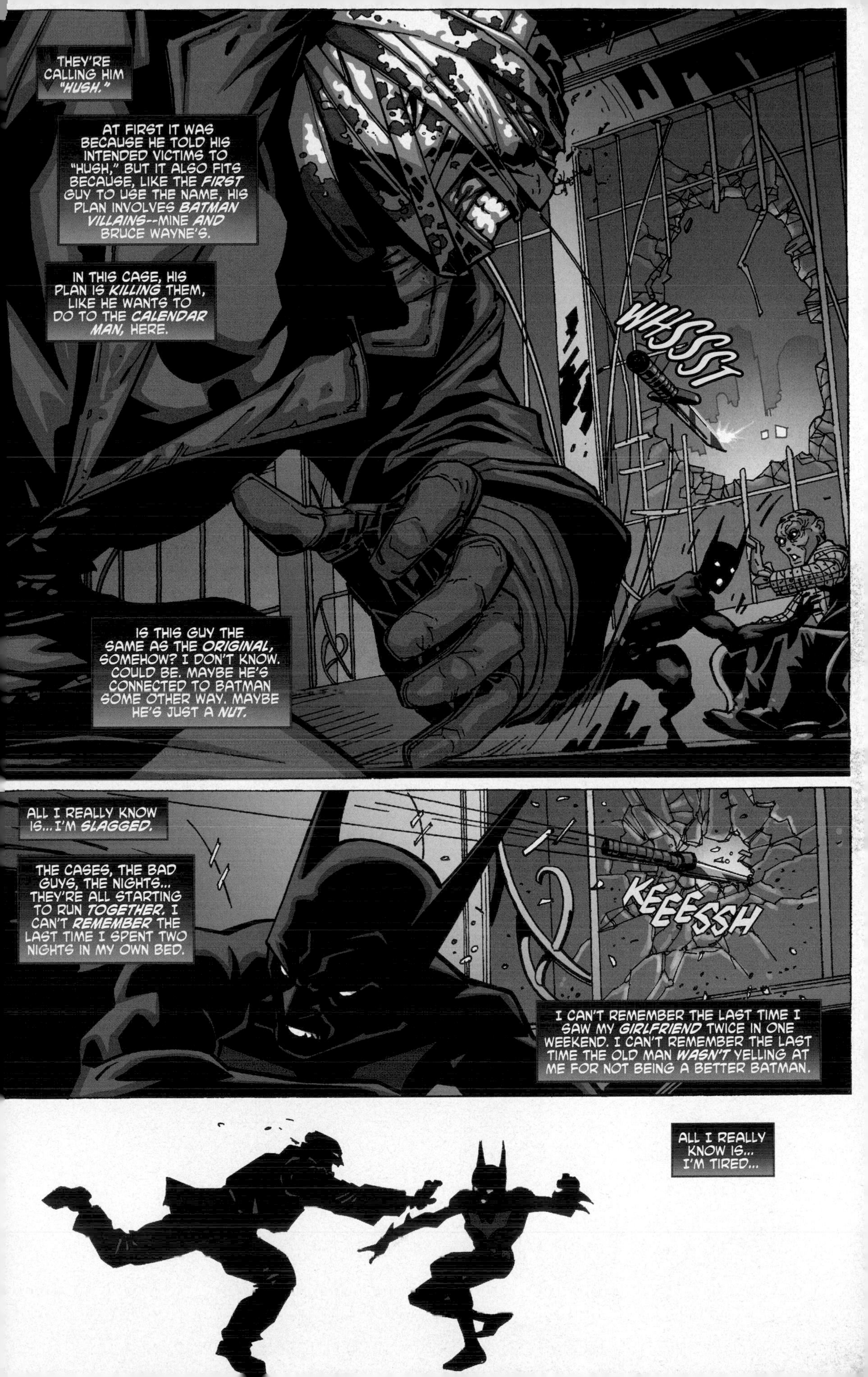

THEY'RE CALLING HIM "HUSH."
AT FIRST IT WAS BECAUSE HE TOLD HIS INTENDED VICTIMS TO "HUSH," BUT IT ALSO FITS BECAUSE, LIKE THE FIRST GUY TO USE THE NAME, HIS PLAN INVOLVES BATMAN VILLAINS--MINE AND BRUCE WAYNE'S.
IN THIS CASE, HIS PLAN IS KILLING THEM, LIKE HE WANTS TO DO TO THE CALENDAR MAN, HERE.
WHSSSST
IS THIS GUY THE SAME AS THE ORIGINAL, SOMEHOW? I DON'T KNOW. COULD BE. MAYBE HE'S CONNECTED TO BATMAN SOME OTHER WAY. MAYBE HE'S JUST A NUT.
ALL I REALLY KNOW IS...I'M SLAGGED.
THE CASES, THE BAD GUYS, THE NIGHTS... THEY'RE ALL STARTING TO RUN TOGETHER. I CAN'T REMEMBER THE LAST TIME I SPENT TWO NIGHTS IN MY OWN BED.
KEEESSH
I CAN'T REMEMBER THE LAST TIME I SAW MY GIRLFRIEND TWICE IN ONE WEEKEND. I CAN'T REMEMBER THE LAST TIME THE OLD MAN WASN'T YELLING AT ME FOR NOT BEING A BETTER BATMAN.
ALL I REALLY KNOW IS... I'M TIRED...

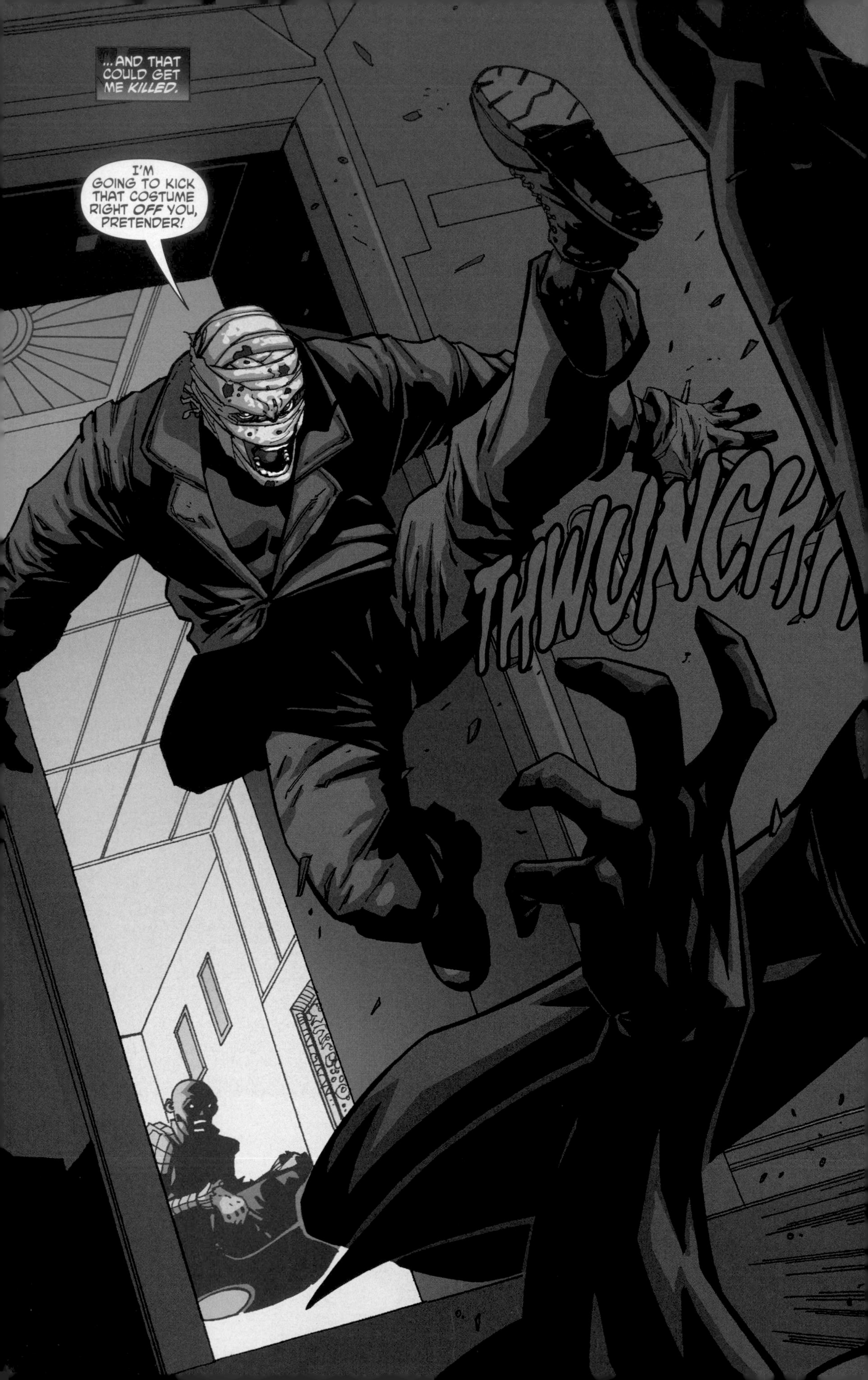
...AND THAT COULD GET ME KILLED.
I'M GOING TO KICK THAT COSTUME RIGHT OFF YOU, PRETENDER!
THWUNCH

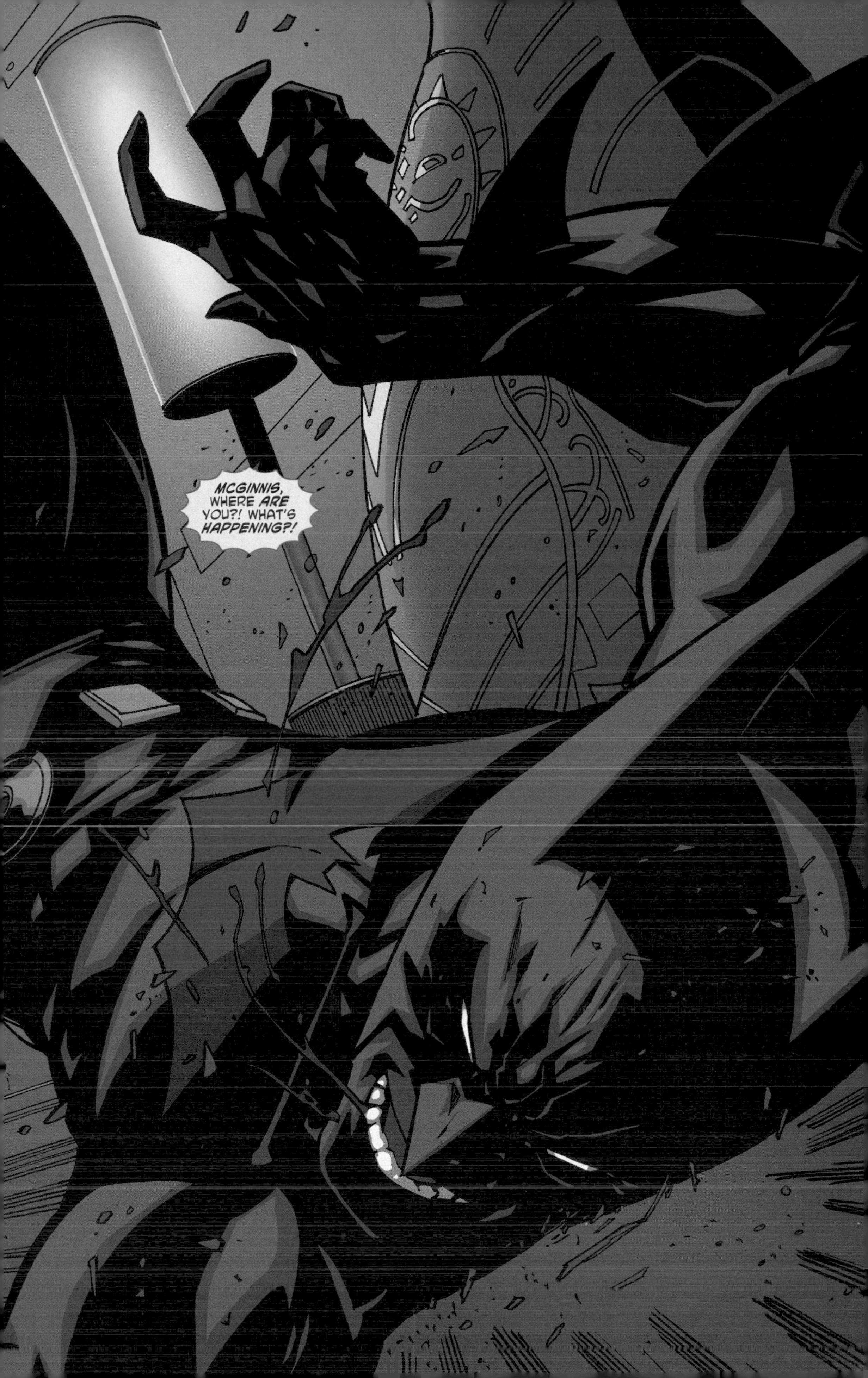
MCGINNIS, WHERE ARE YOU?! WHAT'S HAPPENING?!

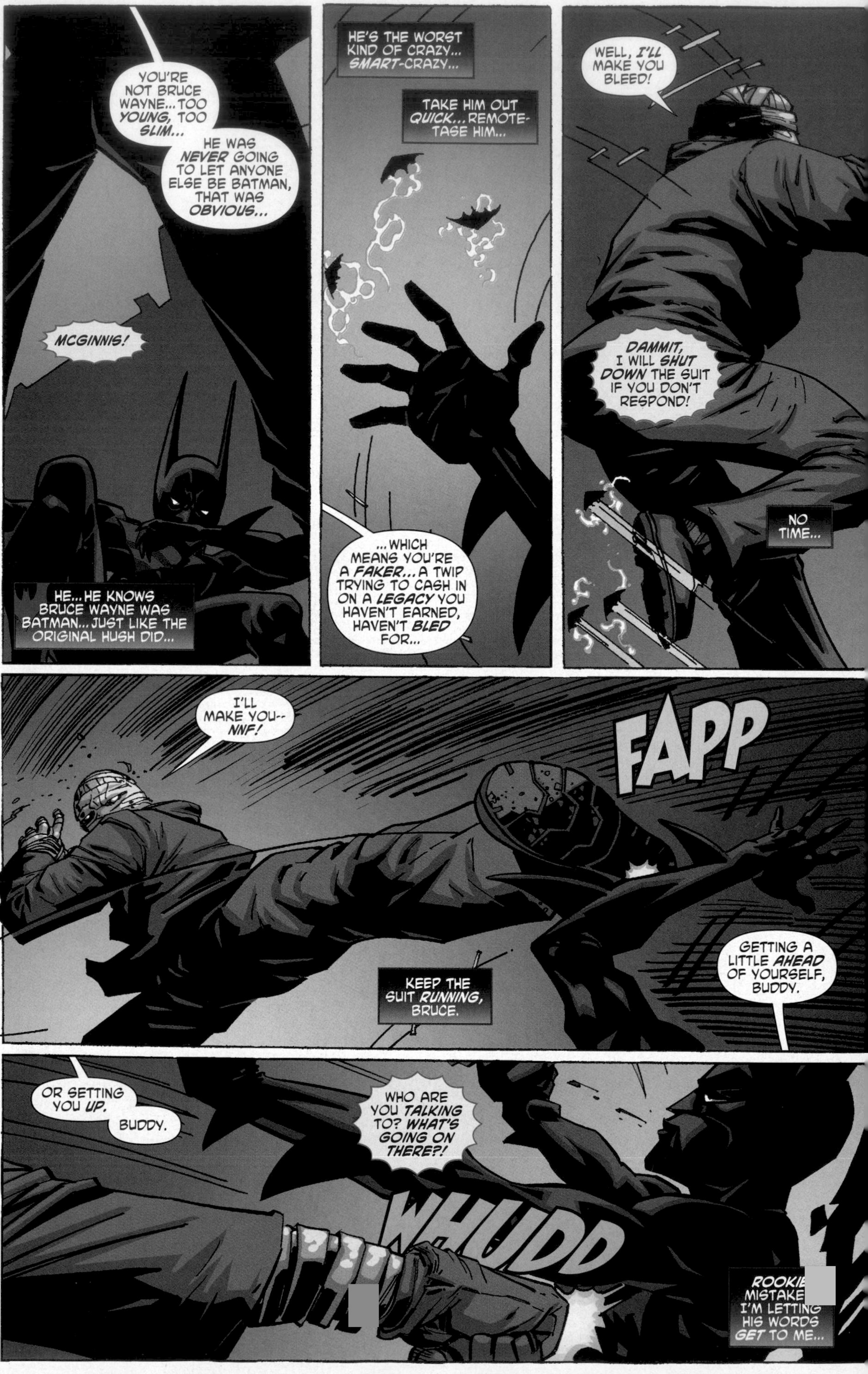

YOU'RE NOT BRUCE WAYNE... TOO *YOUNG*, TOO *SLIM*...
HE WAS *NEVER* GOING TO LET ANYONE ELSE BE BATMAN, THAT WAS *OBVIOUS*...
MCGINNIS!
HE... HE KNOWS BRUCE WAYNE WAS BATMAN... JUST LIKE THE ORIGINAL HUSH DID...
HE'S THE WORST KIND OF CRAZY... *SMART*-CRAZY...
TAKE HIM OUT *QUICK*... REMOTE-TASE HIM...
...WHICH MEANS YOU'RE A *FAKER*... A TWIP TRYING TO CASH IN ON A *LEGACY* YOU HAVEN'T EARNED, HAVEN'T *BLED* FOR...
WELL, *I'LL* MAKE YOU BLEED!
DAMMIT, I WILL *SHUT DOWN* THE SUIT IF YOU DON'T RESPOND!
NO TIME...
I'LL MAKE YOU-- *NNF!*
FAPP
KEEP THE SUIT *RUNNING*, BRUCE.
GETTING A LITTLE *AHEAD* OF YOURSELF, BUDDY.
OR SETTING YOU *UP*.
BUDDY.
WHO ARE YOU *TALKING* TO? *WHAT'S GOING ON THERE?!*
WHUDD
ROOKIE MISTAKE I'M LETTING HIS WORDS *GET* TO ME...

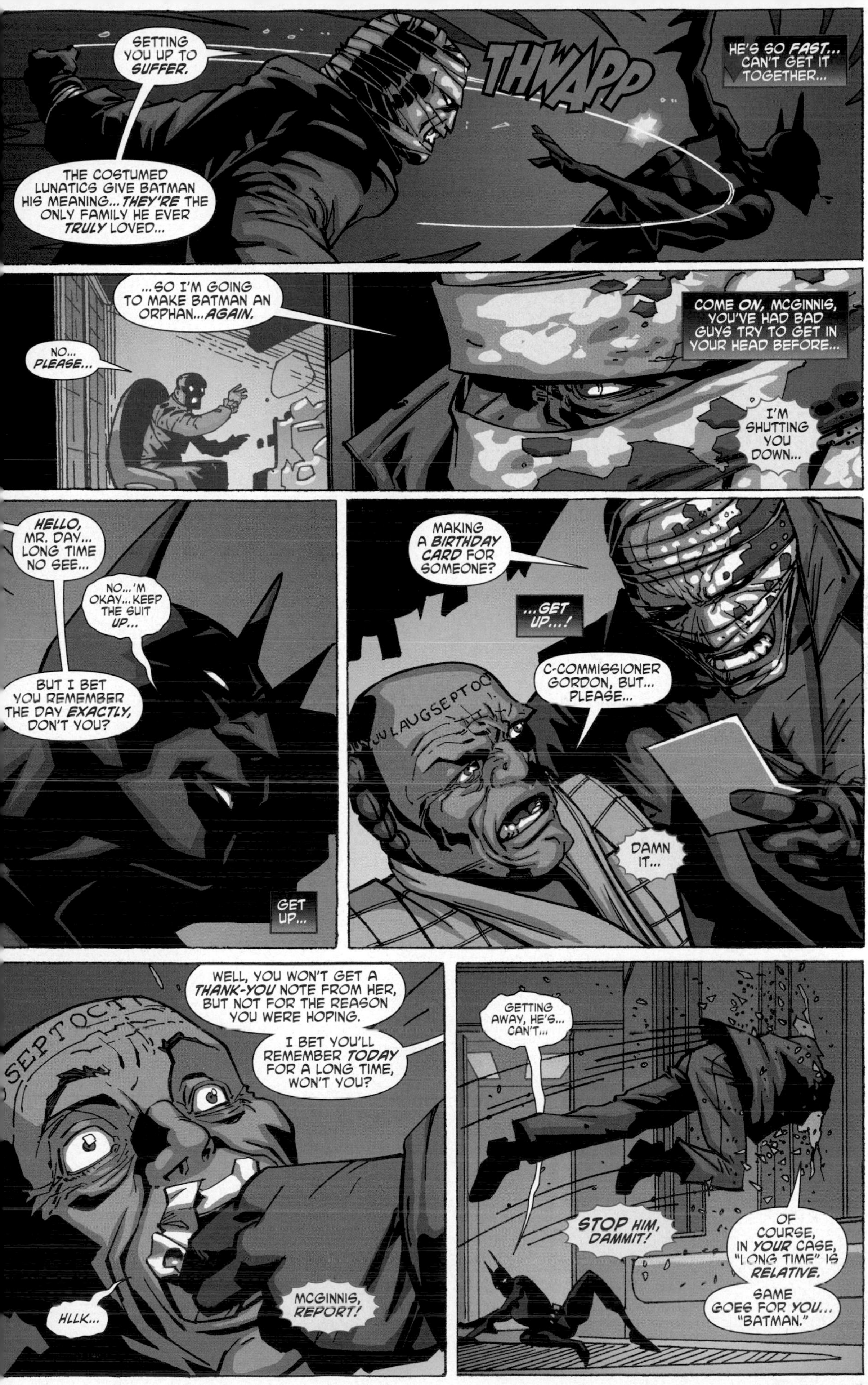
SETTING YOU UP TO SUFFER.
THWAPP
HE'S SO FAST... CAN'T GET IT TOGETHER...
THE COSTUMED LUNATICS GIVE BATMAN HIS MEANING... THEY'RE THE ONLY FAMILY HE EVER TRULY LOVED...
...SO I'M GOING TO MAKE BATMAN AN ORPHAN... AGAIN.
NO... PLEASE...
COME ON, MCGINNIS, YOU'VE HAD BAD GUYS TRY TO GET IN YOUR HEAD BEFORE...
I'M SHUTTING YOU DOWN...
HELLO, MR. DAY... LONG TIME NO SEE...
NO...'M OKAY... KEEP THE SUIT UP...
BUT I BET YOU REMEMBER THE DAY EXACTLY, DON'T YOU?
GET UP...
MAKING A BIRTHDAY CARD FOR SOMEONE?
...GET UP...!
C-COMMISSIONER GORDON, BUT... PLEASE...
DAMN IT...
WELL, YOU WON'T GET A THANK-YOU NOTE FROM HER, BUT NOT FOR THE REASON YOU WERE HOPING.
I BET YOU'LL REMEMBER TODAY FOR A LONG TIME, WON'T YOU?
HLLK...
MCGINNIS, REPORT!
GETTING AWAY, HE'S... CAN'T...
STOP HIM, DAMMIT!
OF COURSE, IN YOUR CASE, "LONG TIME" IS RELATIVE.
SAME GOES FOR YOU... "BATMAN."

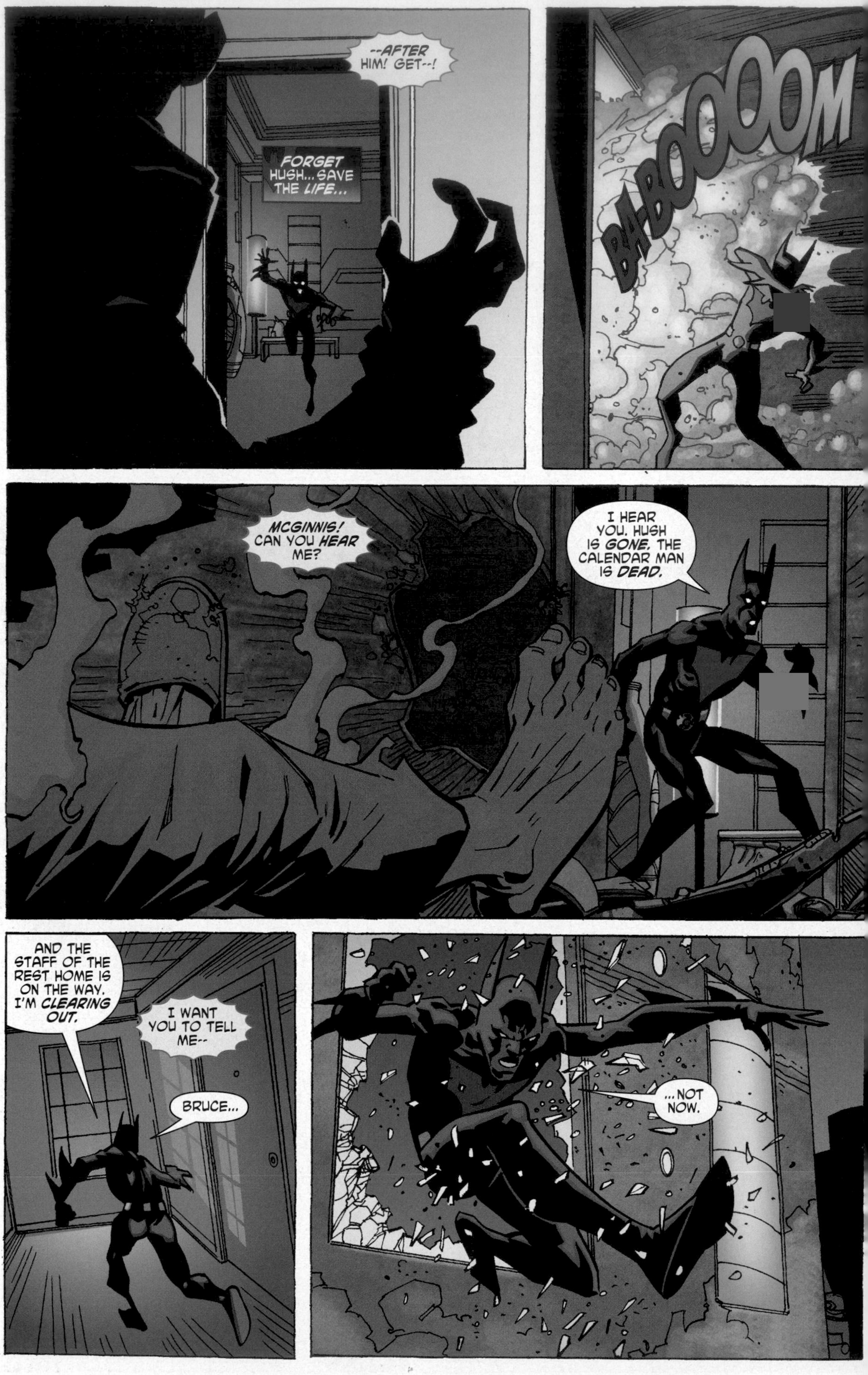
--AFTER HIM! GET--!
FORGET HUSH... SAVE THE LIFE...
BA-BOOOOOM
MCGINNIS! CAN YOU HEAR ME?
I HEAR YOU. HUSH IS GONE. THE CALENDAR MAN IS DEAD.
AND THE STAFF OF THE REST HOME IS ON THE WAY. I'M CLEARING OUT.
I WANT YOU TO TELL ME--
BRUCE...
...NOT NOW.

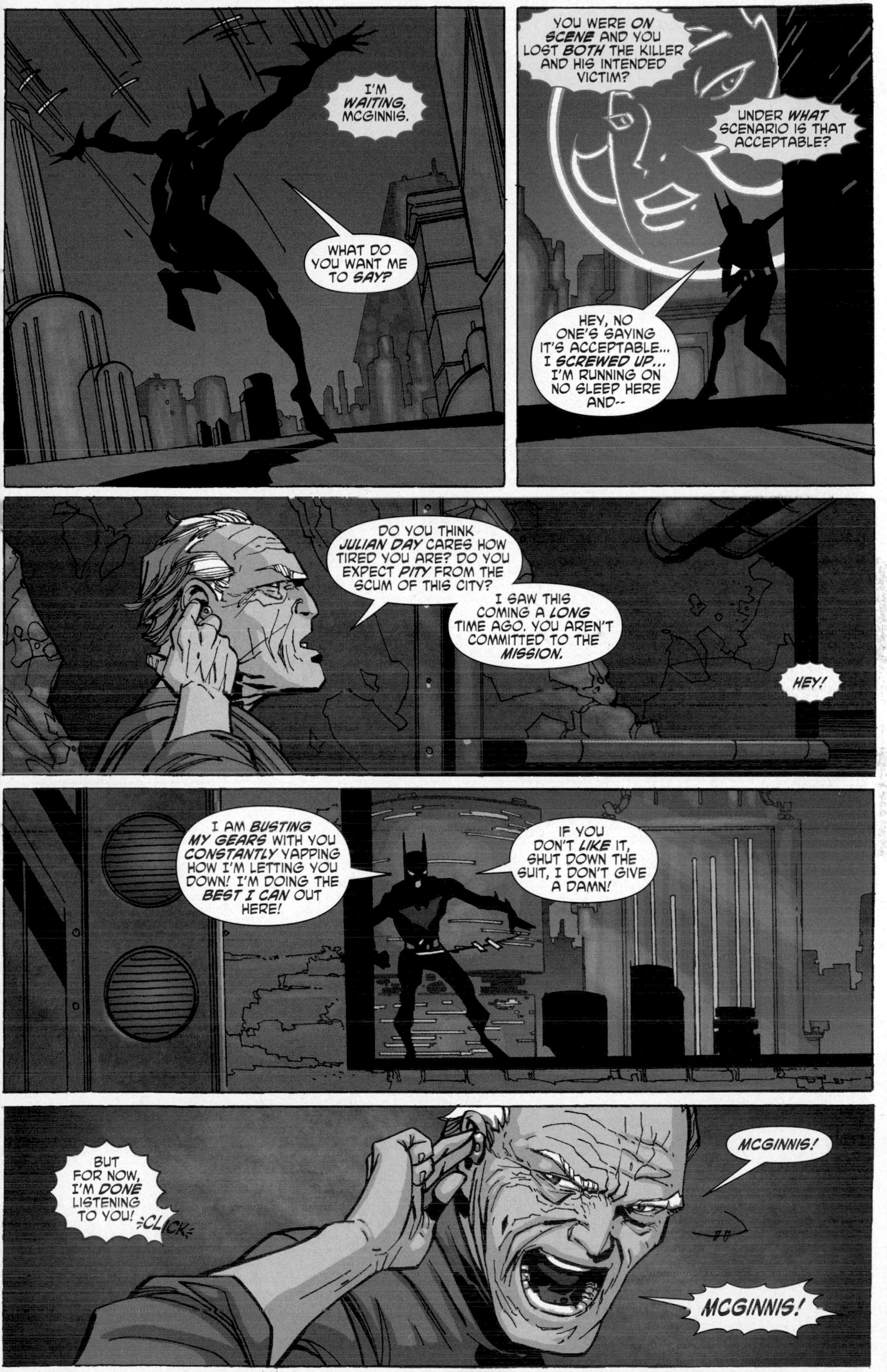
I'M WAITING, MCGINNIS.
WHAT DO YOU WANT ME TO SAY?
YOU WERE ON SCENE AND YOU LOST BOTH THE KILLER AND HIS INTENDED VICTIM?
UNDER WHAT SCENARIO IS THAT ACCEPTABLE?
HEY, NO ONE'S SAYING IT'S ACCEPTABLE... I SCREWED UP... I'M RUNNING ON NO SLEEP HERE AND--
DO YOU THINK JULIAN DAY CARES HOW TIRED YOU ARE? DO YOU EXPECT PITY FROM THE SCUM OF THIS CITY?
I SAW THIS COMING A LONG TIME AGO. YOU AREN'T COMMITTED TO THE MISSION.
HEY!
I AM BUSTING MY GEARS WITH YOU CONSTANTLY YAPPING HOW I'M LETTING YOU DOWN! I'M DOING THE BEST I CAN OUT HERE!
IF YOU DON'T LIKE IT, SHUT DOWN THE SUIT, I DON'T GIVE A DAMN!
BUT FOR NOW, I'M DONE LISTENING TO YOU!
CLICK
MCGINNIS!
MCGINNIS!

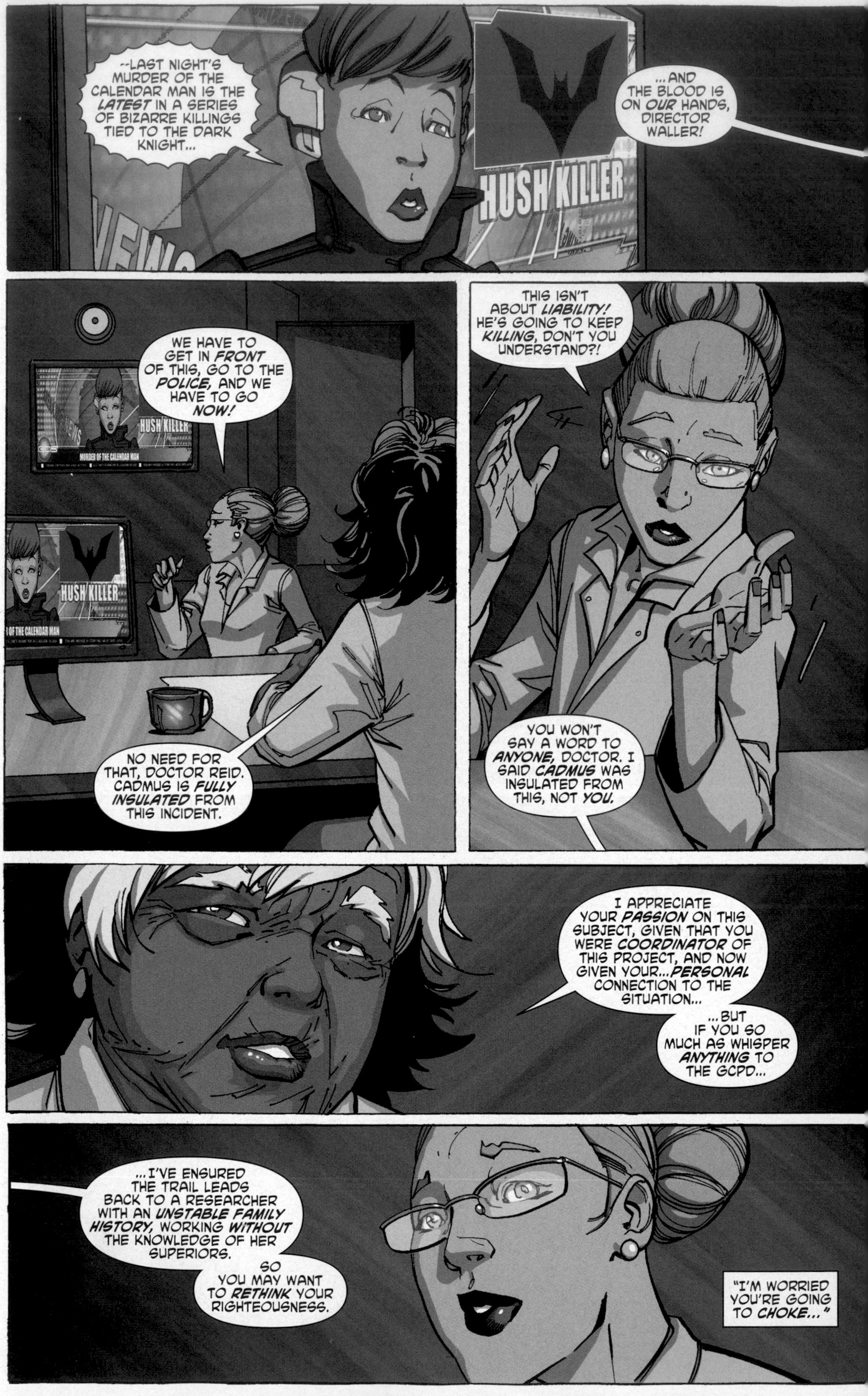
--LAST NIGHT'S MURDER OF THE CALENDAR MAN IS THE *LATEST* IN A SERIES OF BIZARRE KILLINGS TIED TO THE DARK KNIGHT...
HUSH KILLER
...AND THE BLOOD IS ON *OUR* HANDS, DIRECTOR WALLER!
WE HAVE TO GET IN *FRONT* OF THIS, GO TO THE *POLICE*, AND WE HAVE TO GO *NOW!*
HUSH KILLER
MURDER OF THE CALENDAR MAN
HUSH KILLER
NO NEED FOR THAT, DOCTOR REID. CADMUS IS *FULLY INSULATED* FROM THIS INCIDENT.
THIS ISN'T ABOUT *LIABILITY!* HE'S GOING TO KEEP *KILLING*, DON'T YOU UNDERSTAND?!
YOU WON'T SAY A WORD TO *ANYONE*, DOCTOR. I SAID *CADMUS* WAS INSULATED FROM THIS, NOT *YOU.*
I APPRECIATE YOUR *PASSION* ON THIS SUBJECT, GIVEN THAT YOU WERE *COORDINATOR* OF THIS PROJECT, AND NOW GIVEN YOUR...*PERSONAL* CONNECTION TO THE SITUATION...
...BUT IF YOU SO MUCH AS WHISPER *ANYTHING* TO THE GCPD...
...I'VE ENSURED THE TRAIL LEADS BACK TO A RESEARCHER WITH AN *UNSTABLE FAMILY HISTORY*, WORKING *WITHOUT* THE KNOWLEDGE OF HER SUPERIORS.
SO YOU MAY WANT TO *RETHINK* YOUR RIGHTEOUSNESS.
"I'M WORRIED YOU'RE GOING TO *CHOKE...*"

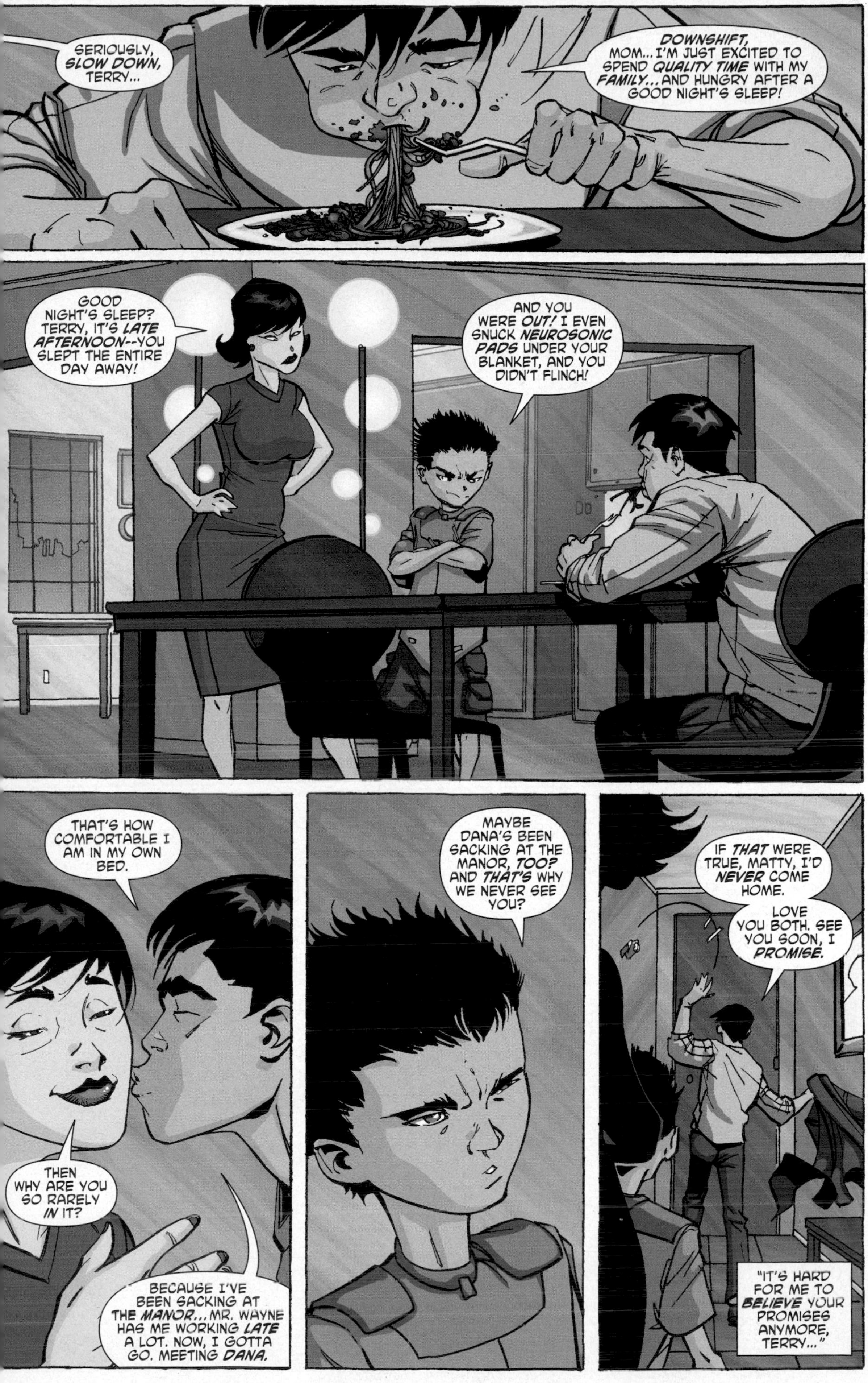
SERIOUSLY, SLOW DOWN, TERRY...
DOWNSHIFT, MOM... I'M JUST EXCITED TO SPEND QUALITY TIME WITH MY FAMILY... AND HUNGRY AFTER A GOOD NIGHT'S SLEEP!
GOOD NIGHT'S SLEEP? TERRY, IT'S LATE AFTERNOON--YOU SLEPT THE ENTIRE DAY AWAY!
AND YOU WERE OUT! I EVEN SNUCK NEUROSONIC PADS UNDER YOUR BLANKET, AND YOU DIDN'T FLINCH!
THAT'S HOW COMFORTABLE I AM IN MY OWN BED.
THEN WHY ARE YOU SO RARELY IN IT?
BECAUSE I'VE BEEN SACKING AT THE MANOR... MR. WAYNE HAS ME WORKING LATE A LOT. NOW, I GOTTA GO. MEETING DANA.
MAYBE DANA'S BEEN SACKING AT THE MANOR, TOO? AND THAT'S WHY WE NEVER SEE YOU?
IF THAT WERE TRUE, MATTY, I'D NEVER COME HOME.
LOVE YOU BOTH. SEE YOU SOON, I PROMISE.
"IT'S HARD FOR ME TO BELIEVE YOUR PROMISES ANYMORE, TERRY..."

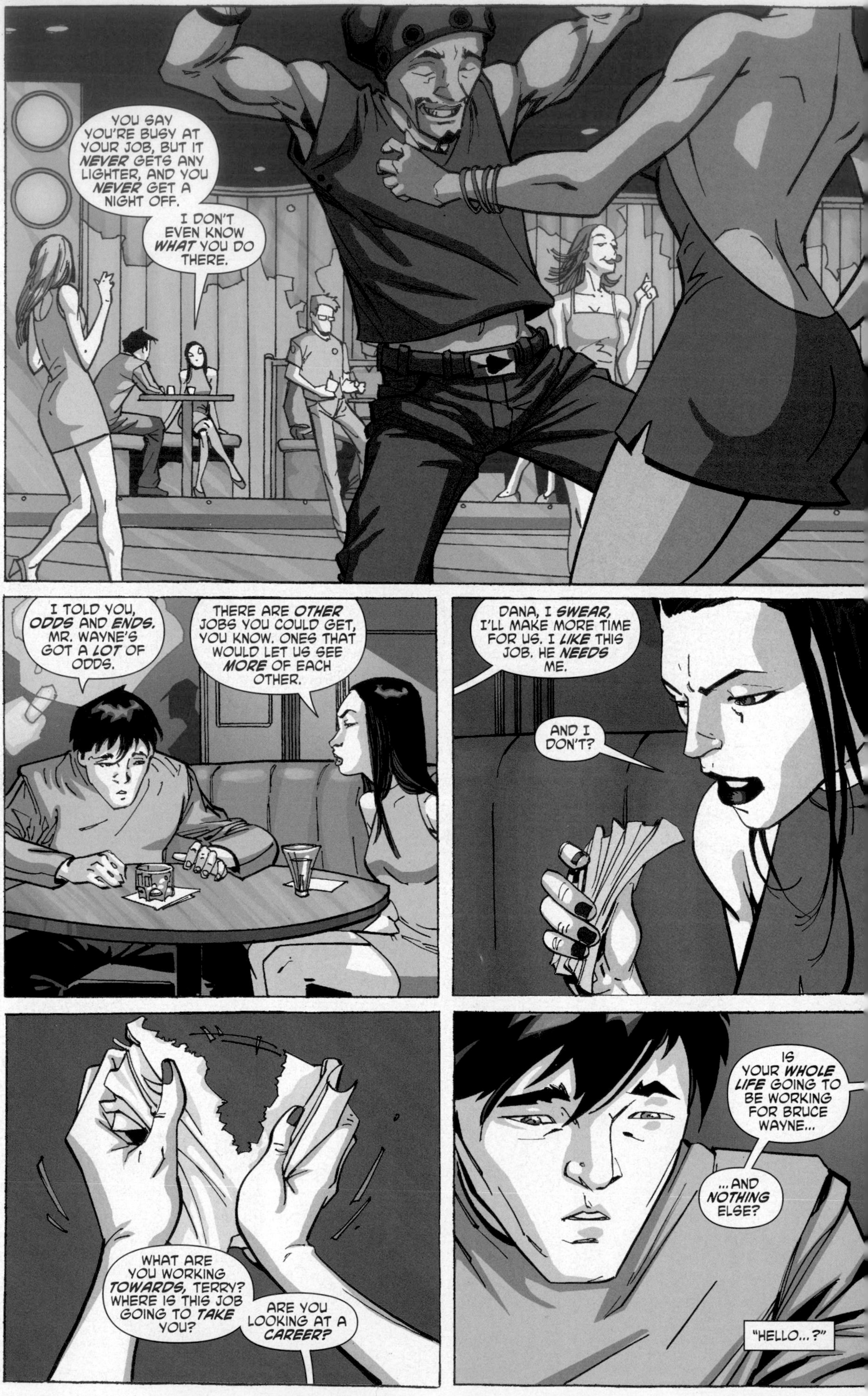

YOU SAY YOU'RE BUSY AT YOUR JOB, BUT IT NEVER GETS ANY LIGHTER, AND YOU NEVER GET A NIGHT OFF.
I DON'T EVEN KNOW WHAT YOU DO THERE.
I TOLD YOU, ODDS AND ENDS. MR. WAYNE'S GOT A LOT OF ODDS.
THERE ARE OTHER JOBS YOU COULD GET, YOU KNOW. ONES THAT WOULD LET US SEE MORE OF EACH OTHER.
DANA, I SWEAR, I'LL MAKE MORE TIME FOR US. I LIKE THIS JOB. HE NEEDS ME.
AND I DON'T?
WHAT ARE YOU WORKING TOWARDS, TERRY? WHERE IS THIS JOB GOING TO TAKE YOU?
ARE YOU LOOKING AT A CAREER?
IS YOUR WHOLE LIFE GOING TO BE WORKING FOR BRUCE WAYNE...
...AND NOTHING ELSE?
"HELLO...?"

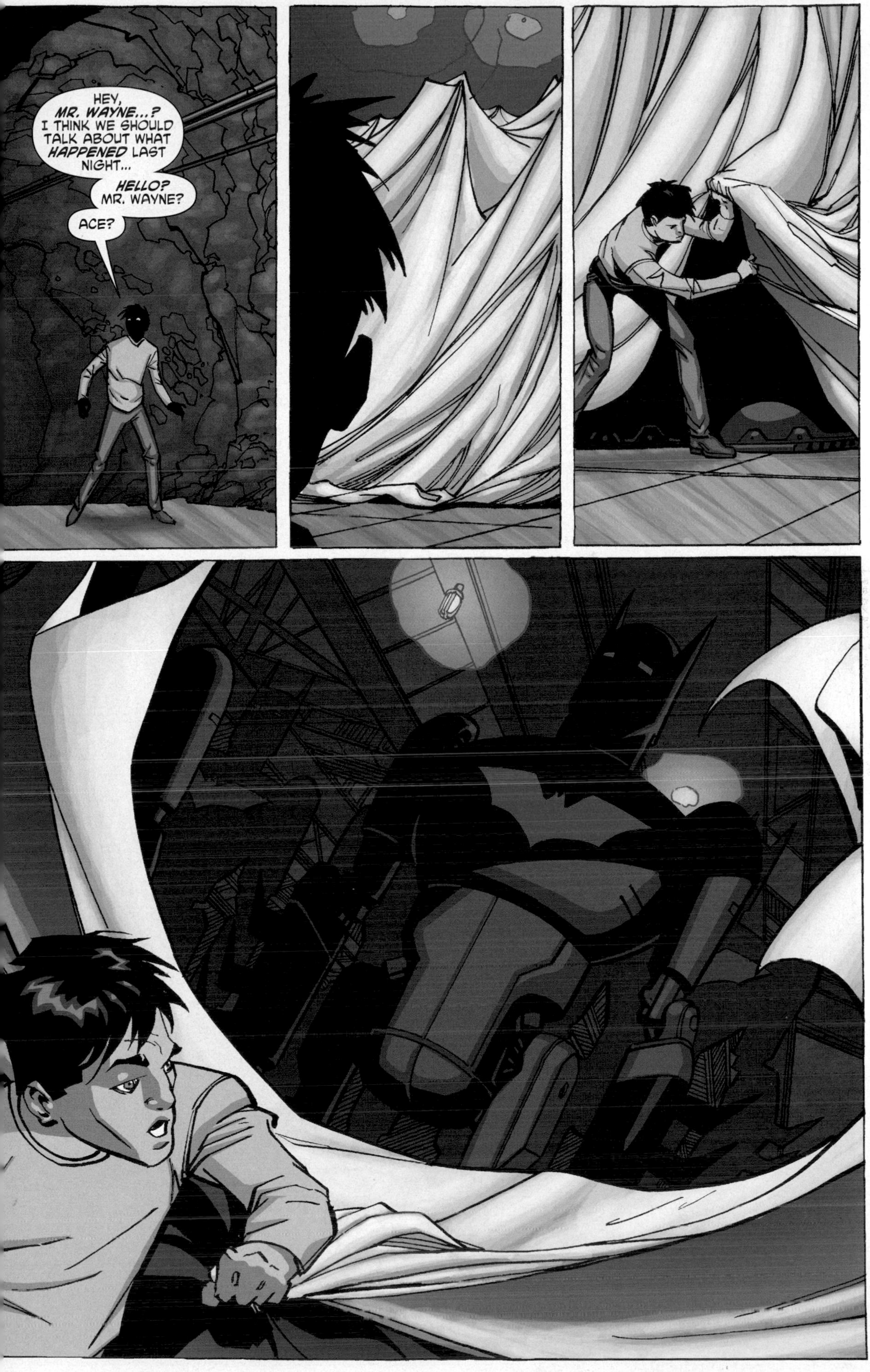
HEY, *MR. WAYNE...?* I THINK WE SHOULD TALK ABOUT WHAT *HAPPENED* LAST NIGHT...
HELLO? MR. WAYNE?
ACE?

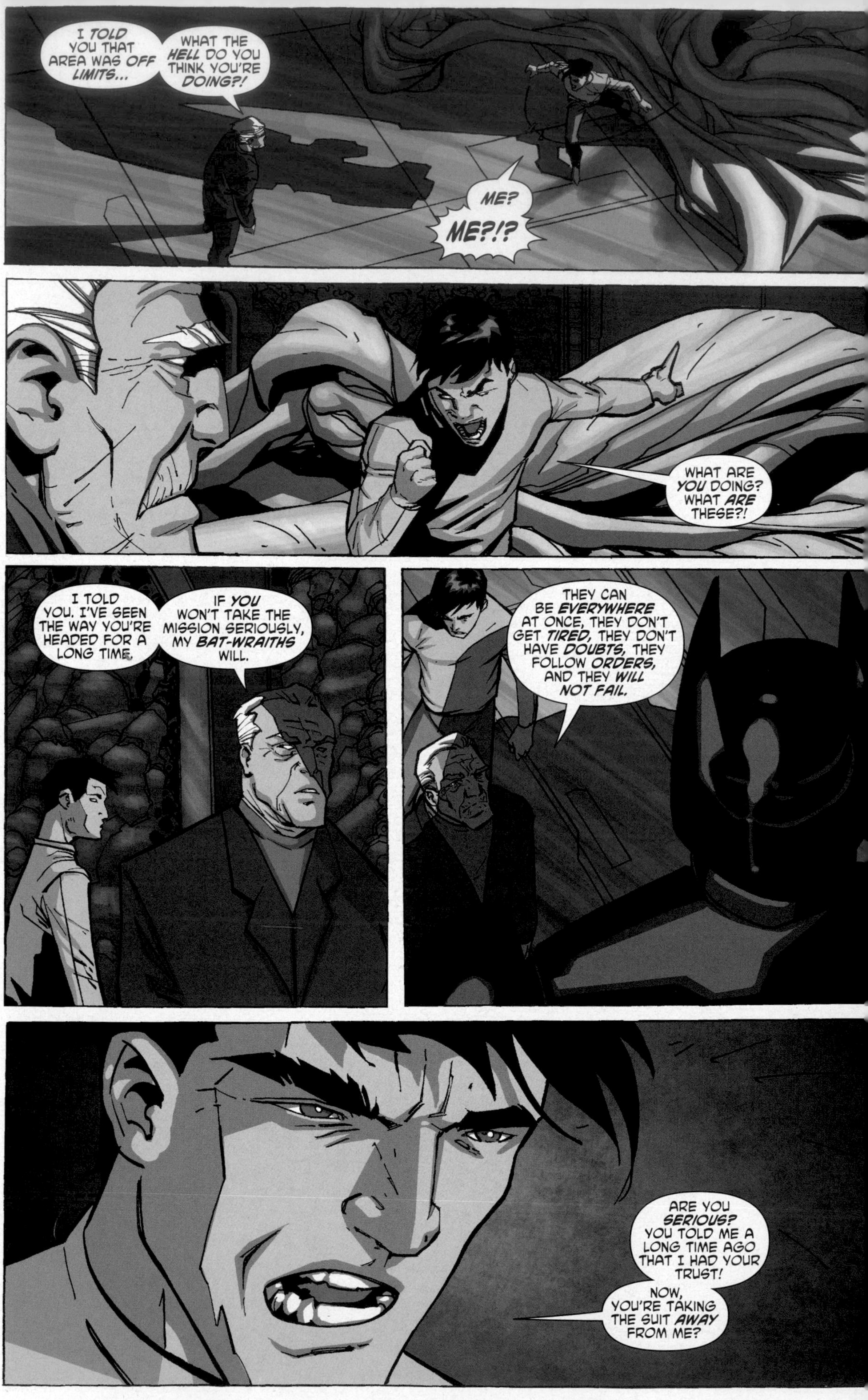
I TOLD YOU THAT AREA WAS OFF LIMITS...
WHAT THE HELL DO YOU THINK YOU'RE DOING?!
ME?
ME?!?
WHAT ARE YOU DOING? WHAT ARE THESE?!
I TOLD YOU. I'VE SEEN THE WAY YOU'RE HEADED FOR A LONG TIME.
IF YOU WON'T TAKE THE MISSION SERIOUSLY, MY BAT-WRAITHS WILL.
THEY CAN BE EVERYWHERE AT ONCE, THEY DON'T GET TIRED, THEY DON'T HAVE DOUBTS, THEY FOLLOW ORDERS, AND THEY WILL NOT FAIL.
ARE YOU SERIOUS? YOU TOLD ME A LONG TIME AGO THAT I HAD YOUR TRUST!
NOW, YOU'RE TAKING THE SUIT AWAY FROM ME?

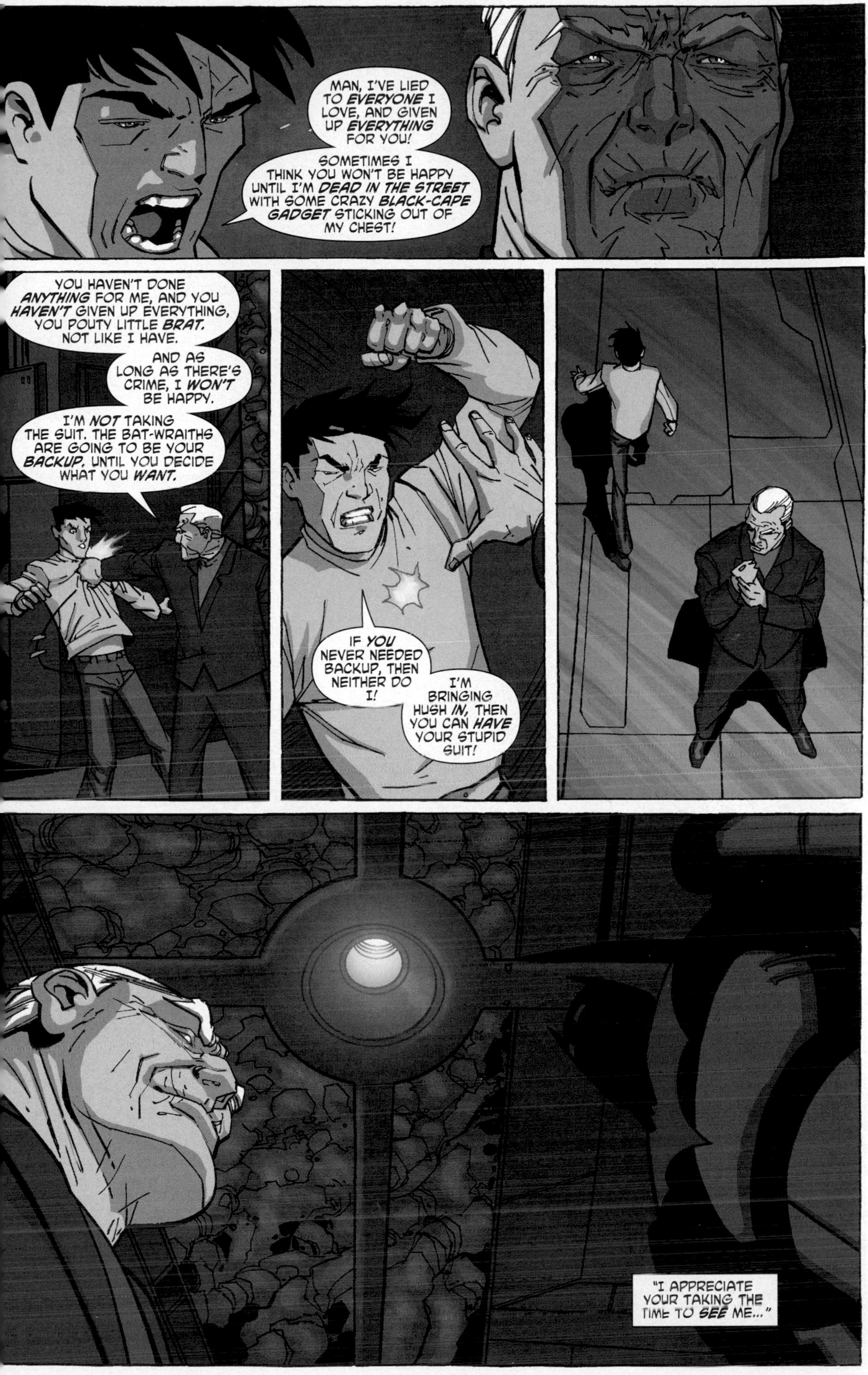
MAN, I'VE LIED TO EVERYONE I LOVE, AND GIVEN UP EVERYTHING FOR YOU!
SOMETIMES I THINK YOU WON'T BE HAPPY UNTIL I'M DEAD IN THE STREET WITH SOME CRAZY BLACK-CAPE GADGET STICKING OUT OF MY CHEST!
YOU HAVEN'T DONE ANYTHING FOR ME, AND YOU HAVEN'T GIVEN UP EVERYTHING, YOU POUTY LITTLE BRAT. NOT LIKE I HAVE.
AND AS LONG AS THERE'S CRIME, I WON'T BE HAPPY.
I'M NOT TAKING THE SUIT. THE BAT-WRAITHS ARE GOING TO BE YOUR BACKUP, UNTIL YOU DECIDE WHAT YOU WANT.
IF YOU NEVER NEEDED BACKUP, THEN NEITHER DO I!
I'M BRINGING HUSH IN, THEN YOU CAN HAVE YOUR STUPID SUIT!
"I APPRECIATE YOUR TAKING THE TIME TO SEE ME..."

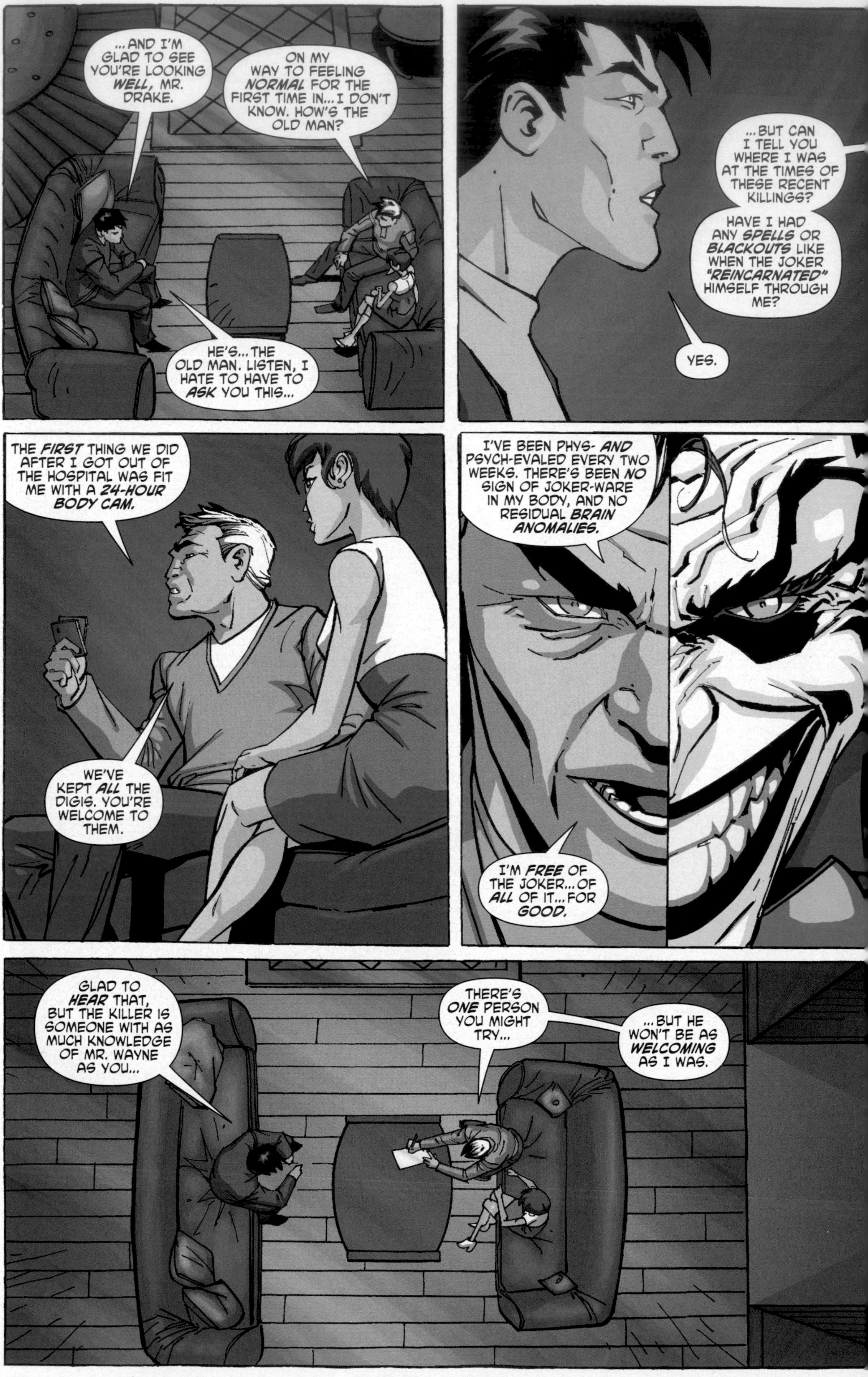
...AND I'M GLAD TO SEE YOU'RE LOOKING WELL, MR. DRAKE.
ON MY WAY TO FEELING NORMAL FOR THE FIRST TIME IN... I DON'T KNOW. HOW'S THE OLD MAN?
HE'S... THE OLD MAN. LISTEN, I HATE TO HAVE TO ASK YOU THIS...
...BUT CAN I TELL YOU WHERE I WAS AT THE TIMES OF THESE RECENT KILLINGS?
HAVE I HAD ANY SPELLS OR BLACKOUTS LIKE WHEN THE JOKER "REINCARNATED" HIMSELF THROUGH ME?
YES.
THE FIRST THING WE DID AFTER I GOT OUT OF THE HOSPITAL WAS FIT ME WITH A 24-HOUR BODY CAM.
WE'VE KEPT ALL THE DIGIS. YOU'RE WELCOME TO THEM.
I'VE BEEN PHYS- AND PSYCH-EVALED EVERY TWO WEEKS. THERE'S BEEN NO SIGN OF JOKER-WARE IN MY BODY, AND NO RESIDUAL BRAIN ANOMALIES.
I'M FREE OF THE JOKER... OF ALL OF IT... FOR GOOD.
GLAD TO HEAR THAT, BUT THE KILLER IS SOMEONE WITH AS MUCH KNOWLEDGE OF MR. WAYNE AS YOU...
THERE'S ONE PERSON YOU MIGHT TRY...
...BUT HE WON'T BE AS WELCOMING AS I WAS.

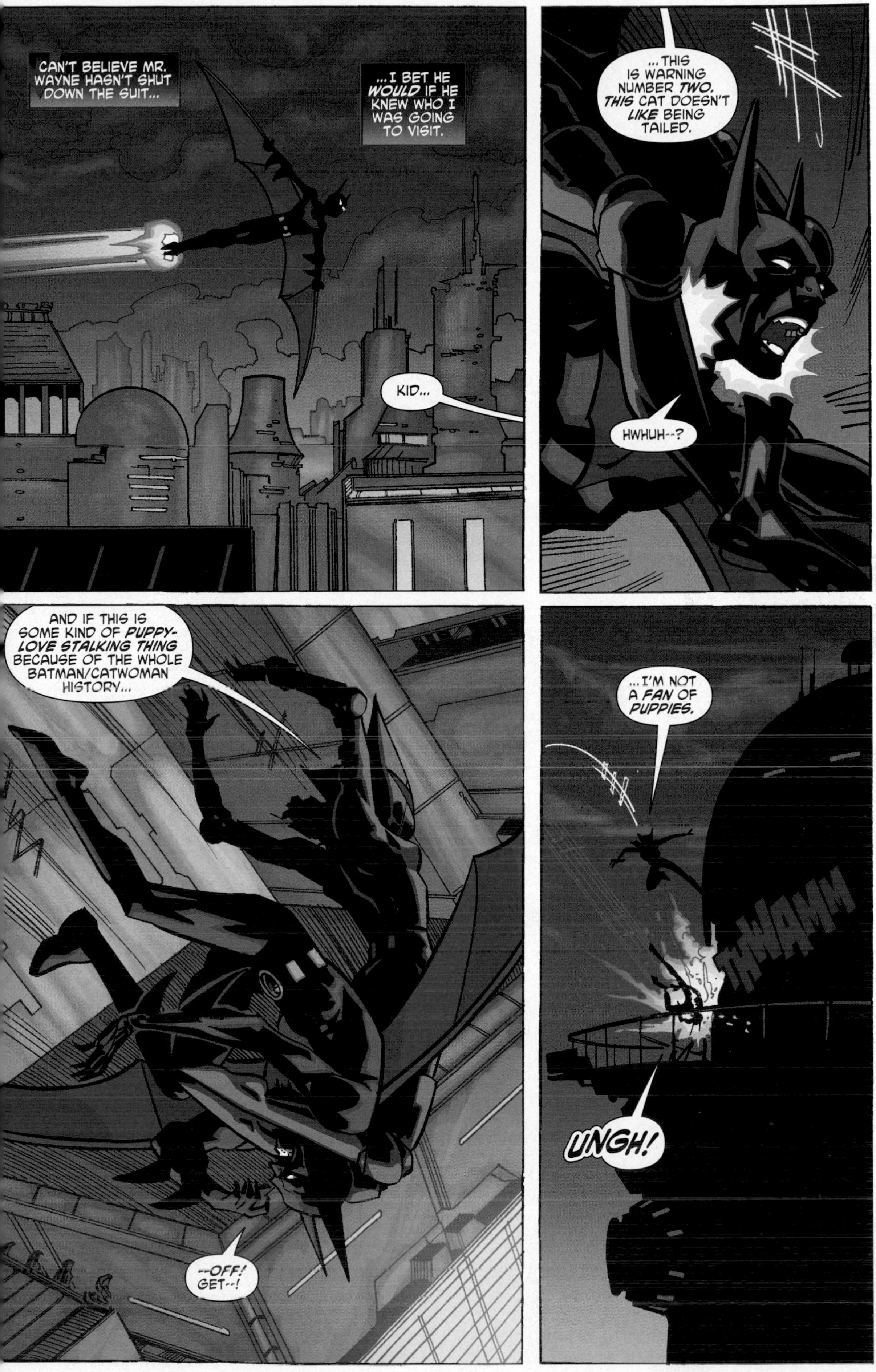
CAN'T BELIEVE MR. WAYNE HASN'T SHUT DOWN THE SUIT...
...I BET HE WOULD IF HE KNEW WHO I WAS GOING TO VISIT.
KID...
...THIS IS WARNING NUMBER TWO. THIS CAT DOESN'T LIKE BEING TAILED.
HWHUH--?
AND IF THIS IS SOME KIND OF PUPPY-LOVE STALKING THING BECAUSE OF THE WHOLE BATMAN/CATWOMAN HISTORY...
--OFF! GET--!
...I'M NOT A FAN OF PUPPIES.
THWAMM
UNGH!

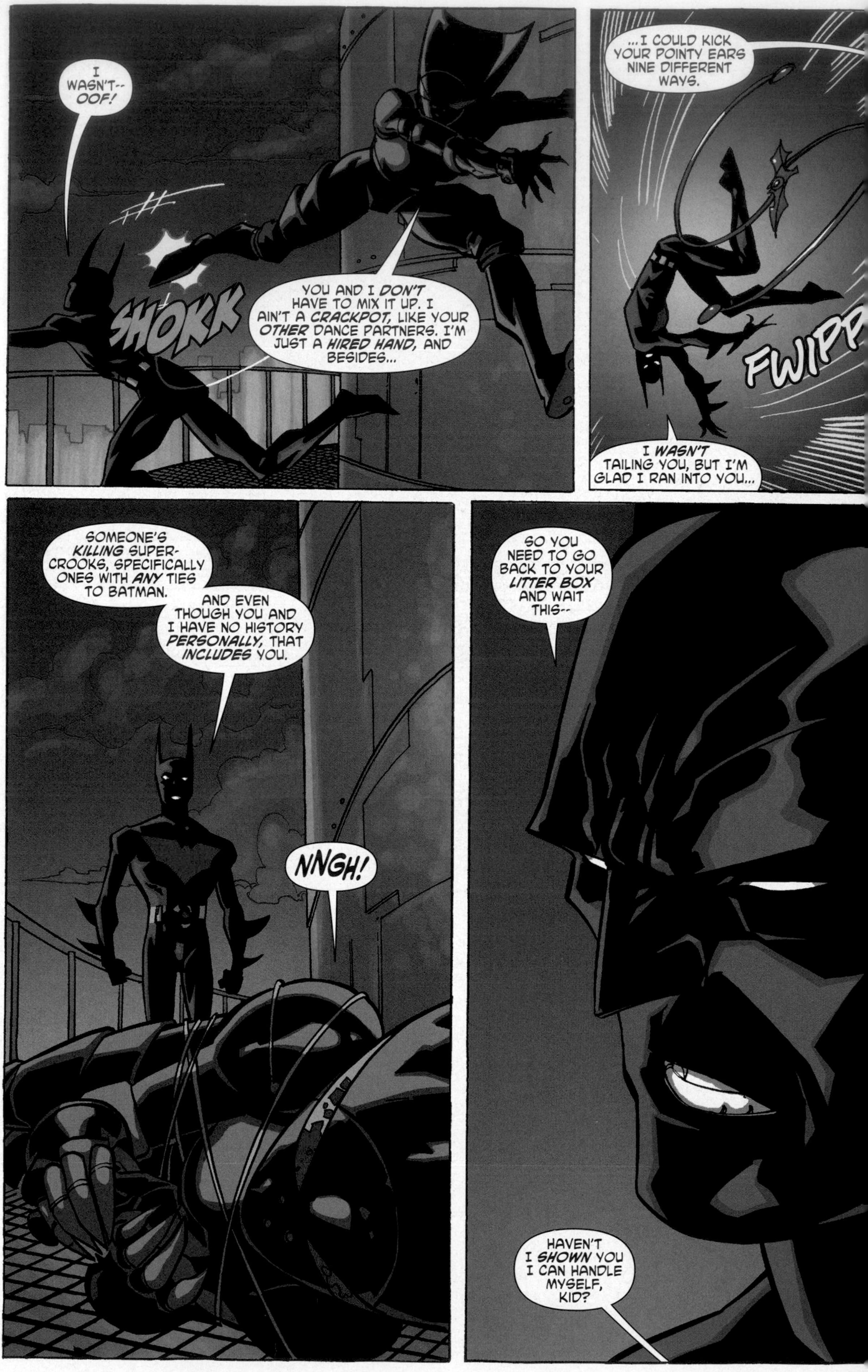
I WASN'T-- OOF!
SHOKK
YOU AND I DON'T HAVE TO MIX IT UP. I AIN'T A CRACKPOT, LIKE YOUR OTHER DANCE PARTNERS. I'M JUST A HIRED HAND, AND BESIDES...
...I COULD KICK YOUR POINTY EARS NINE DIFFERENT WAYS.
FWIPP
I WASN'T TAILING YOU, BUT I'M GLAD I RAN INTO YOU...
SOMEONE'S KILLING SUPER-CROOKS, SPECIFICALLY ONES WITH ANY TIES TO BATMAN.
AND EVEN THOUGH YOU AND I HAVE NO HISTORY PERSONALLY, THAT INCLUDES YOU.
NNGH!
SO YOU NEED TO GO BACK TO YOUR LITTER BOX AND WAIT THIS--
HAVEN'T I SHOWN YOU I CAN HANDLE MYSELF, KID?

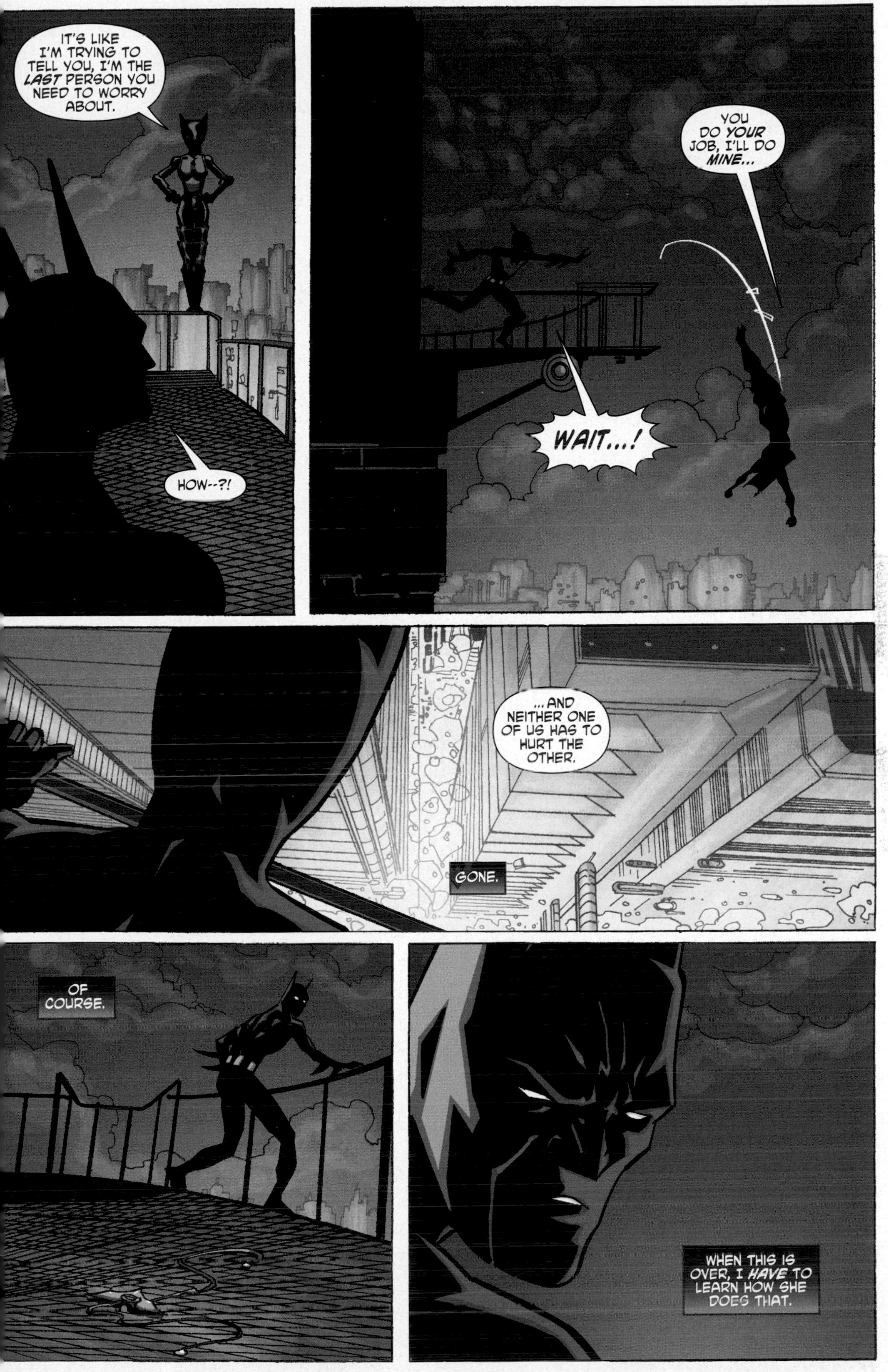
IT'S LIKE I'M TRYING TO TELL YOU, I'M THE LAST PERSON YOU NEED TO WORRY ABOUT.
HOW--?!
YOU DO YOUR JOB, I'LL DO MINE...
WAIT...!
...AND NEITHER ONE OF US HAS TO HURT THE OTHER.
GONE.
OF COURSE.
WHEN THIS IS OVER, I HAVE TO LEARN HOW SHE DOES THAT.

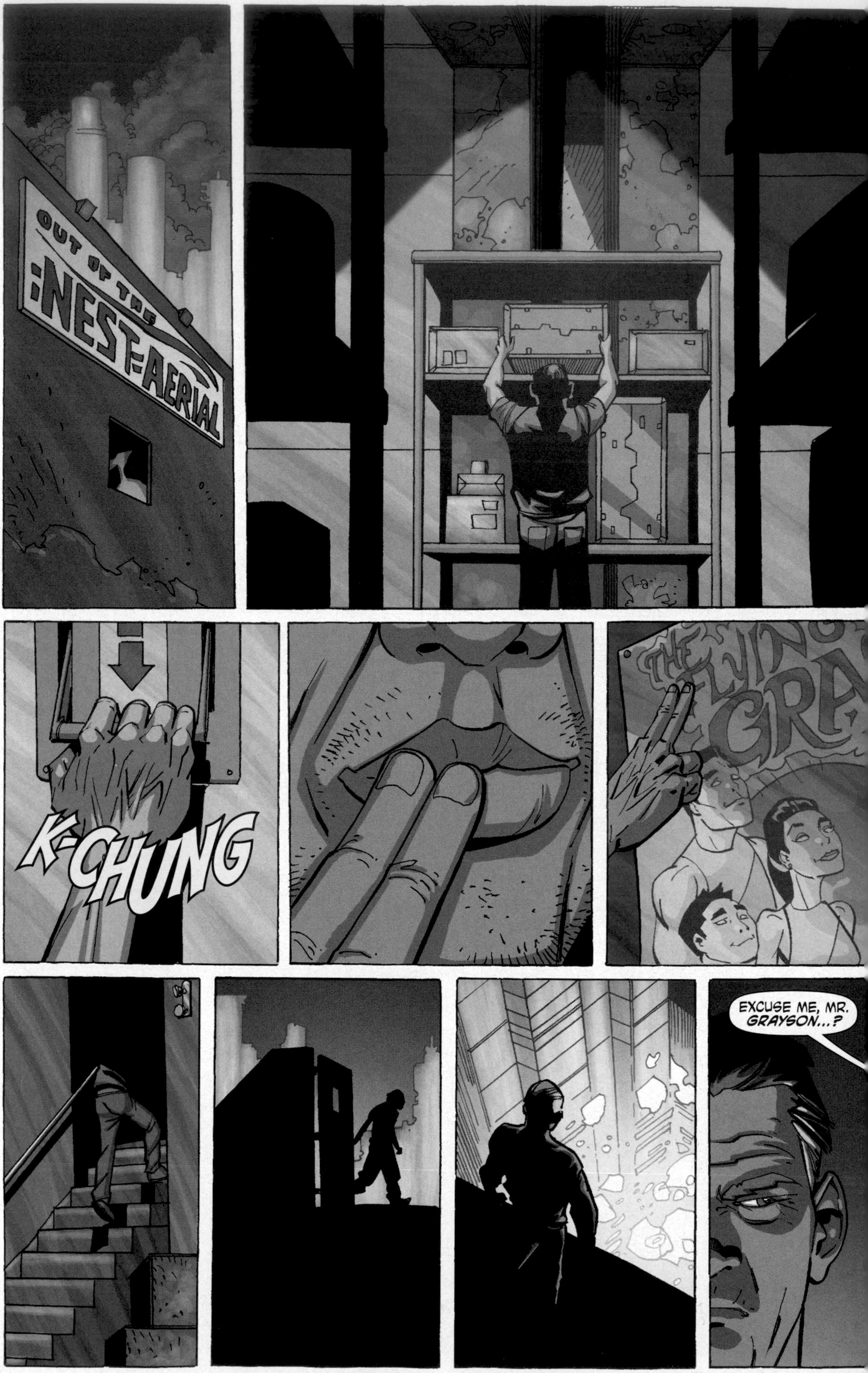
OUT OF THE
NEST AERIAL
K-CHUNG
EXCUSE ME, MR. GRAYSON...?

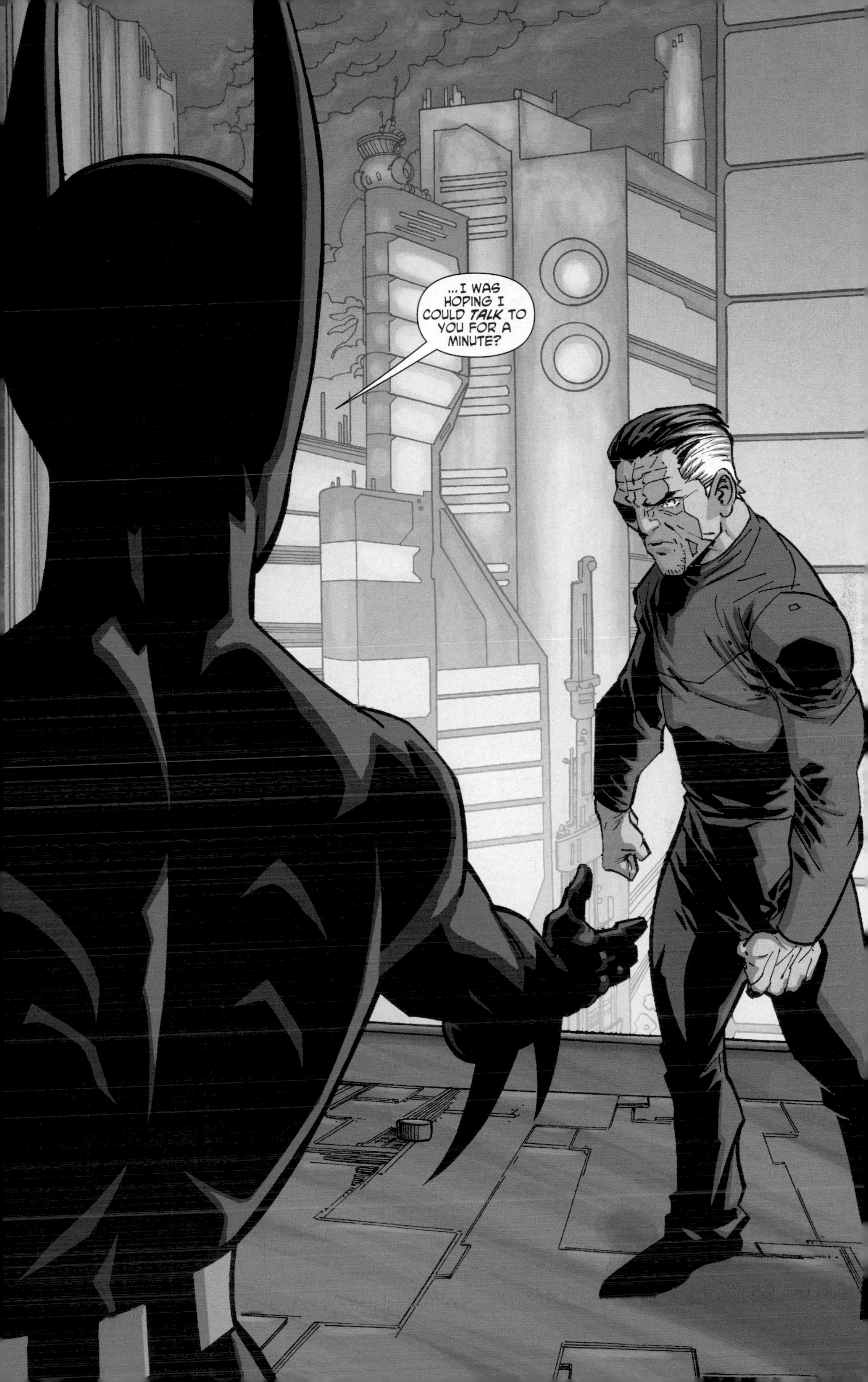
...I WAS HOPING I COULD *TALK* TO YOU FOR A MINUTE?

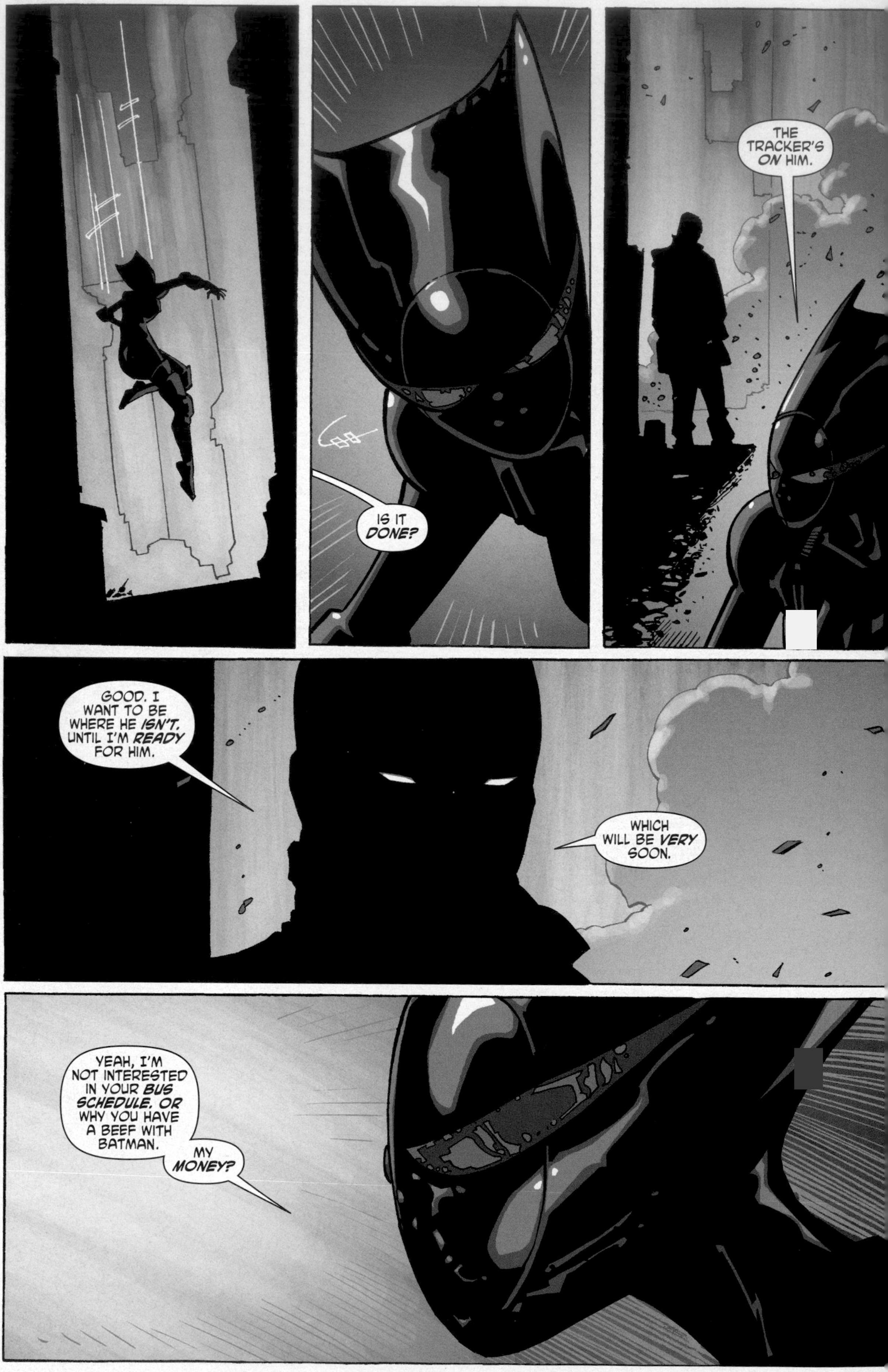
IS IT DONE?
THE TRACKER'S ON HIM.
GOOD. I WANT TO BE WHERE HE ISN'T. UNTIL I'M READY FOR HIM.
WHICH WILL BE VERY SOON.
YEAH, I'M NOT INTERESTED IN YOUR BUS SCHEDULE. OR WHY YOU HAVE A BEEF WITH BATMAN.
MY MONEY?

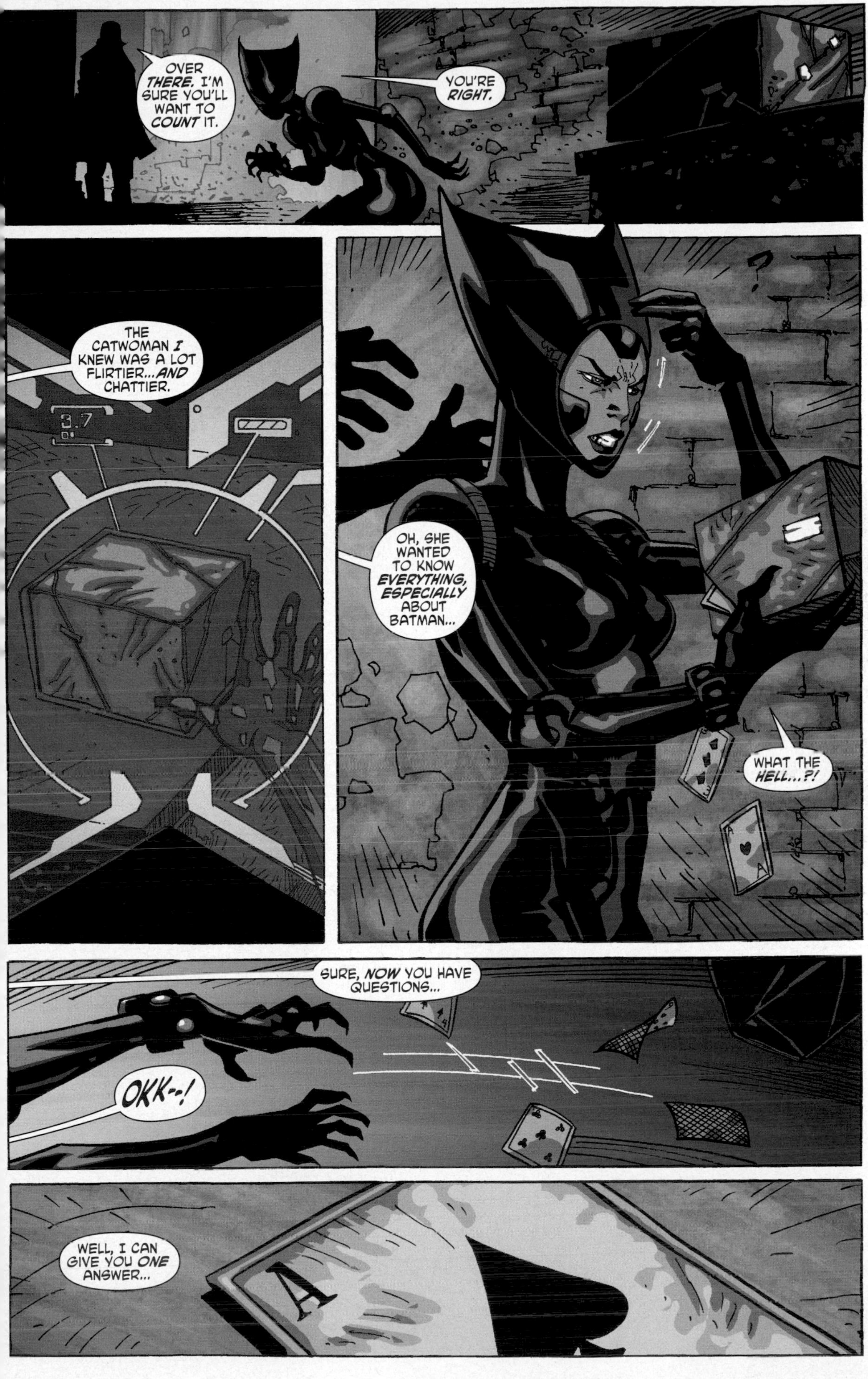
OVER THERE. I'M SURE YOU'LL WANT TO COUNT IT.
YOU'RE RIGHT.
THE CATWOMAN I KNEW WAS A LOT FLIRTIER...AND CHATTIER.
3.7
OH, SHE WANTED TO KNOW EVERYTHING, ESPECIALLY ABOUT BATMAN...
WHAT THE HELL...?!
SURE, NOW YOU HAVE QUESTIONS...
OKK--!
WELL, I CAN GIVE YOU ONE ANSWER...

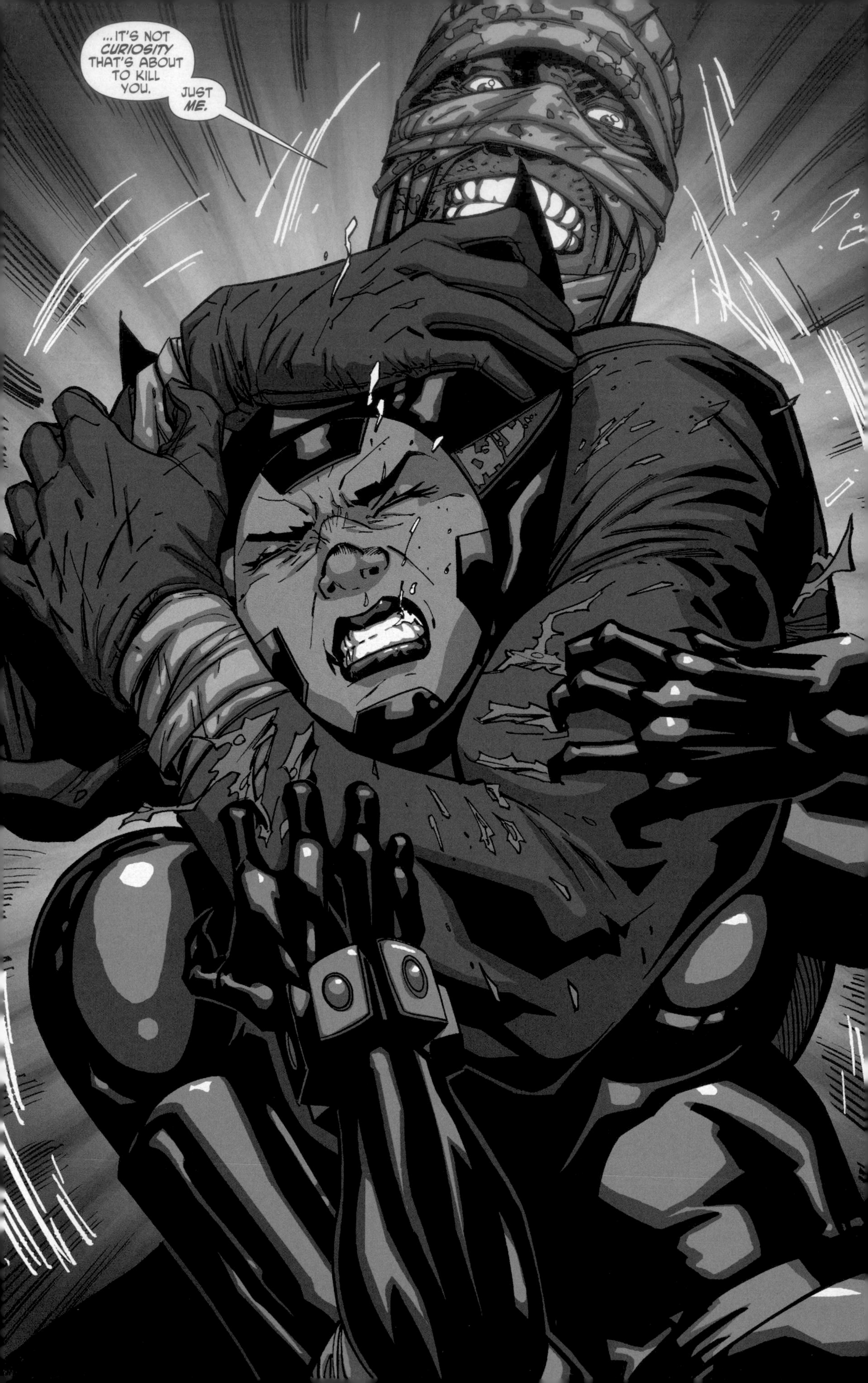
...IT'S NOT *CURIOSITY* THAT'S ABOUT TO KILL YOU.
JUST *ME.*

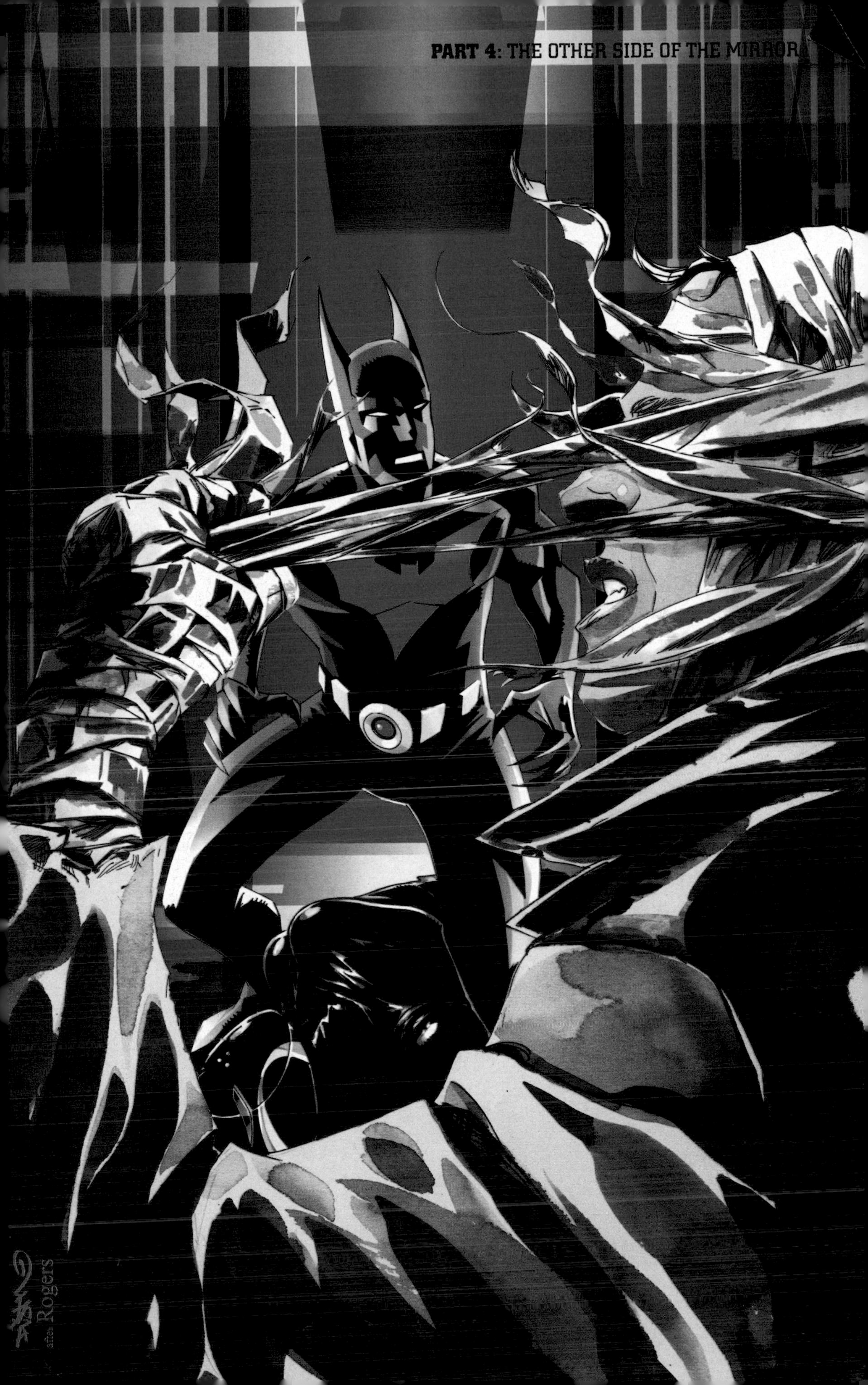
PART 4: THE OTHER SIDE OF THE MIRROR
after Rogers

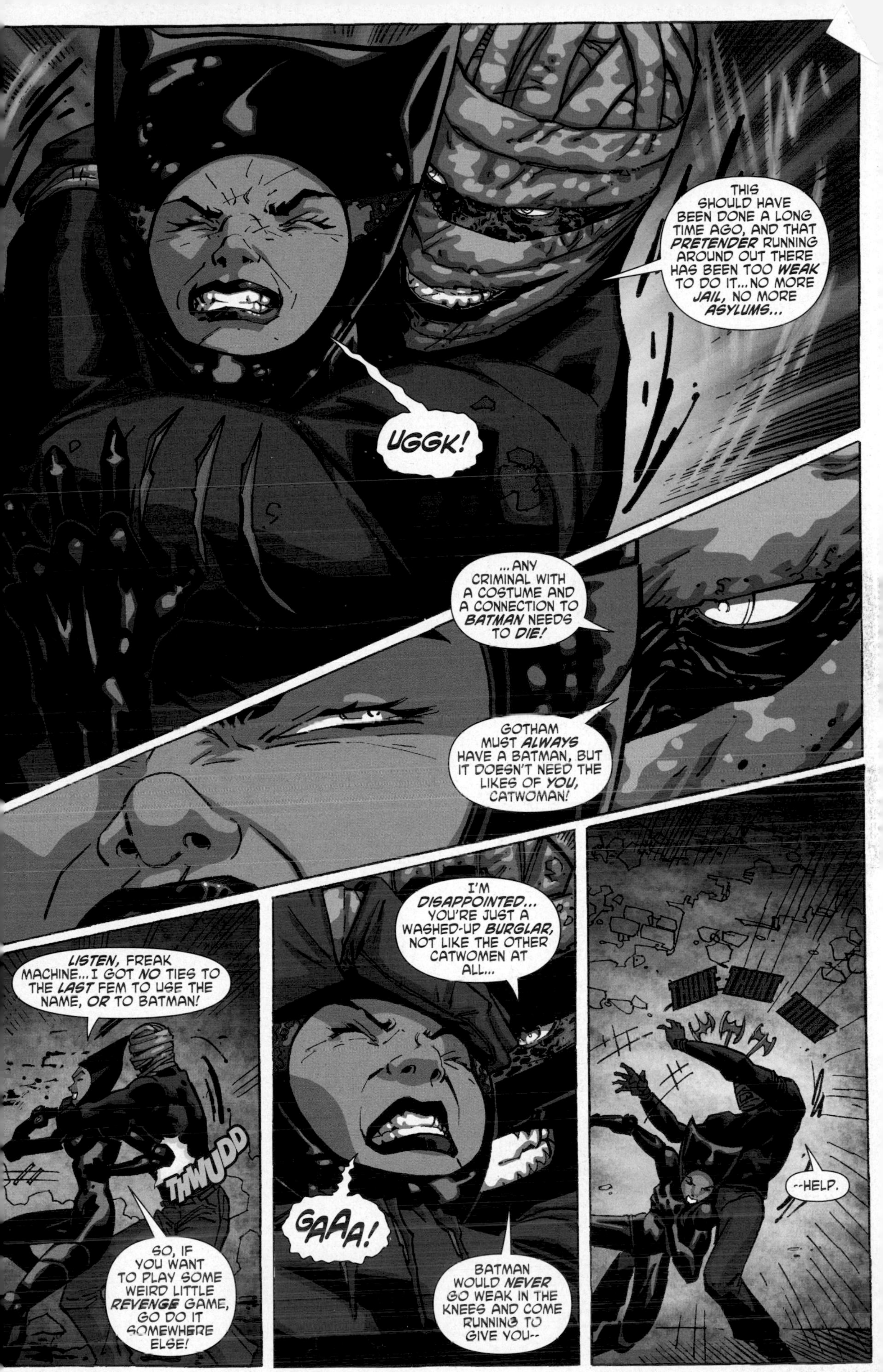
THIS SHOULD HAVE BEEN DONE A LONG TIME AGO, AND THAT PRETENDER RUNNING AROUND OUT THERE HAS BEEN TOO WEAK TO DO IT... NO MORE JAIL, NO MORE ASYLUMS...
UGGK!
...ANY CRIMINAL WITH A COSTUME AND A CONNECTION TO BATMAN NEEDS TO DIE!
GOTHAM MUST ALWAYS HAVE A BATMAN, BUT IT DOESN'T NEED THE LIKES OF YOU, CATWOMAN!
LISTEN, FREAK MACHINE... I GOT NO TIES TO THE LAST FEM TO USE THE NAME, OR TO BATMAN!
THWUDD
SO, IF YOU WANT TO PLAY SOME WEIRD LITTLE REVENGE GAME, GO DO IT SOMEWHERE ELSE!
I'M DISAPPOINTED... YOU'RE JUST A WASHED-UP BURGLAR, NOT LIKE THE OTHER CATWOMEN AT ALL...
GAAA!
BATMAN WOULD NEVER GO WEAK IN THE KNEES AND COME RUNNING TO GIVE YOU--
--HELP.

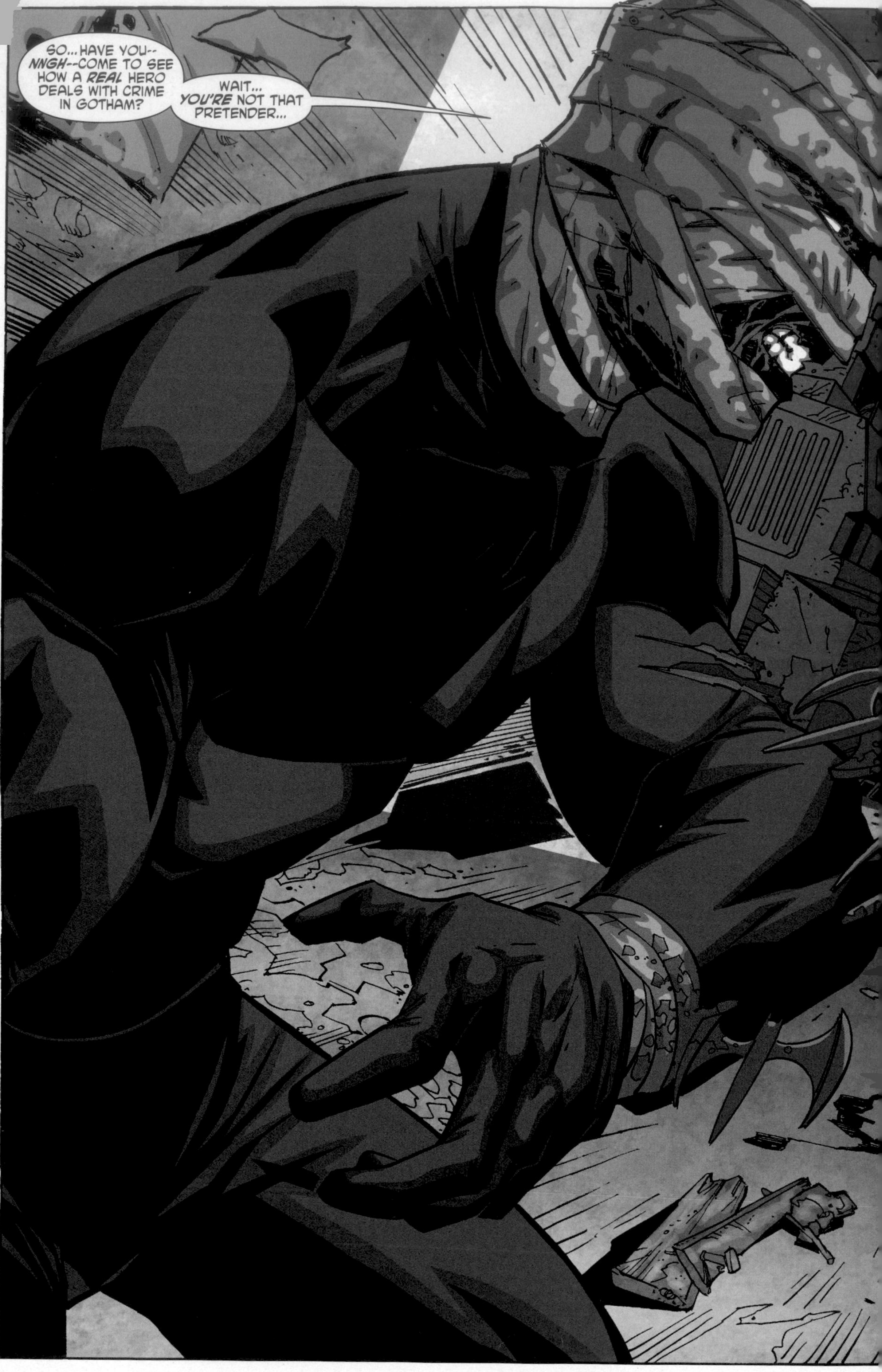
SO... HAVE YOU--
NNGH--COME TO SEE HOW A REAL HERO DEALS WITH CRIME IN GOTHAM?
WAIT... YOU'RE NOT THAT PRETENDER...

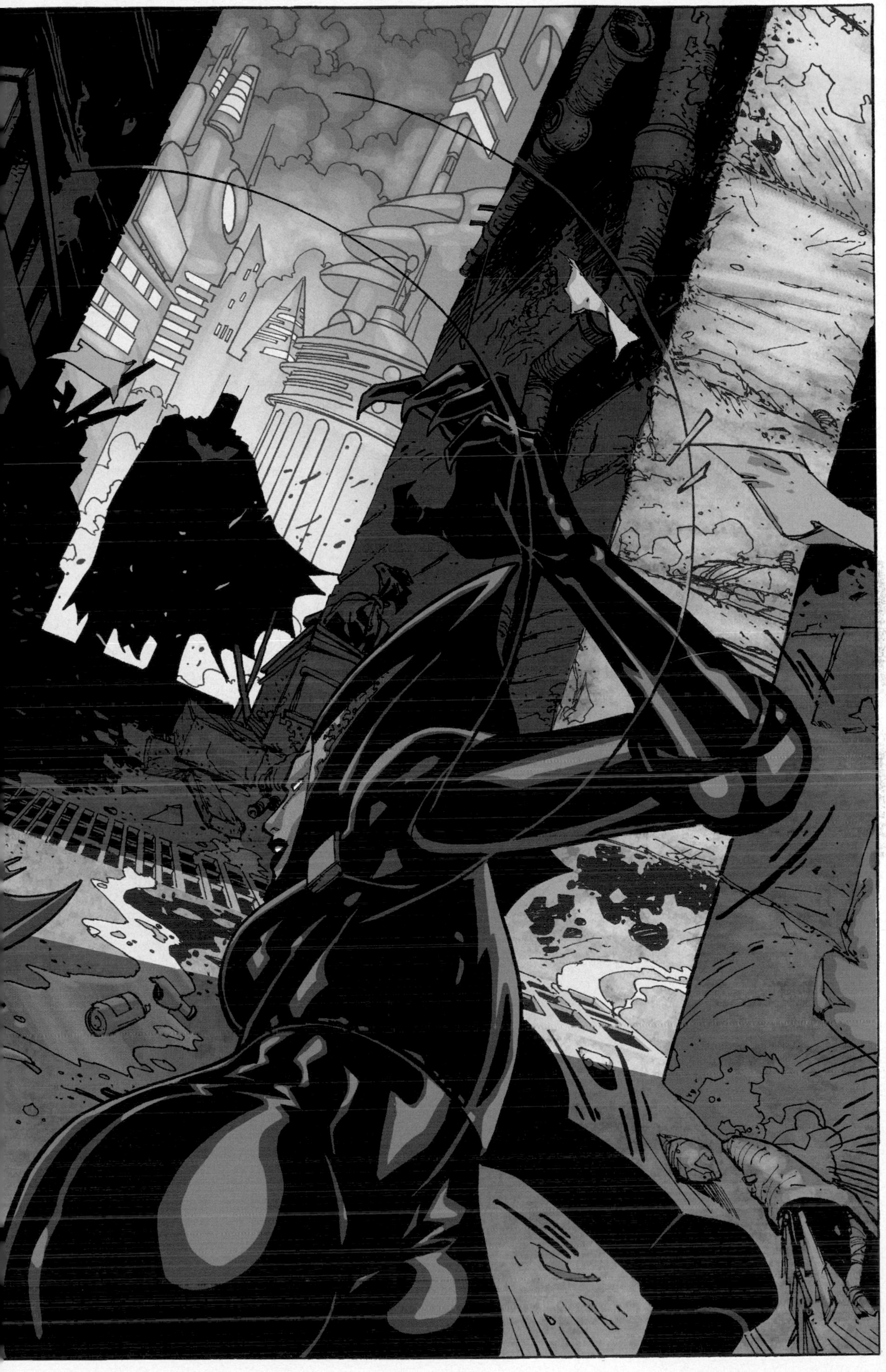

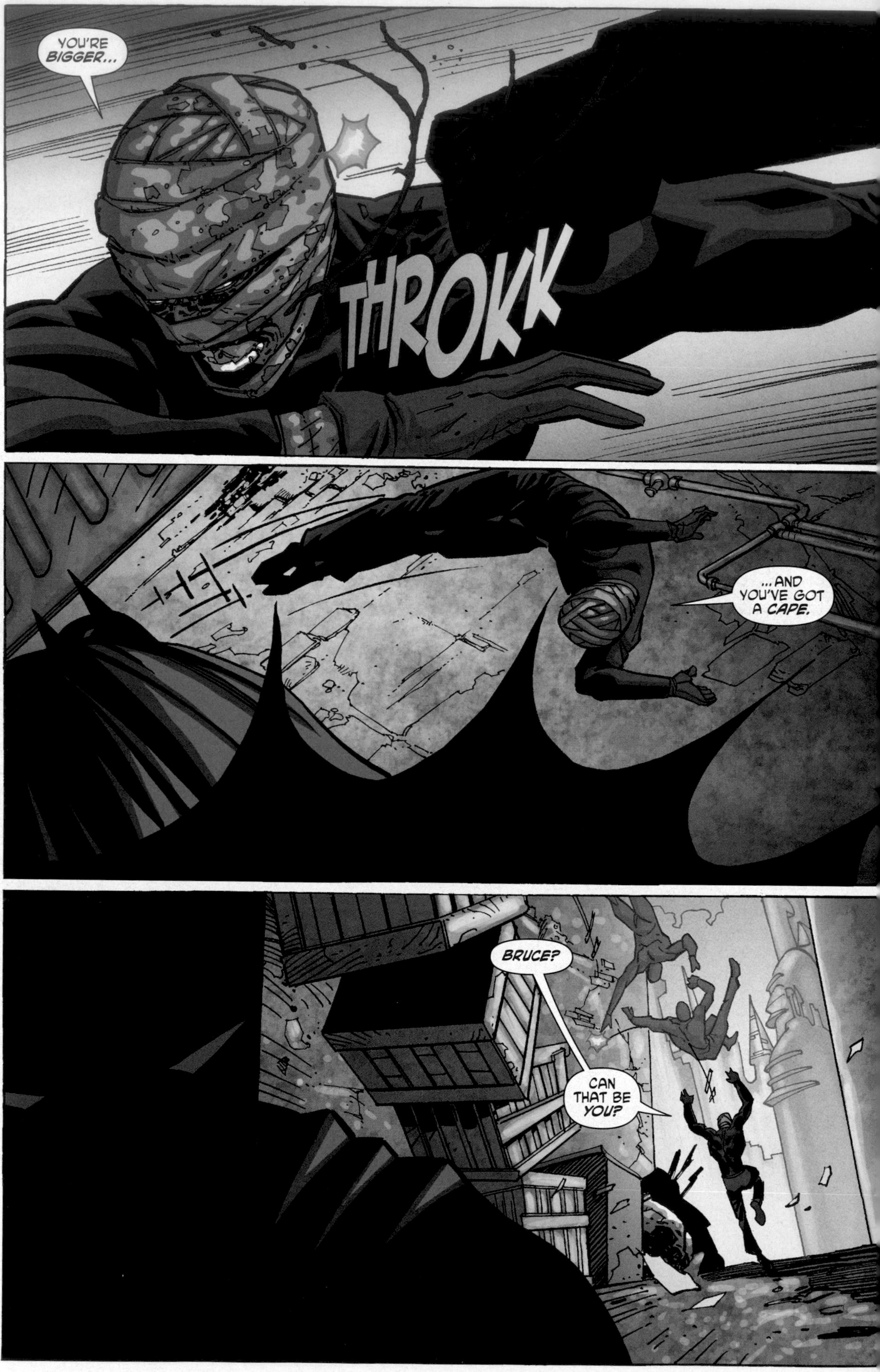
YOU'RE BIGGER...
THROKK
...AND YOU'VE GOT A CAPE.
BRUCE?
CAN THAT BE YOU?

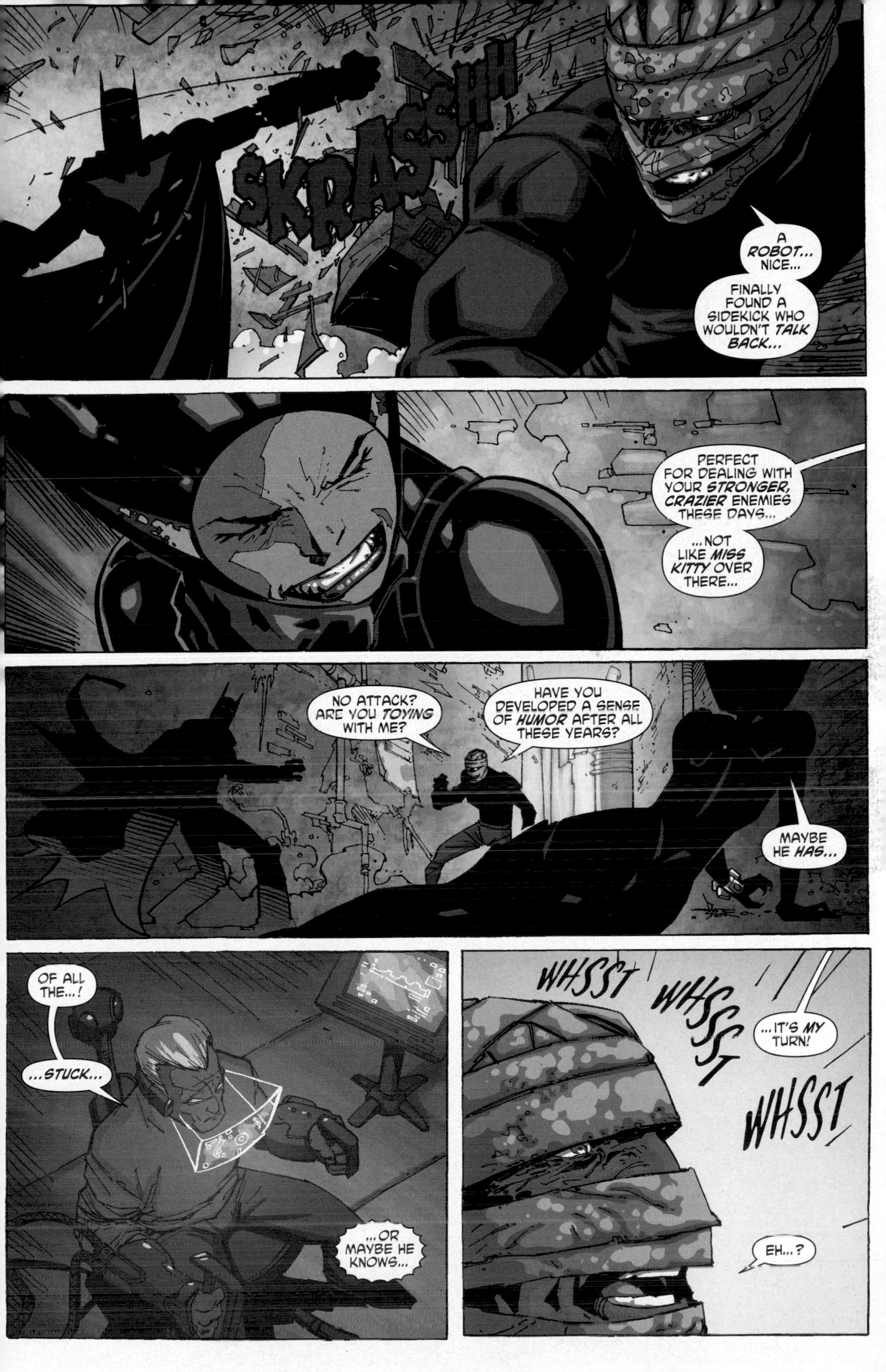
SKRASSHH
A ROBOT... NICE...
FINALLY FOUND A SIDEKICK WHO WOULDN'T TALK BACK...
PERFECT FOR DEALING WITH YOUR STRONGER, CRAZIER ENEMIES THESE DAYS...
...NOT LIKE MISS KITTY OVER THERE...
NO ATTACK? ARE YOU TOYING WITH ME?
HAVE YOU DEVELOPED A SENSE OF HUMOR AFTER ALL THESE YEARS?
MAYBE HE HAS...
OF ALL THE...!
...STUCK...
...OR MAYBE HE KNOWS...
WHSST
WHSSST
...IT'S MY TURN!
WHSST
EH...?

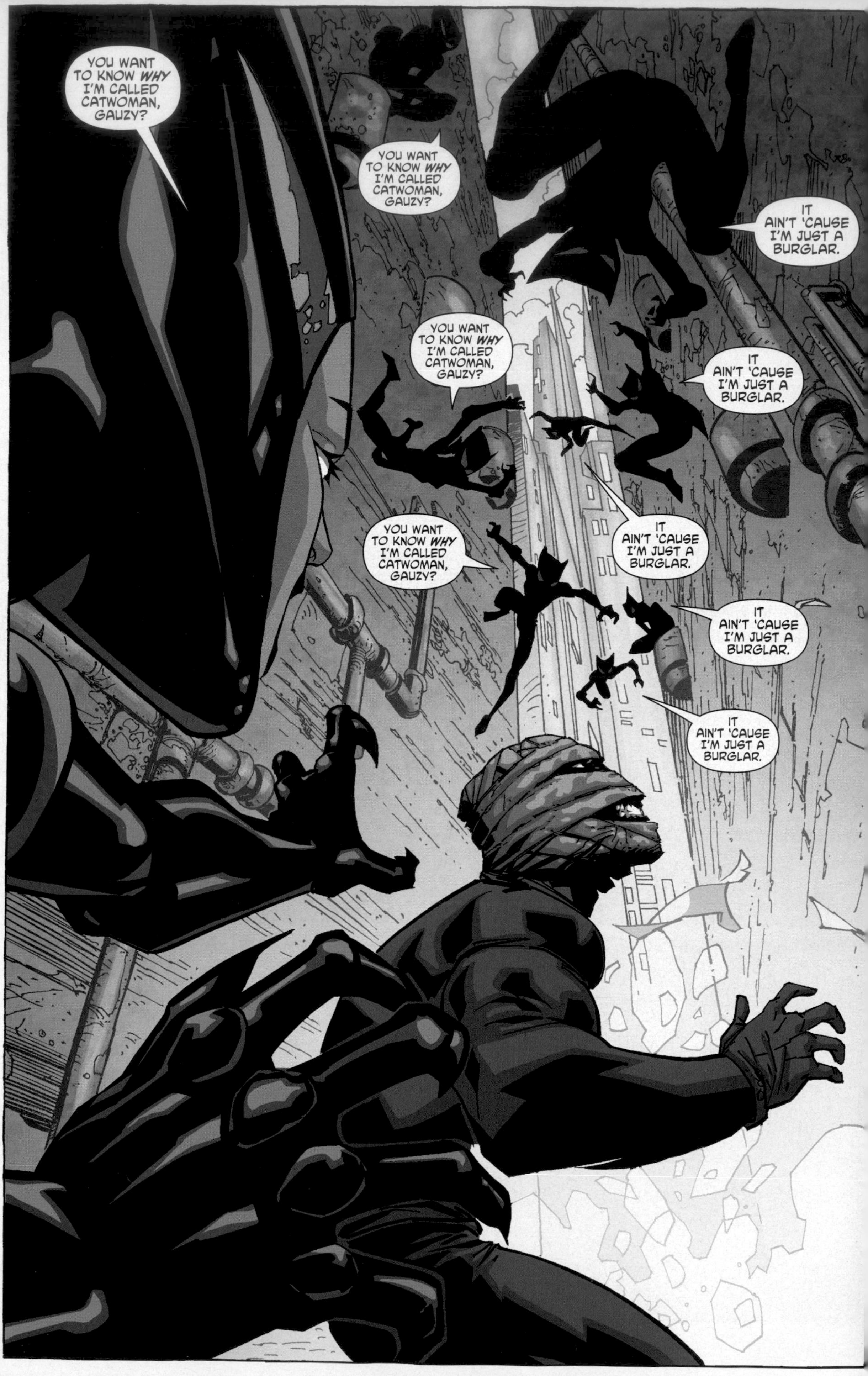
YOU WANT TO KNOW *WHY* I'M CALLED CATWOMAN, GAUZY?
YOU WANT TO KNOW *WHY* I'M CALLED CATWOMAN, GAUZY?
IT AIN'T 'CAUSE I'M JUST A BURGLAR.
YOU WANT TO KNOW *WHY* I'M CALLED CATWOMAN, GAUZY?
IT AIN'T 'CAUSE I'M JUST A BURGLAR.
YOU WANT TO KNOW *WHY* I'M CALLED CATWOMAN, GAUZY?
IT AIN'T 'CAUSE I'M JUST A BURGLAR.
IT AIN'T 'CAUSE I'M JUST A BURGLAR.
IT AIN'T 'CAUSE I'M JUST A BURGLAR.

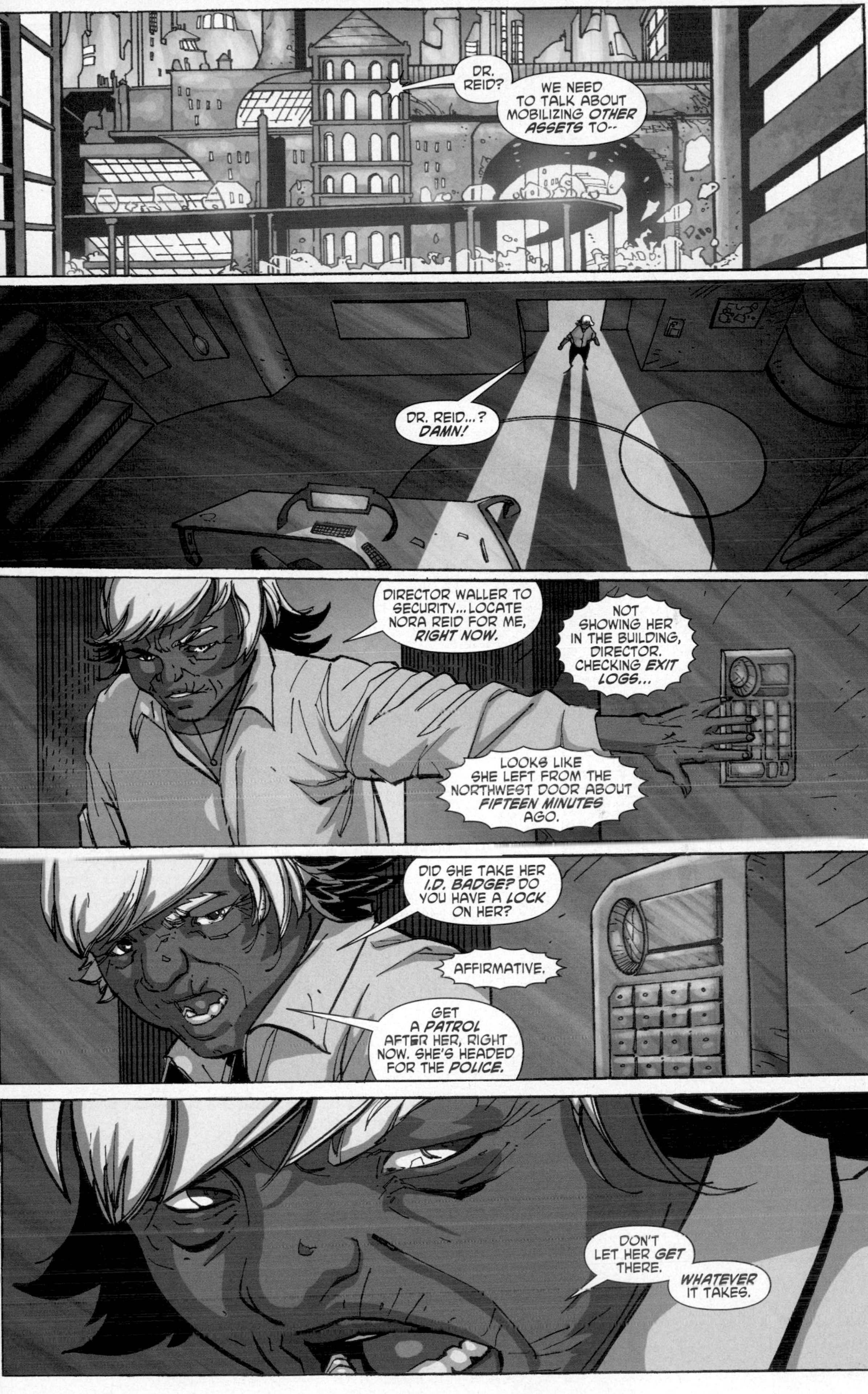
DR. REID?
WE NEED TO TALK ABOUT MOBILIZING OTHER ASSETS TO--
DR. REID...? DAMN!
DIRECTOR WALLER TO SECURITY...LOCATE NORA REID FOR ME, RIGHT NOW.
NOT SHOWING HER IN THE BUILDING, DIRECTOR. CHECKING EXIT LOGS...
LOOKS LIKE SHE LEFT FROM THE NORTHWEST DOOR ABOUT FIFTEEN MINUTES AGO.
DID SHE TAKE HER I.D. BADGE? DO YOU HAVE A LOCK ON HER?
AFFIRMATIVE.
GET A PATROL AFTER HER, RIGHT NOW. SHE'S HEADED FOR THE POLICE.
DON'T LET HER GET THERE. WHATEVER IT TAKES.

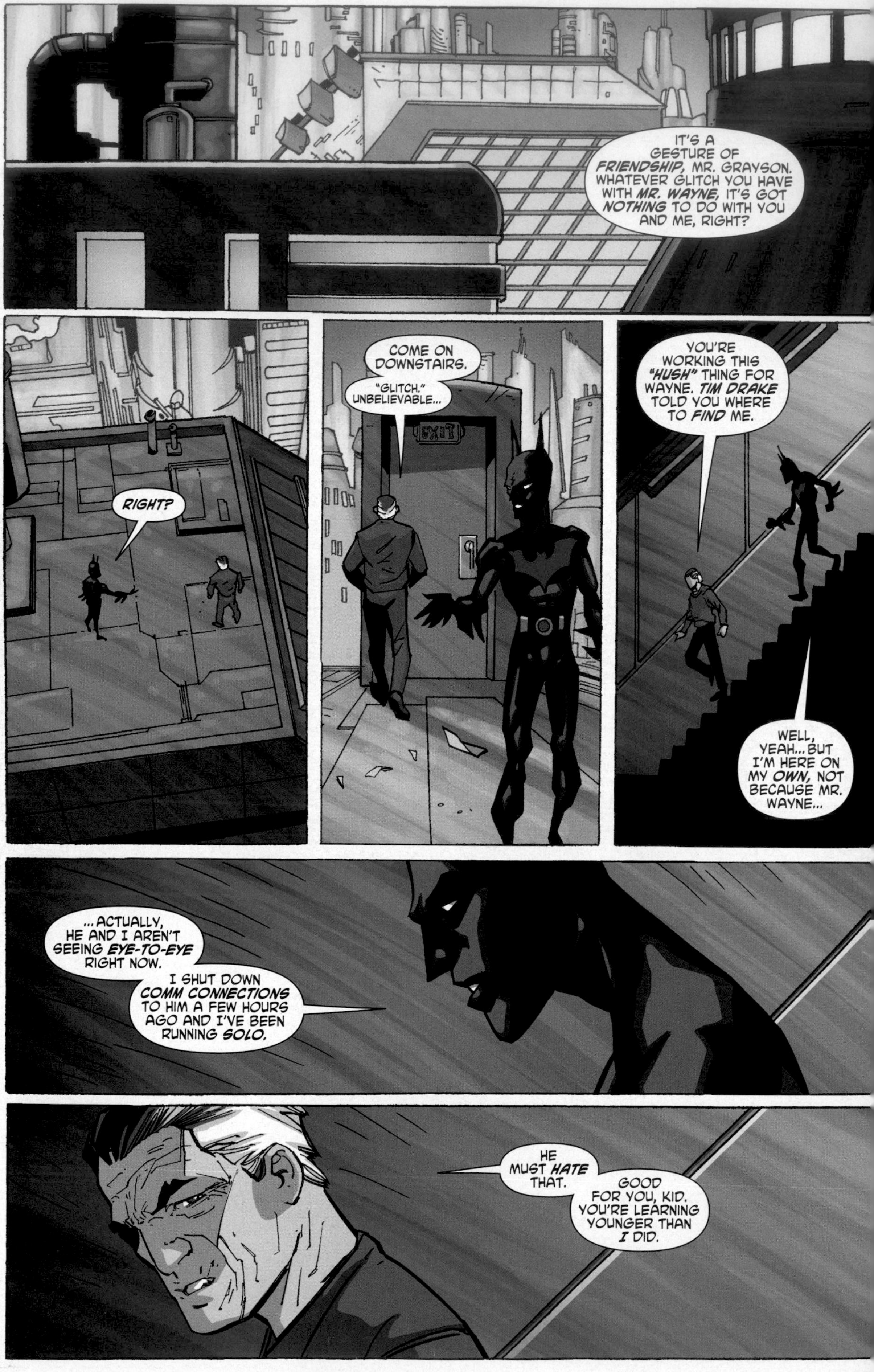
IT'S A GESTURE OF FRIENDSHIP, MR. GRAYSON. WHATEVER GLITCH YOU HAVE WITH MR. WAYNE, IT'S GOT NOTHING TO DO WITH YOU AND ME, RIGHT?
RIGHT?
COME ON DOWNSTAIRS.
"GLITCH." UNBELIEVABLE...
EXIT
YOU'RE WORKING THIS "HUSH" THING FOR WAYNE. TIM DRAKE TOLD YOU WHERE TO FIND ME.
WELL, YEAH... BUT I'M HERE ON MY OWN, NOT BECAUSE MR. WAYNE...
...ACTUALLY, HE AND I AREN'T SEEING EYE-TO-EYE RIGHT NOW.
I SHUT DOWN COMM CONNECTIONS TO HIM A FEW HOURS AGO AND I'VE BEEN RUNNING SOLO.
HE MUST HATE THAT.
GOOD FOR YOU, KID. YOU'RE LEARNING YOUNGER THAN I DID.

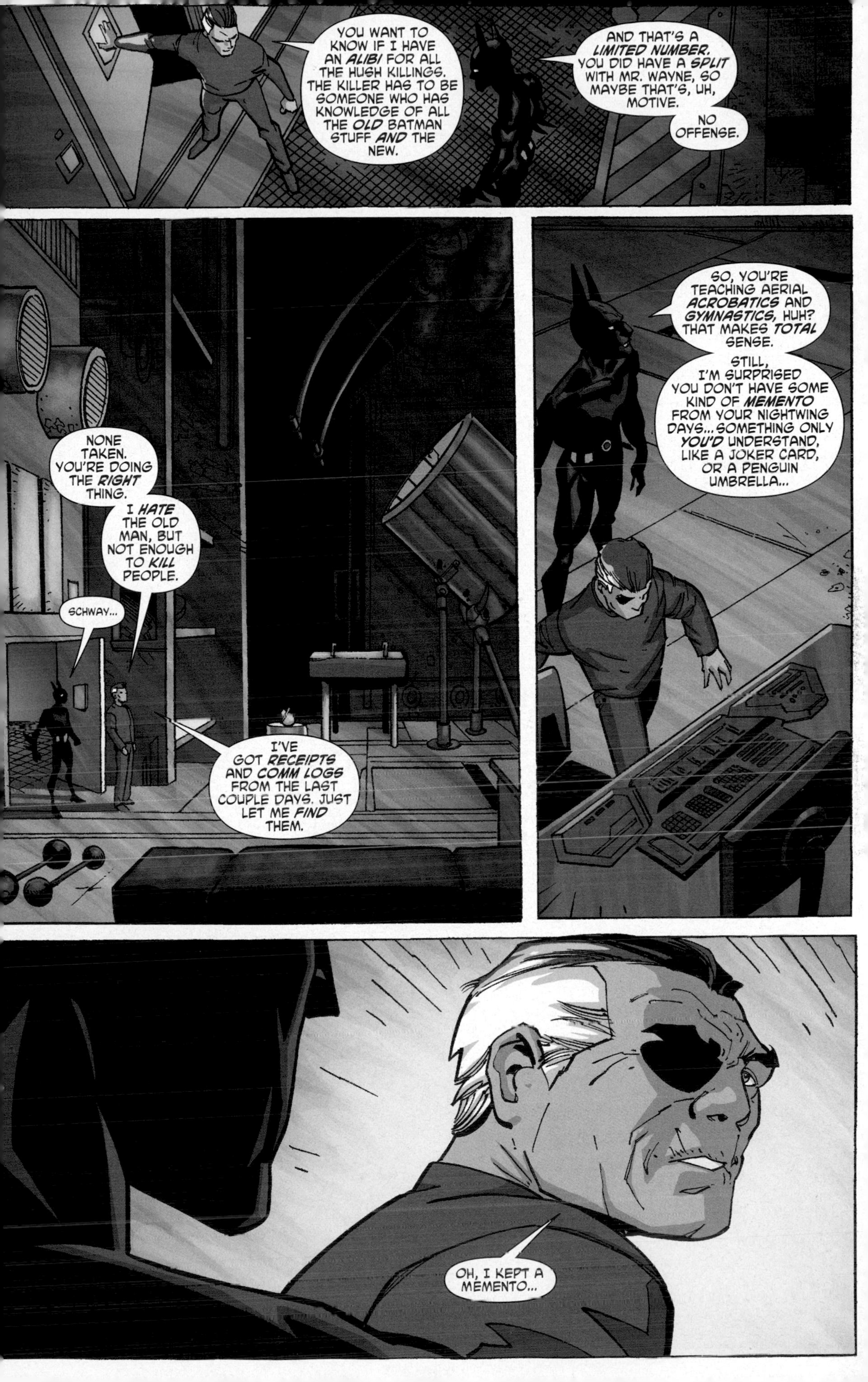
YOU WANT TO KNOW IF I HAVE AN ALIBI FOR ALL THE HUSH KILLINGS. THE KILLER HAS TO BE SOMEONE WHO HAS KNOWLEDGE OF ALL THE OLD BATMAN STUFF AND THE NEW.
AND THAT'S A LIMITED NUMBER. YOU DID HAVE A SPLIT WITH MR. WAYNE, SO MAYBE THAT'S, UH, MOTIVE.
NO OFFENSE.
NONE TAKEN. YOU'RE DOING THE RIGHT THING.
I HATE THE OLD MAN, BUT NOT ENOUGH TO KILL PEOPLE.
SCHWAY...
I'VE GOT RECEIPTS AND COMM LOGS FROM THE LAST COUPLE DAYS. JUST LET ME FIND THEM.
SO, YOU'RE TEACHING AERIAL ACROBATICS AND GYMNASTICS, HUH? THAT MAKES TOTAL SENSE.
STILL, I'M SURPRISED YOU DON'T HAVE SOME KIND OF MEMENTO FROM YOUR NIGHTWING DAYS...SOMETHING ONLY YOU'D UNDERSTAND, LIKE A JOKER CARD, OR A PENGUIN UMBRELLA...
OH, I KEPT A MEMENTO...

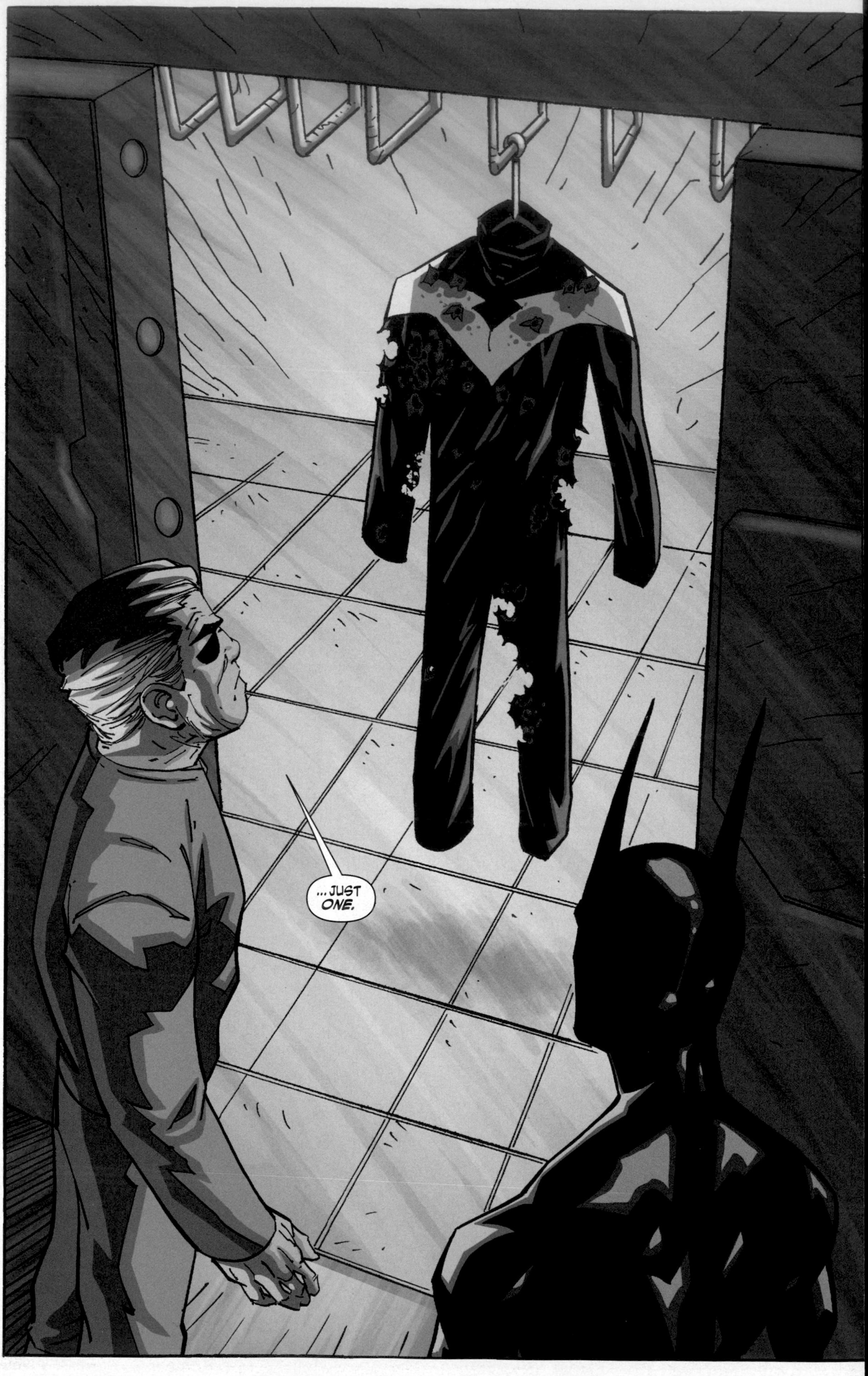
...JUST ONE.

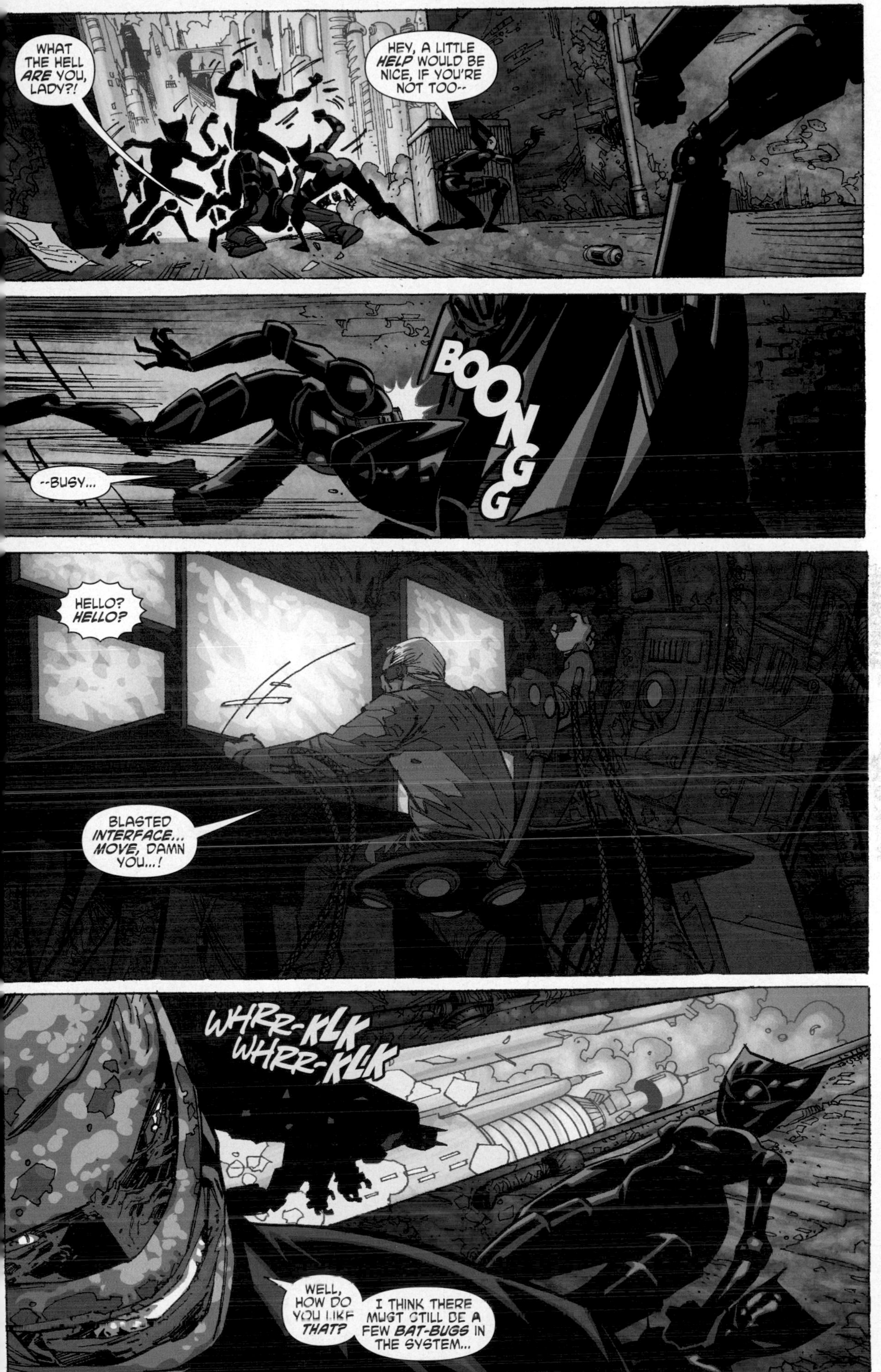
WHAT THE HELL ARE YOU, LADY?!
HEY, A LITTLE HELP WOULD BE NICE, IF YOU'RE NOT TOO--
BOONGG
--BUSY...
HELLO? HELLO?
BLASTED INTERFACE... MOVE, DAMN YOU...!
WHRR-KLK WHRR-KLK
WELL, HOW DO YOU LIKE THAT?
I THINK THERE MUST STILL BE A FEW BAT-BUGS IN THE SYSTEM...

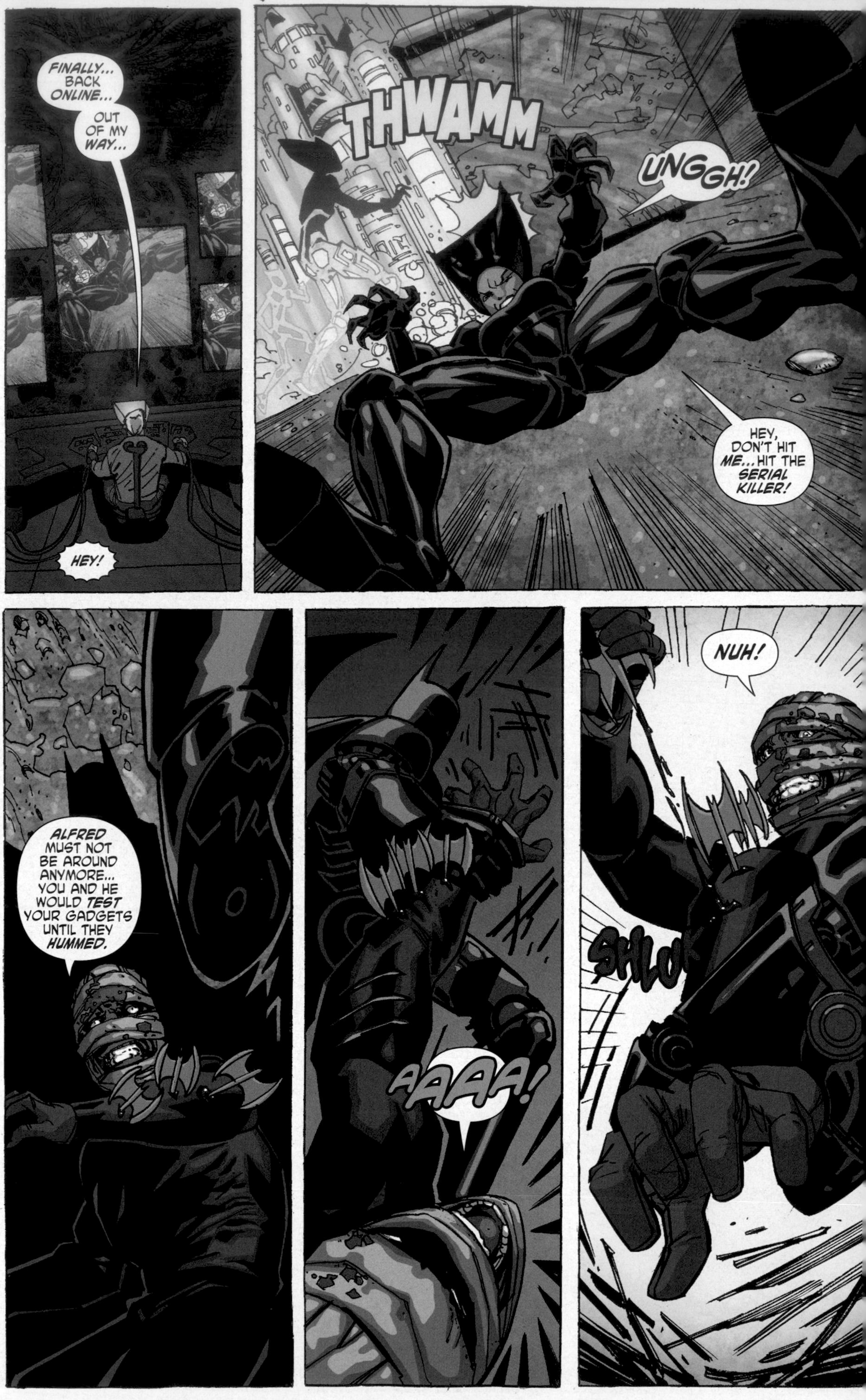
FINALLY... BACK ONLINE...
OUT OF MY WAY...
HEY!
THWAMM
UNGGH!
HEY, DON'T HIT ME... HIT THE SERIAL KILLER!
ALFRED MUST NOT BE AROUND ANYMORE... YOU AND HE WOULD TEST YOUR GADGETS UNTIL THEY HUMMED.
AAAA!
NUH!
SHLU

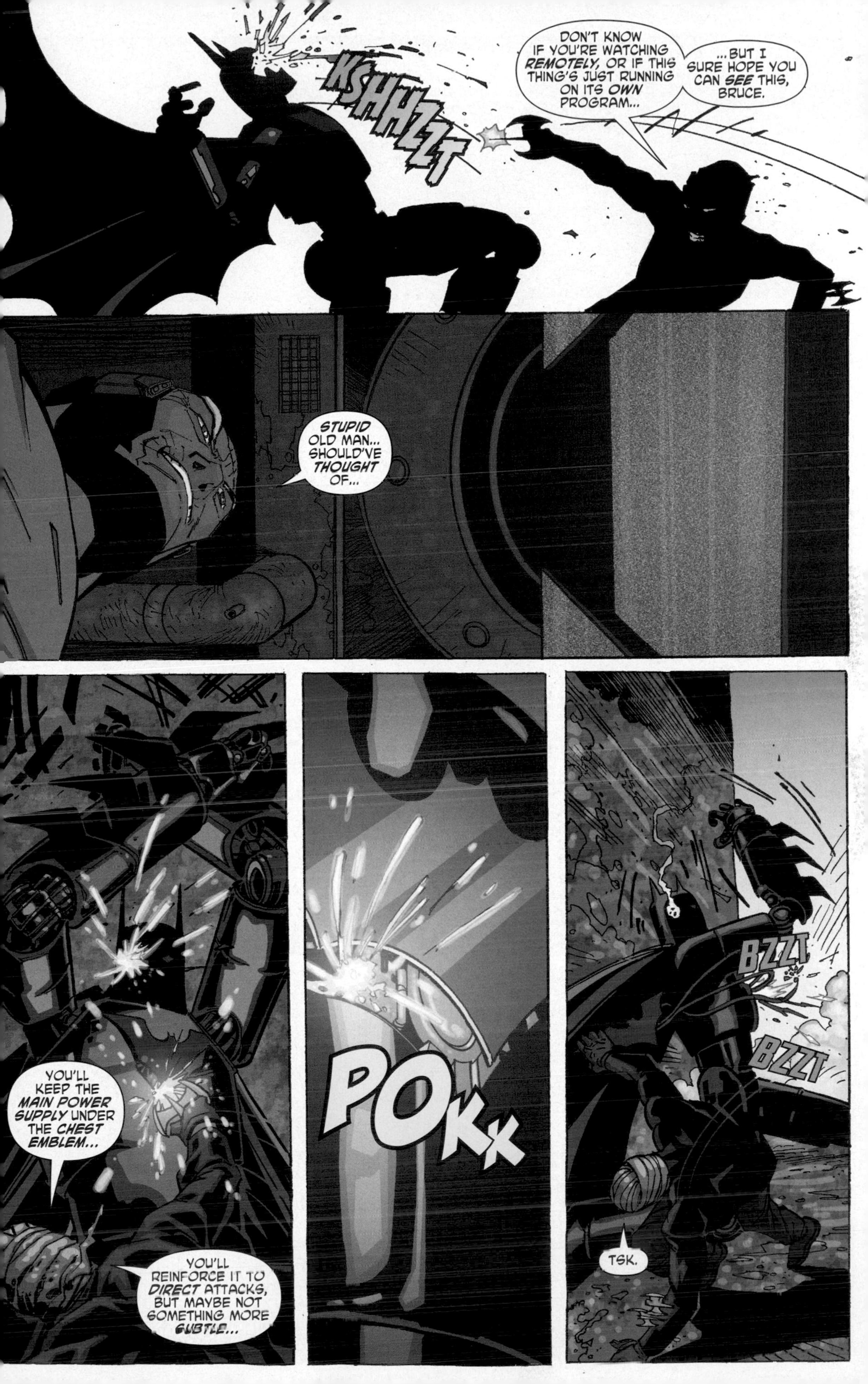
KSHHZZT
DON'T KNOW IF YOU'RE WATCHING *REMOTELY*, OR IF THIS THING'S JUST RUNNING ON ITS *OWN* PROGRAM...
...BUT I SURE HOPE YOU CAN *SEE* THIS, BRUCE.
STUPID OLD MAN... SHOULD'VE *THOUGHT* OF...
YOU'LL KEEP THE *MAIN POWER SUPPLY* UNDER THE *CHEST EMBLEM*...
YOU'LL REINFORCE IT TO *DIRECT* ATTACKS, BUT MAYBE NOT SOMETHING MORE *SUBTLE*...
POKK
BZZZT
BZZZT
TSK.

NO...NO! CAN'T LET HIM HAVE THE WRAITH FOR *STUDY*...

...BEFORE THE POWER *COMPLETELY* GOES, CATCH HIM IN THE *BLAST*...

...WAYNE INDUSTRIES BUILT THINGS *BETTER* IN MY DAY...

WHA-BOOOM

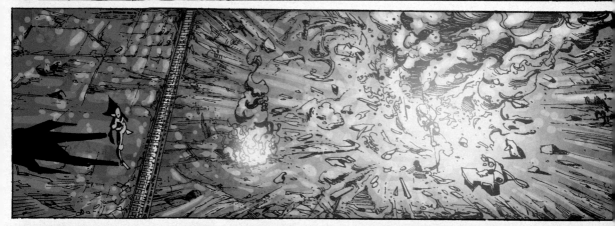

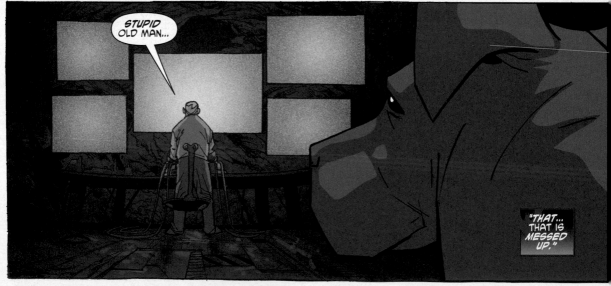

STUPID OLD MAN...

"*THAT*... THAT IS *MESSED UP.*"

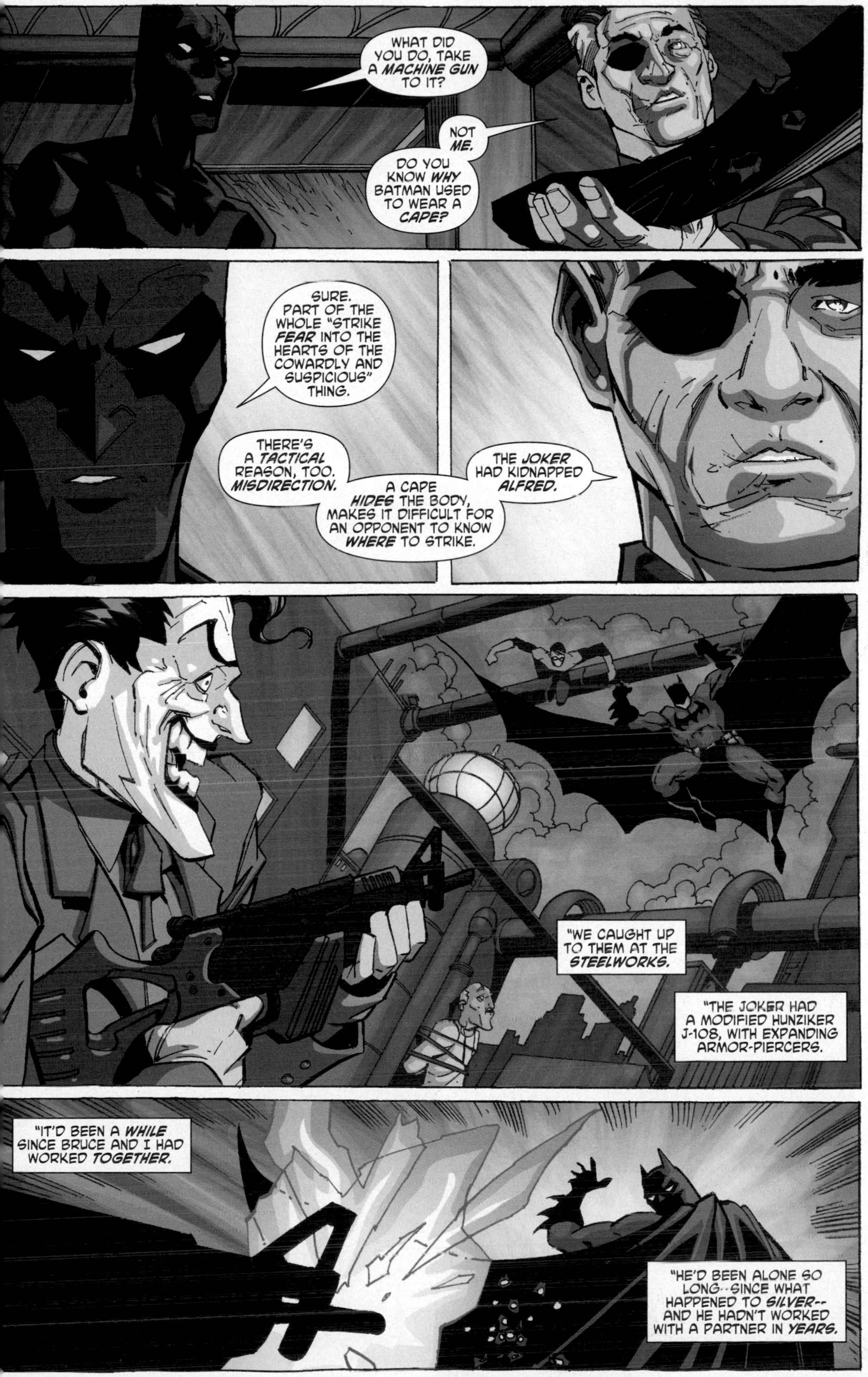
WHAT DID YOU DO, TAKE A MACHINE GUN TO IT?
NOT ME.
DO YOU KNOW WHY BATMAN USED TO WEAR A CAPE?
SURE. PART OF THE WHOLE "STRIKE FEAR INTO THE HEARTS OF THE COWARDLY AND SUSPICIOUS" THING.
THERE'S A TACTICAL REASON, TOO. MISDIRECTION.
A CAPE HIDES THE BODY, MAKES IT DIFFICULT FOR AN OPPONENT TO KNOW WHERE TO STRIKE.
THE JOKER HAD KIDNAPPED ALFRED.
"WE CAUGHT UP TO THEM AT THE STEELWORKS.
"THE JOKER HAD A MODIFIED HUNZIKER J-108, WITH EXPANDING ARMOR-PIERCERS.
"IT'D BEEN A WHILE SINCE BRUCE AND I HAD WORKED TOGETHER.
"HE'D BEEN ALONE SO LONG--SINCE WHAT HAPPENED TO SILVER--AND HE HADN'T WORKED WITH A PARTNER IN YEARS.

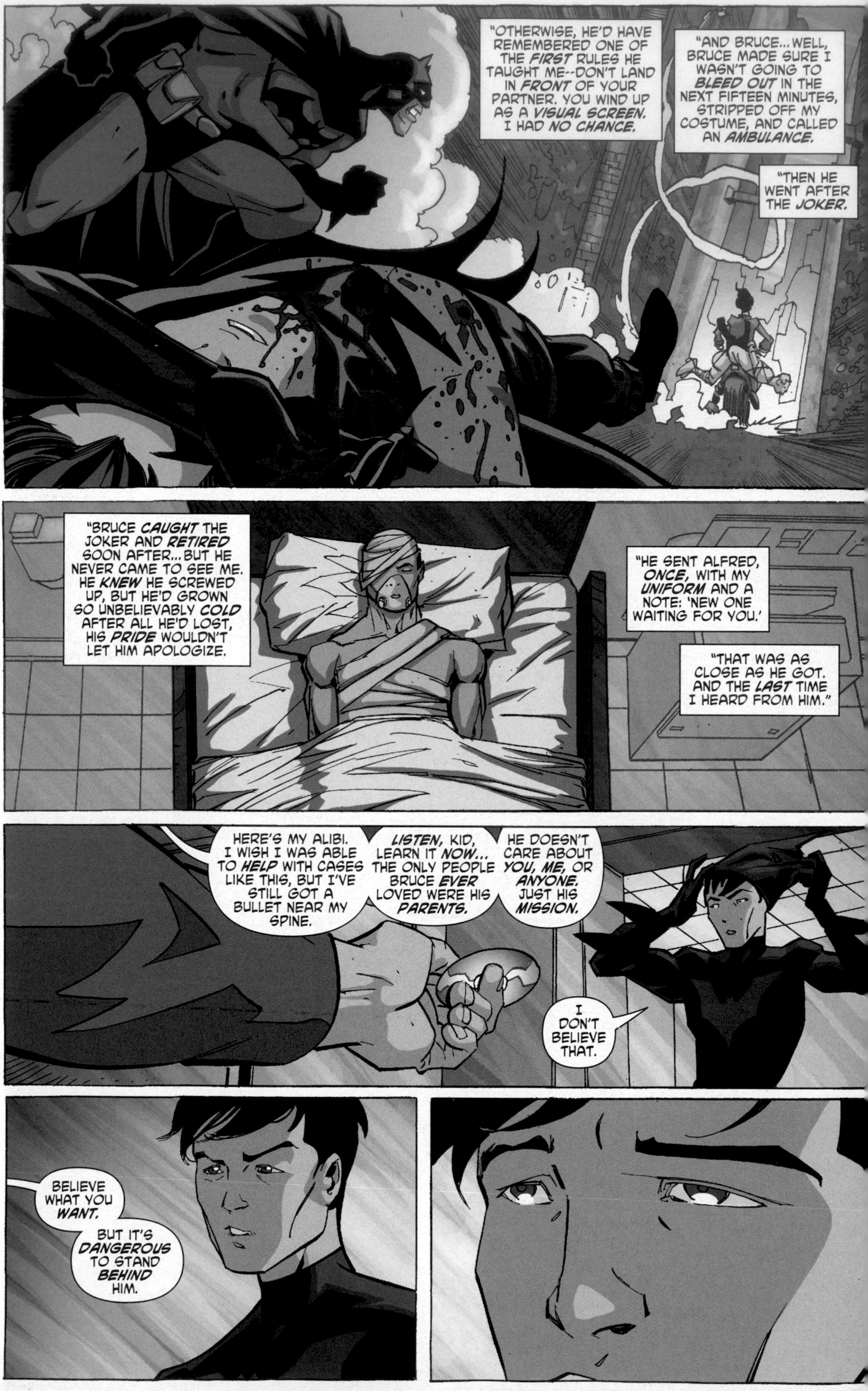
"OTHERWISE, HE'D HAVE REMEMBERED ONE OF THE FIRST RULES HE TAUGHT ME--DON'T LAND IN FRONT OF YOUR PARTNER. YOU WIND UP AS A VISUAL SCREEN. I HAD NO CHANCE.
"AND BRUCE...WELL, BRUCE MADE SURE I WASN'T GOING TO BLEED OUT IN THE NEXT FIFTEEN MINUTES, STRIPPED OFF MY COSTUME, AND CALLED AN AMBULANCE.
"THEN HE WENT AFTER THE JOKER.
"BRUCE CAUGHT THE JOKER AND RETIRED SOON AFTER...BUT HE NEVER CAME TO SEE ME. HE KNEW HE SCREWED UP, BUT HE'D GROWN SO UNBELIEVABLY COLD AFTER ALL HE'D LOST, HIS PRIDE WOULDN'T LET HIM APOLOGIZE.
"HE SENT ALFRED, ONCE, WITH MY UNIFORM AND A NOTE: 'NEW ONE WAITING FOR YOU.'
"THAT WAS AS CLOSE AS HE GOT. AND THE LAST TIME I HEARD FROM HIM."
HERE'S MY ALIBI. I WISH I WAS ABLE TO HELP WITH CASES LIKE THIS, BUT I'VE STILL GOT A BULLET NEAR MY SPINE.
LISTEN, KID, LEARN IT NOW... THE ONLY PEOPLE BRUCE EVER LOVED WERE HIS PARENTS.
HE DOESN'T CARE ABOUT YOU, ME, OR ANYONE. JUST HIS MISSION.
I DON'T BELIEVE THAT.
BELIEVE WHAT YOU WANT.
BUT IT'S DANGEROUS TO STAND BEHIND HIM.

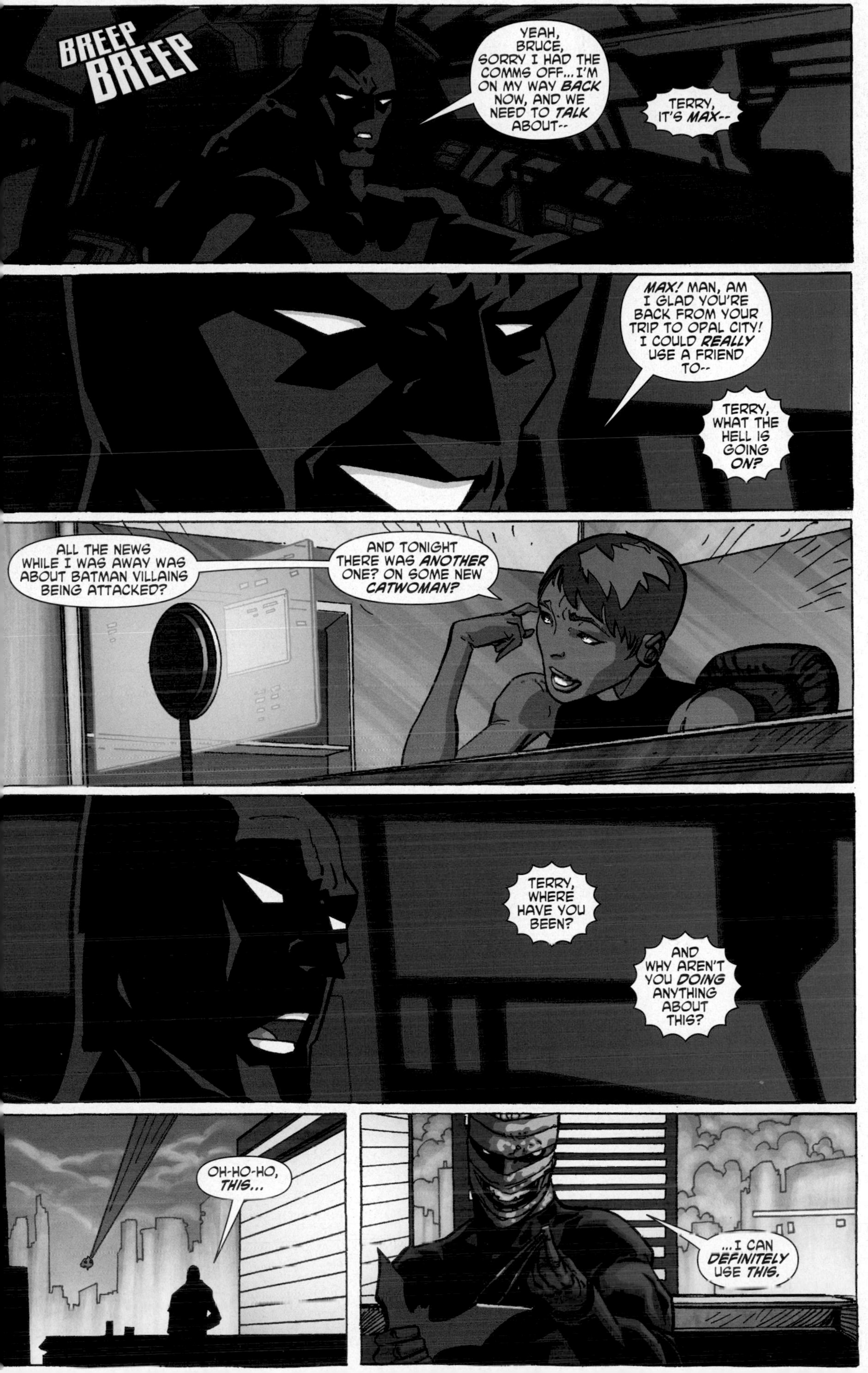
BREEP BREEP
YEAH, BRUCE, SORRY I HAD THE COMMS OFF... I'M ON MY WAY BACK NOW, AND WE NEED TO TALK ABOUT--
TERRY, IT'S MAX--
MAX! MAN, AM I GLAD YOU'RE BACK FROM YOUR TRIP TO OPAL CITY! I COULD REALLY USE A FRIEND TO--
TERRY, WHAT THE HELL IS GOING ON?
ALL THE NEWS WHILE I WAS AWAY WAS ABOUT BATMAN VILLAINS BEING ATTACKED?
AND TONIGHT THERE WAS ANOTHER ONE? ON SOME NEW CATWOMAN?
TERRY, WHERE HAVE YOU BEEN?
AND WHY AREN'T YOU DOING ANYTHING ABOUT THIS?
OH-HO-HO, THIS...
...I CAN DEFINITELY USE THIS.

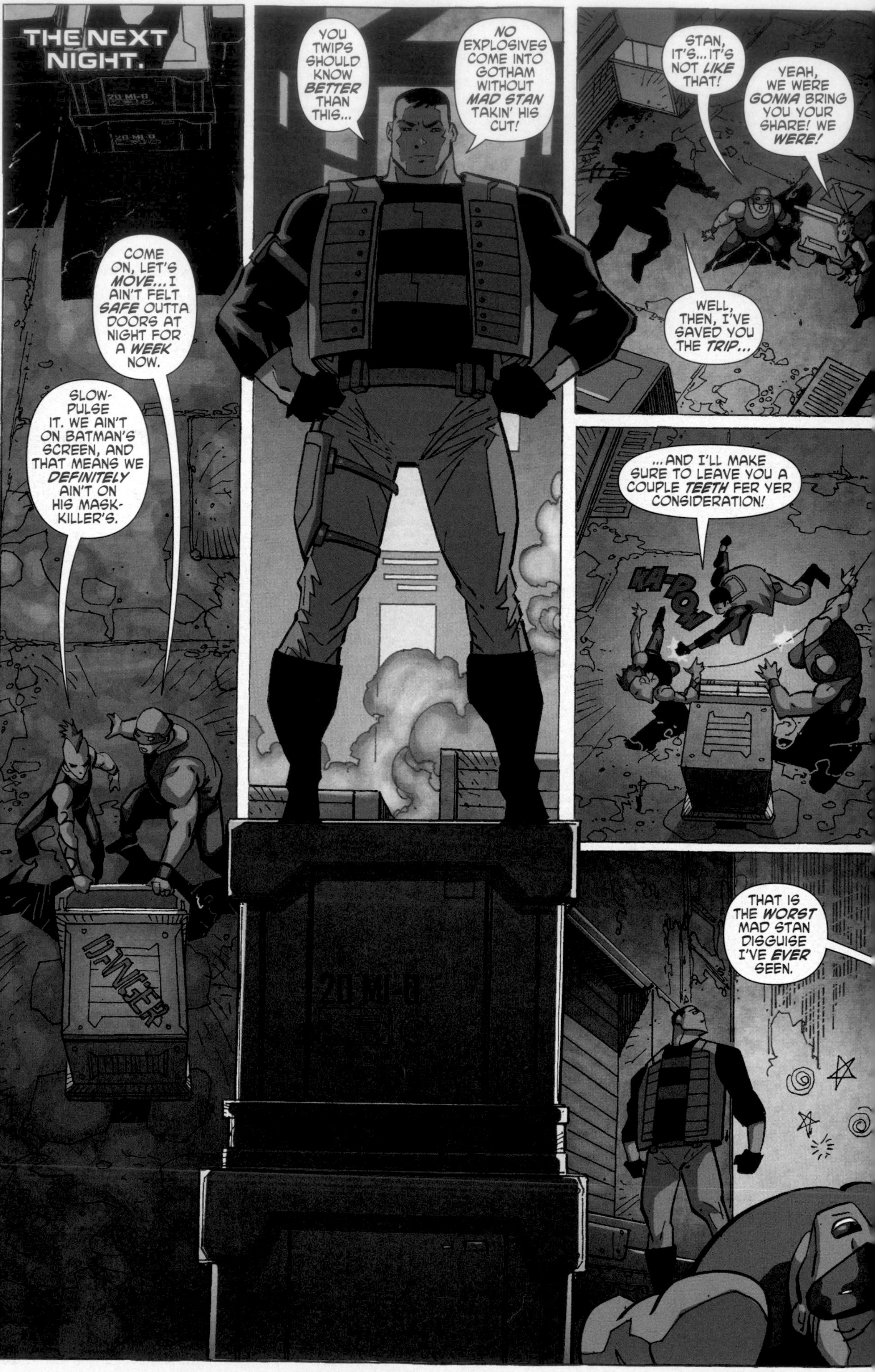
THE NEXT NIGHT.
COME ON, LET'S MOVE... I AIN'T FELT SAFE OUTTA DOORS AT NIGHT FOR A WEEK NOW.
SLOW-PULSE IT. WE AIN'T ON BATMAN'S SCREEN, AND THAT MEANS WE DEFINITELY AIN'T ON HIS MASK-KILLER'S.
DANGER
YOU TWIPS SHOULD KNOW BETTER THAN THIS...
NO EXPLOSIVES COME INTO GOTHAM WITHOUT MAD STAN TAKIN' HIS CUT!
STAN, IT'S... IT'S NOT LIKE THAT!
YEAH, WE WERE GONNA BRING YOU YOUR SHARE! WE WERE!
WELL, THEN, I'VE SAVED YOU THE TRIP...
...AND I'LL MAKE SURE TO LEAVE YOU A COUPLE TEETH FER YER CONSIDERATION!
KA-POW
THAT IS THE WORST MAD STAN DISGUISE I'VE EVER SEEN.

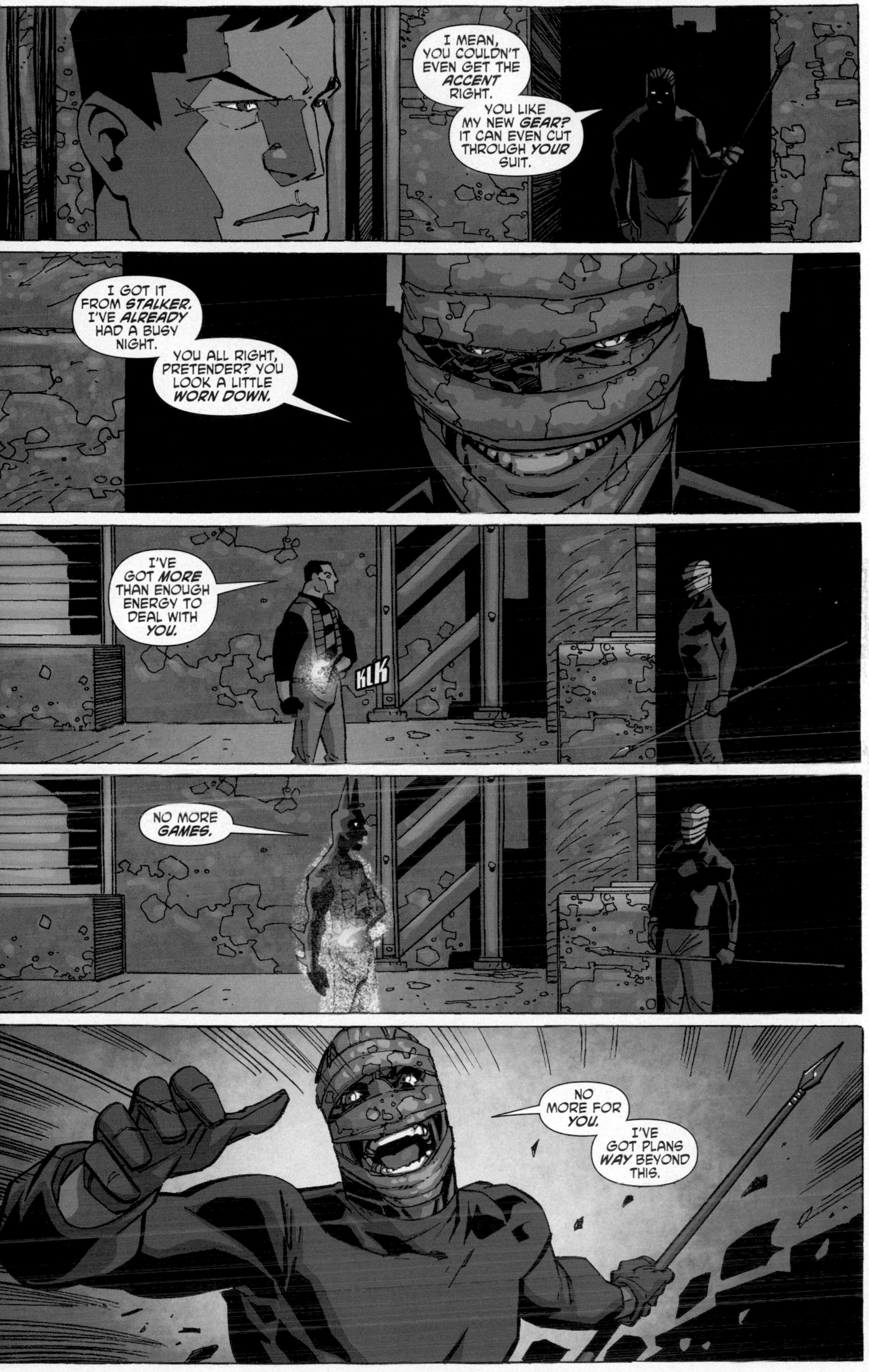
I MEAN, YOU COULDN'T EVEN GET THE ACCENT RIGHT.
YOU LIKE MY NEW GEAR? IT CAN EVEN CUT THROUGH YOUR SUIT.
I GOT IT FROM STALKER. I'VE ALREADY HAD A BUSY NIGHT.
YOU ALL RIGHT, PRETENDER? YOU LOOK A LITTLE WORN DOWN.
I'VE GOT MORE THAN ENOUGH ENERGY TO DEAL WITH YOU.
KLK
NO MORE GAMES.
NO MORE FOR YOU.
I'VE GOT PLANS WAY BEYOND THIS.

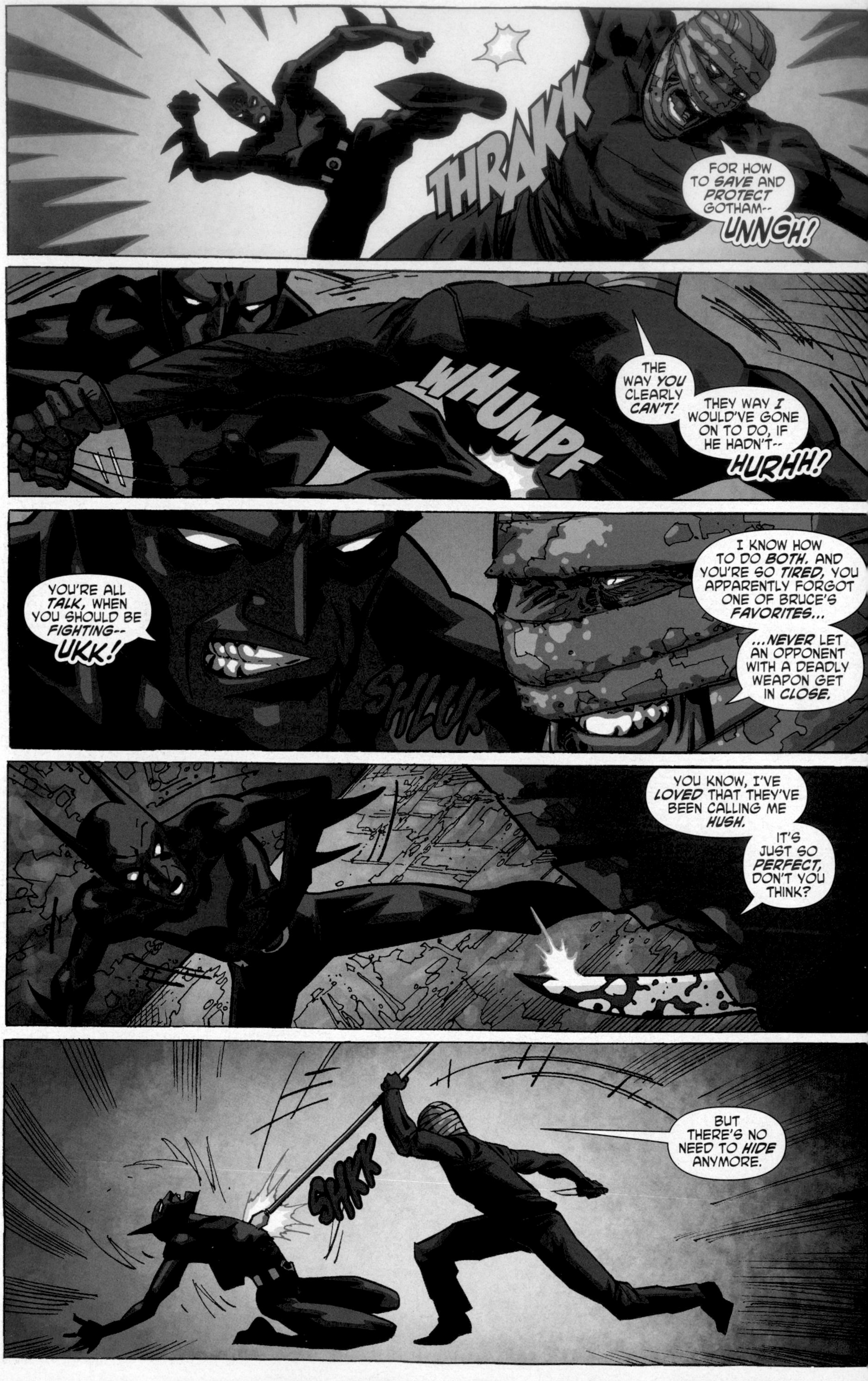
THRAKK
FOR HOW TO SAVE AND PROTECT GOTHAM-- UNNGH!
WHUMPF
THE WAY YOU CLEARLY CAN'T!
THEY WAY I WOULD'VE GONE ON TO DO, IF HE HADN'T-- HURHH!
YOU'RE ALL TALK, WHEN YOU SHOULD BE FIGHTING-- UKK!
SHLUK
I KNOW HOW TO DO BOTH. AND YOU'RE SO TIRED, YOU APPARENTLY FORGOT ONE OF BRUCE'S FAVORITES...
...NEVER LET AN OPPONENT WITH A DEADLY WEAPON GET IN CLOSE.
YOU KNOW, I'VE LOVED THAT THEY'VE BEEN CALLING ME HUSH.
IT'S JUST SO PERFECT, DON'T YOU THINK?
BUT THERE'S NO NEED TO HIDE ANYMORE.
SHKK

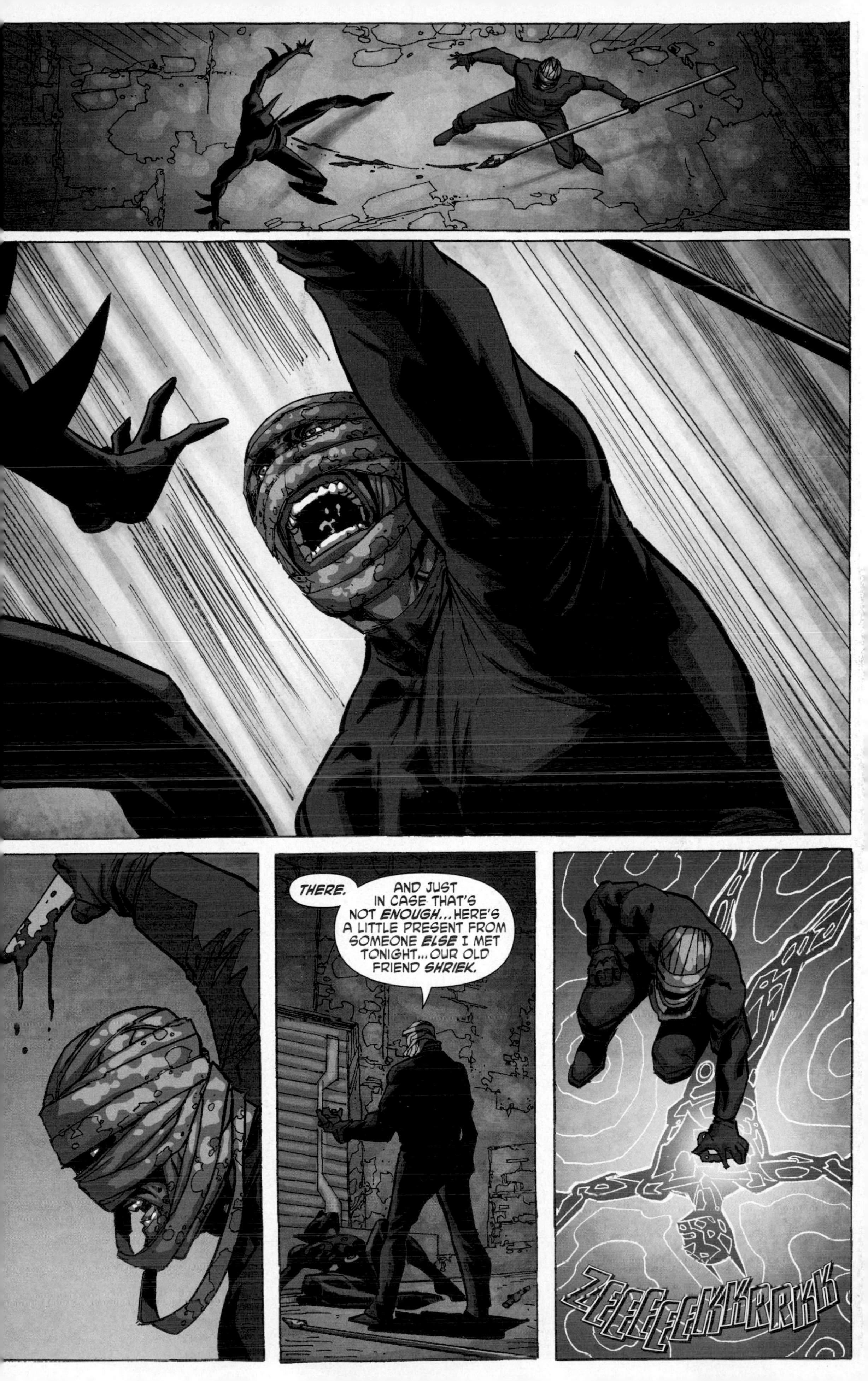
THERE.
AND JUST IN CASE THAT'S NOT ENOUGH... HERE'S A LITTLE PRESENT FROM SOMEONE ELSE I MET TONIGHT... OUR OLD FRIEND SHRIEK.
ZZEEEEEKKRRKK

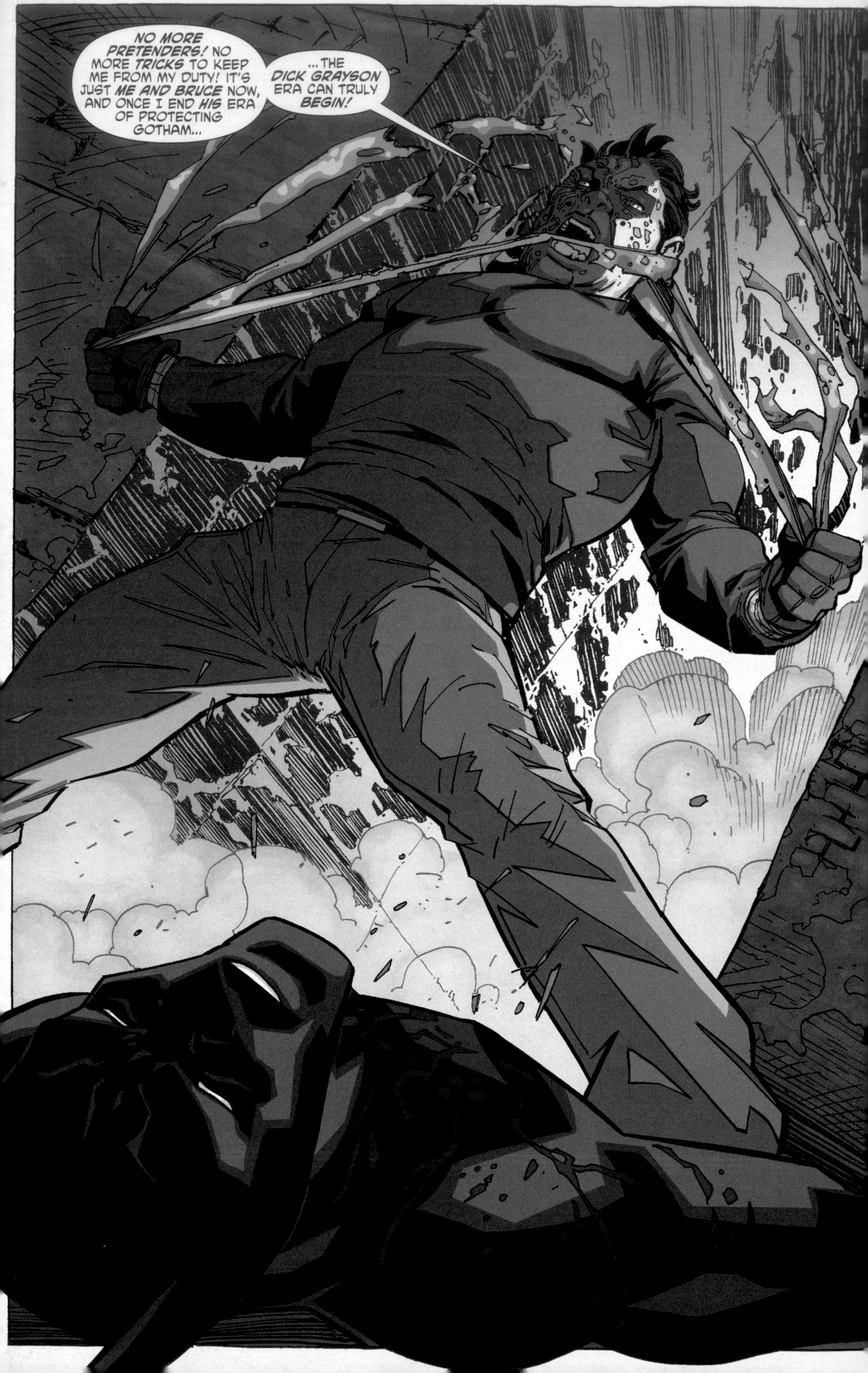
NO MORE PRETENDERS! NO MORE TRICKS TO KEEP ME FROM MY DUTY! IT'S JUST ME AND BRUCE NOW, AND ONCE I END HIS ERA OF PROTECTING GOTHAM...
...THE DICK GRAYSON ERA CAN TRULY BEGIN!

PART 5: BLOOD IN BACK ALLEYS

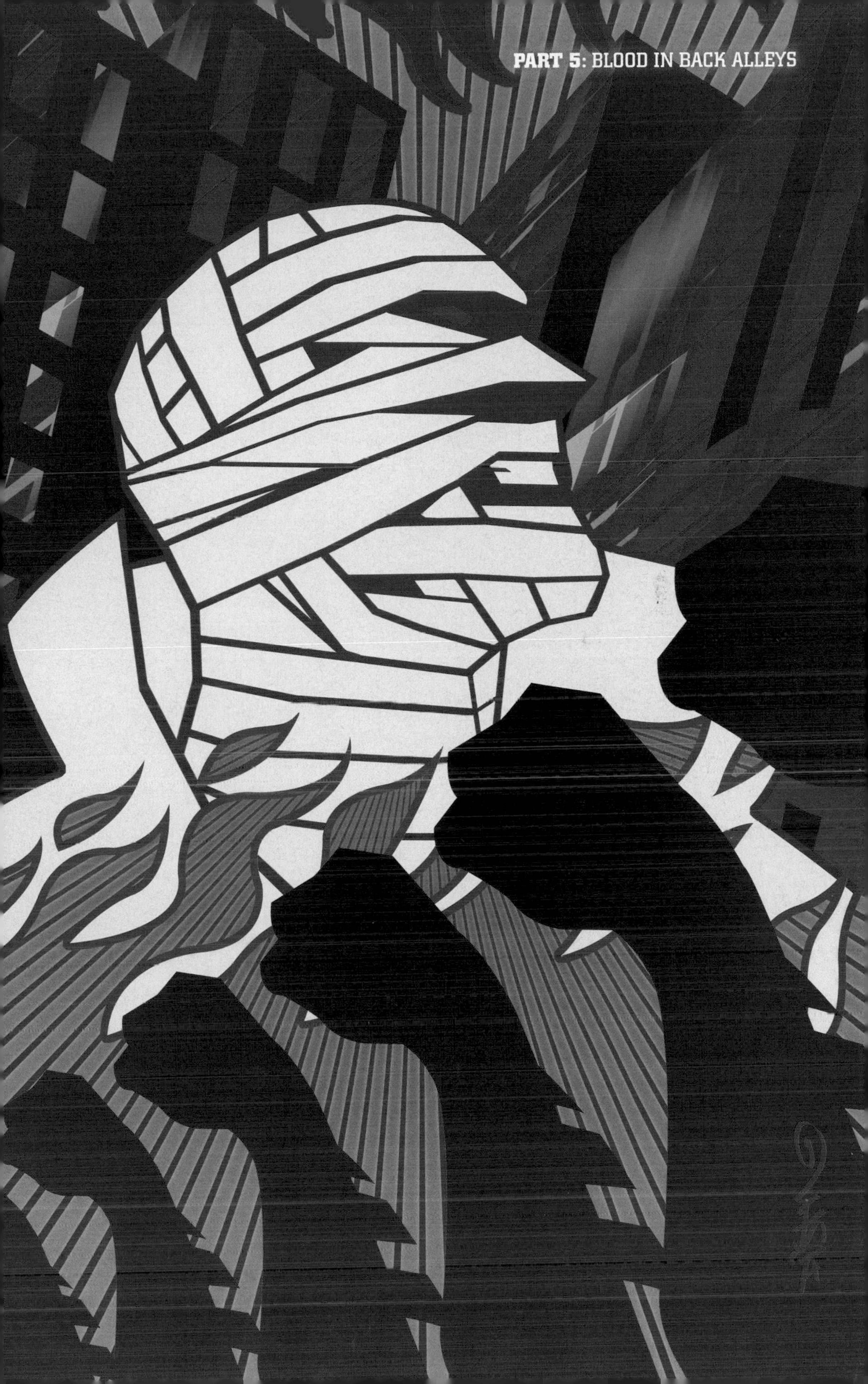

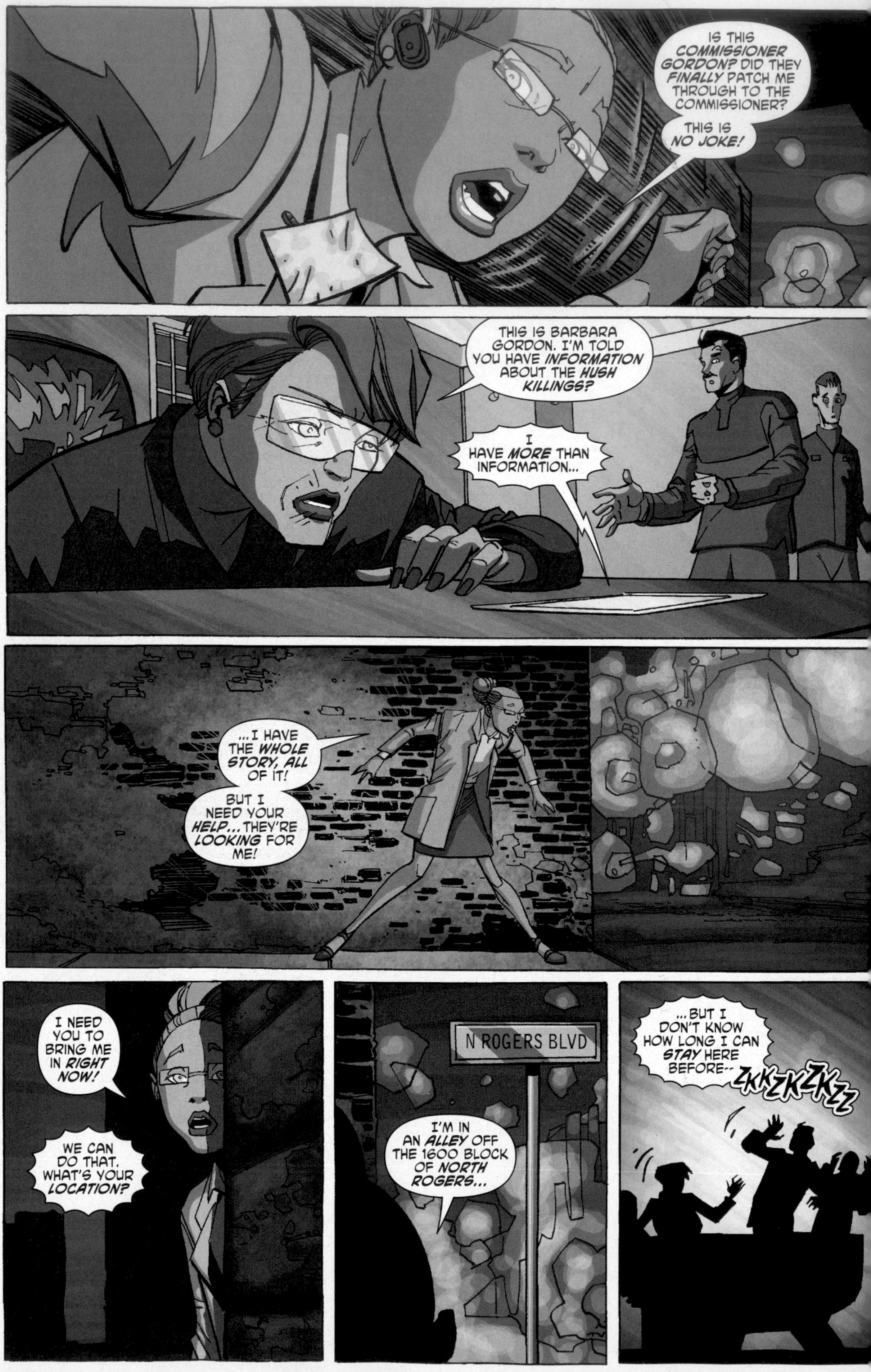
IS THIS COMMISSIONER GORDON? DID THEY FINALLY PATCH ME THROUGH TO THE COMMISSIONER?
THIS IS NO JOKE!
THIS IS BARBARA GORDON. I'M TOLD YOU HAVE INFORMATION ABOUT THE HUSH KILLINGS?
I HAVE MORE THAN INFORMATION...
...I HAVE THE WHOLE STORY, ALL OF IT!
BUT I NEED YOUR HELP... THEY'RE LOOKING FOR ME!
I NEED YOU TO BRING ME IN RIGHT NOW!
WE CAN DO THAT. WHAT'S YOUR LOCATION?
N ROGERS BLVD
I'M IN AN ALLEY OFF THE 1600 BLOCK OF NORTH ROGERS...
...BUT I DON'T KNOW HOW LONG I CAN STAY HERE BEFORE--
ZKKZKZKZZ

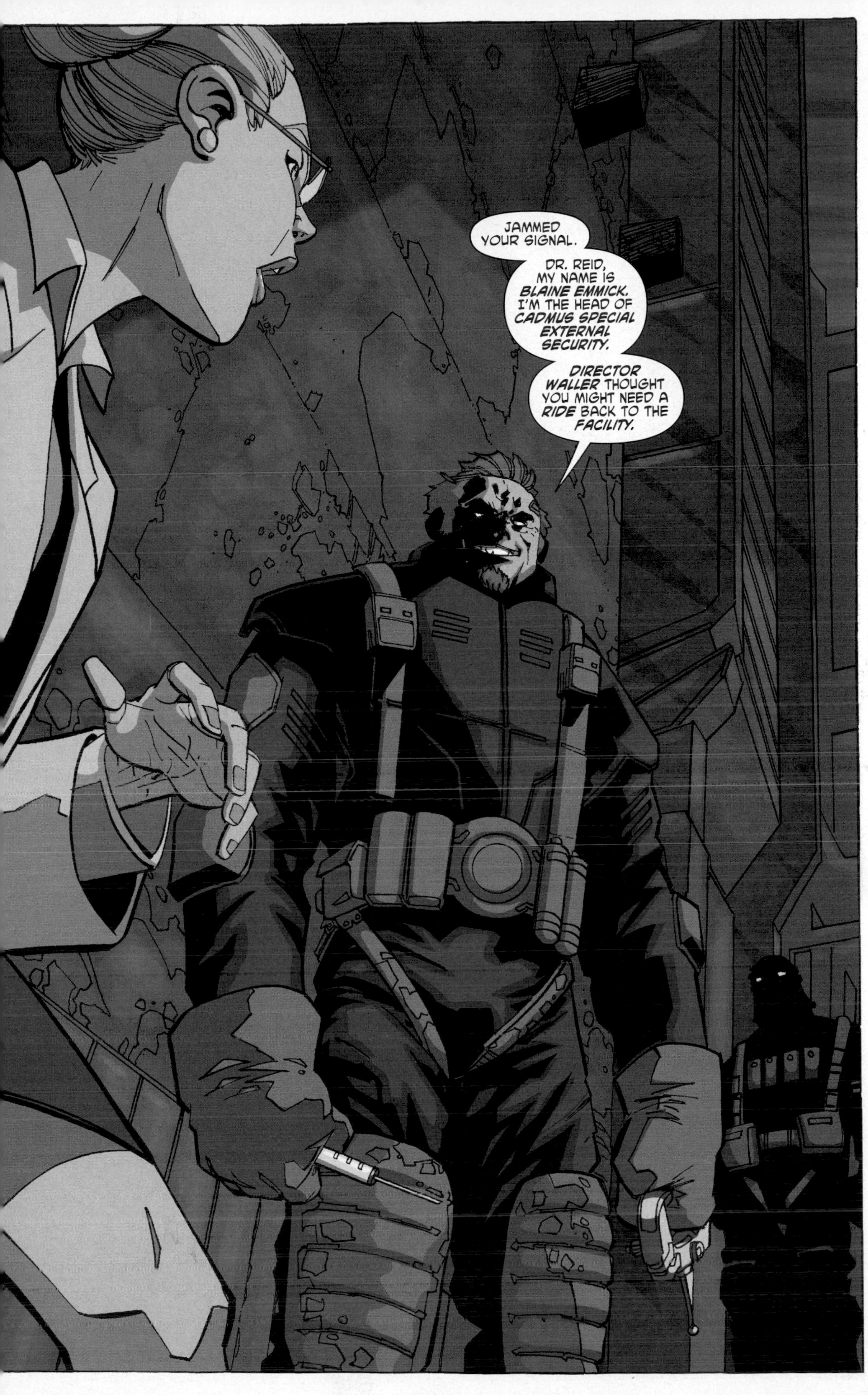
JAMMED YOUR SIGNAL.
DR. REID, MY NAME IS BLAINE EMMICK. I'M THE HEAD OF CADMUS SPECIAL EXTERNAL SECURITY.
DIRECTOR WALLER THOUGHT YOU MIGHT NEED A RIDE BACK TO THE FACILITY.

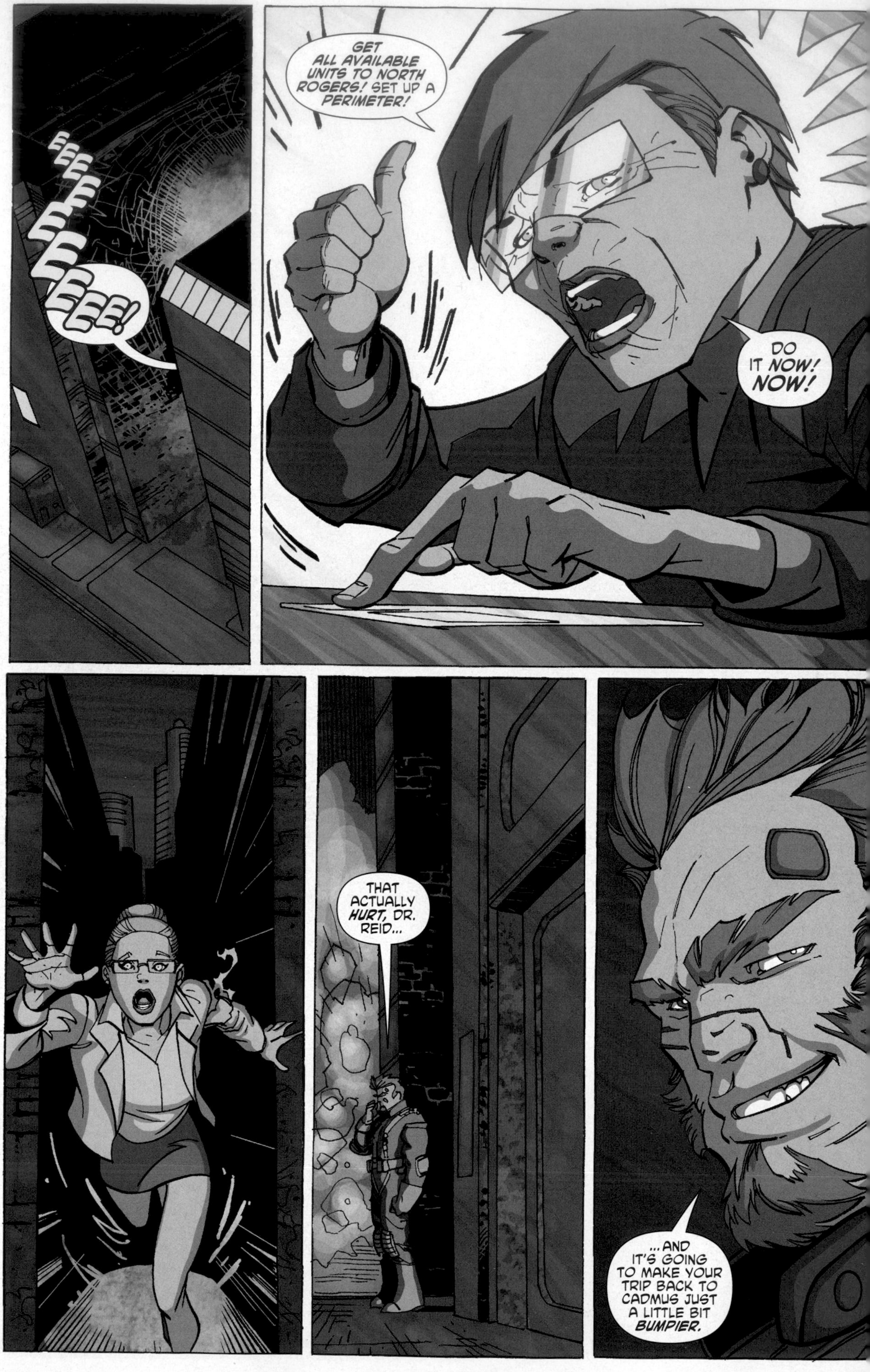
EEEEEEEEEE!
GET ALL AVAILABLE UNITS TO NORTH ROGERS! SET UP A PERIMETER!
DO IT NOW! NOW!
THAT ACTUALLY HURT, DR. REID...
...AND IT'S GOING TO MAKE YOUR TRIP BACK TO CADMUS JUST A LITTLE BIT BUMPIER.

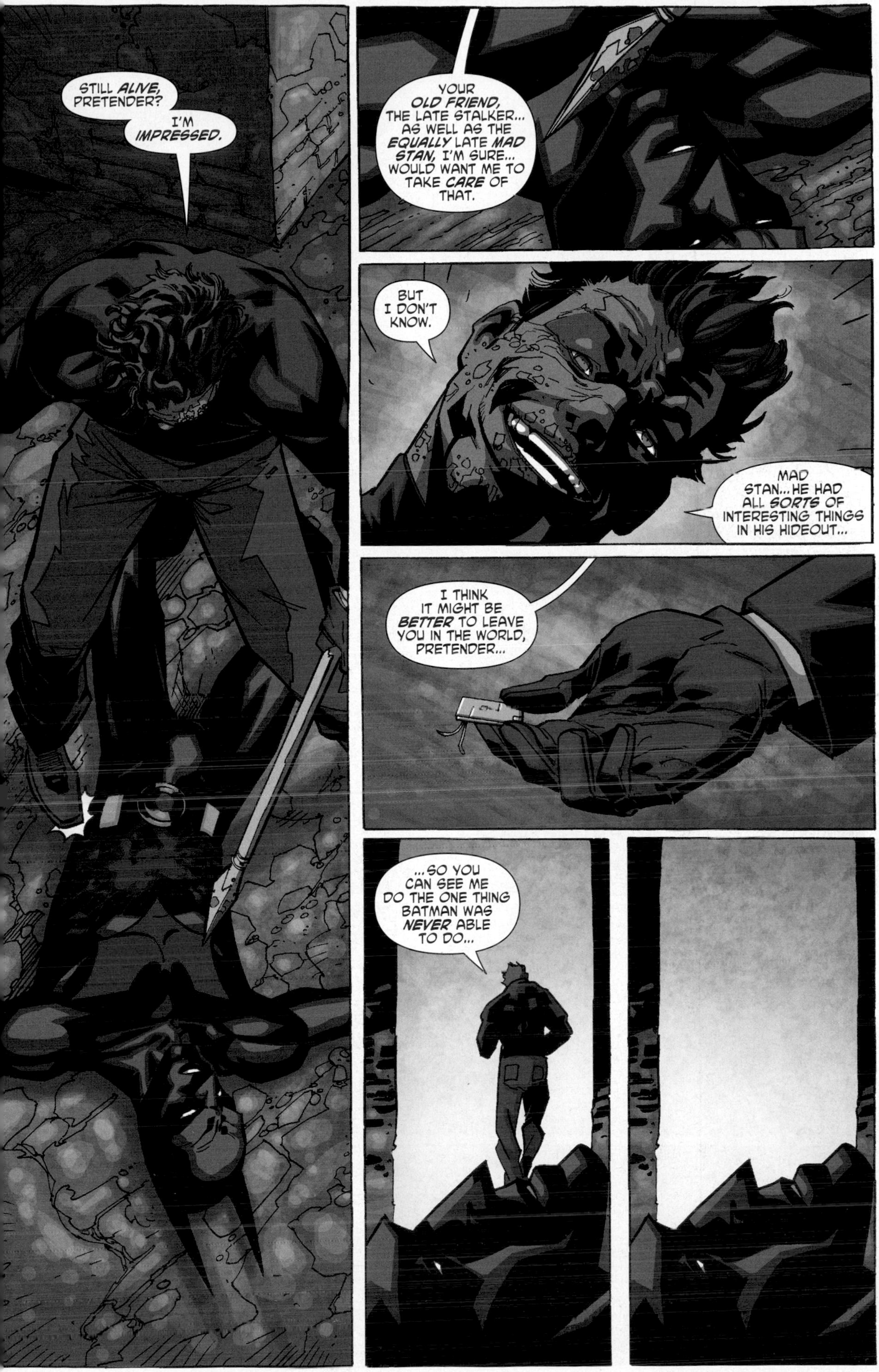
STILL ALIVE, PRETENDER?
I'M IMPRESSED.
YOUR OLD FRIEND, THE LATE STALKER... AS WELL AS THE EQUALLY LATE MAD STAN, I'M SURE... WOULD WANT ME TO TAKE CARE OF THAT.
BUT I DON'T KNOW.
MAD STAN... HE HAD ALL SORTS OF INTERESTING THINGS IN HIS HIDEOUT...
I THINK IT MIGHT BE BETTER TO LEAVE YOU IN THE WORLD, PRETENDER...
...SO YOU CAN SEE ME DO THE ONE THING BATMAN WAS NEVER ABLE TO DO...

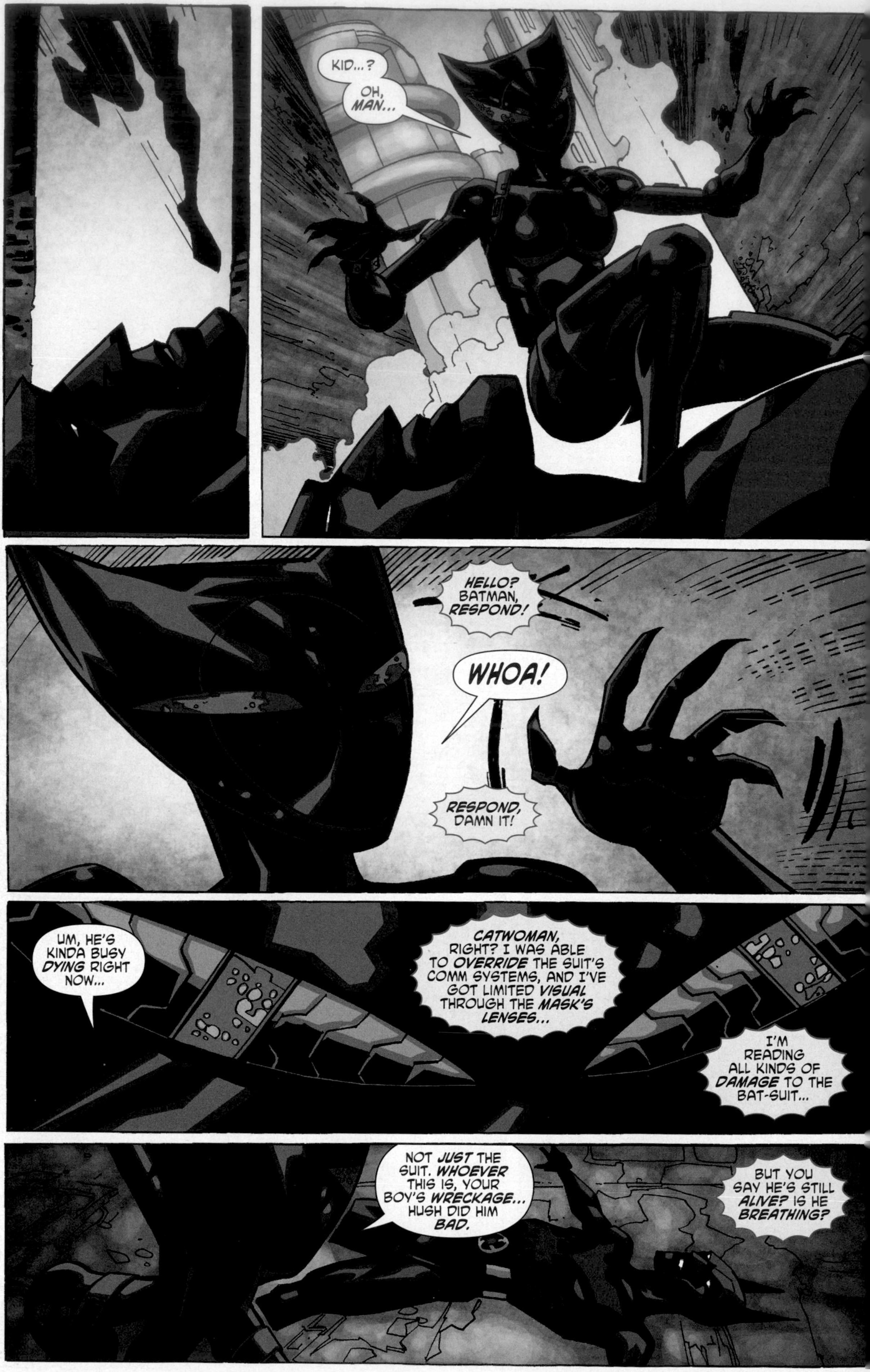
KID...?
OH, MAN...
HELLO? BATMAN, RESPOND!
WHOA!
RESPOND, DAMN IT!
UM, HE'S KINDA BUSY DYING RIGHT NOW...
CATWOMAN, RIGHT? I WAS ABLE TO OVERRIDE THE SUIT'S COMM SYSTEMS, AND I'VE GOT LIMITED VISUAL THROUGH THE MASK'S LENSES...
I'M READING ALL KINDS OF DAMAGE TO THE BAT-SUIT...
NOT JUST THE SUIT. WHOEVER THIS IS, YOUR BOY'S WRECKAGE... HUSH DID HIM BAD.
BUT YOU SAY HE'S STILL ALIVE? IS HE BREATHING?

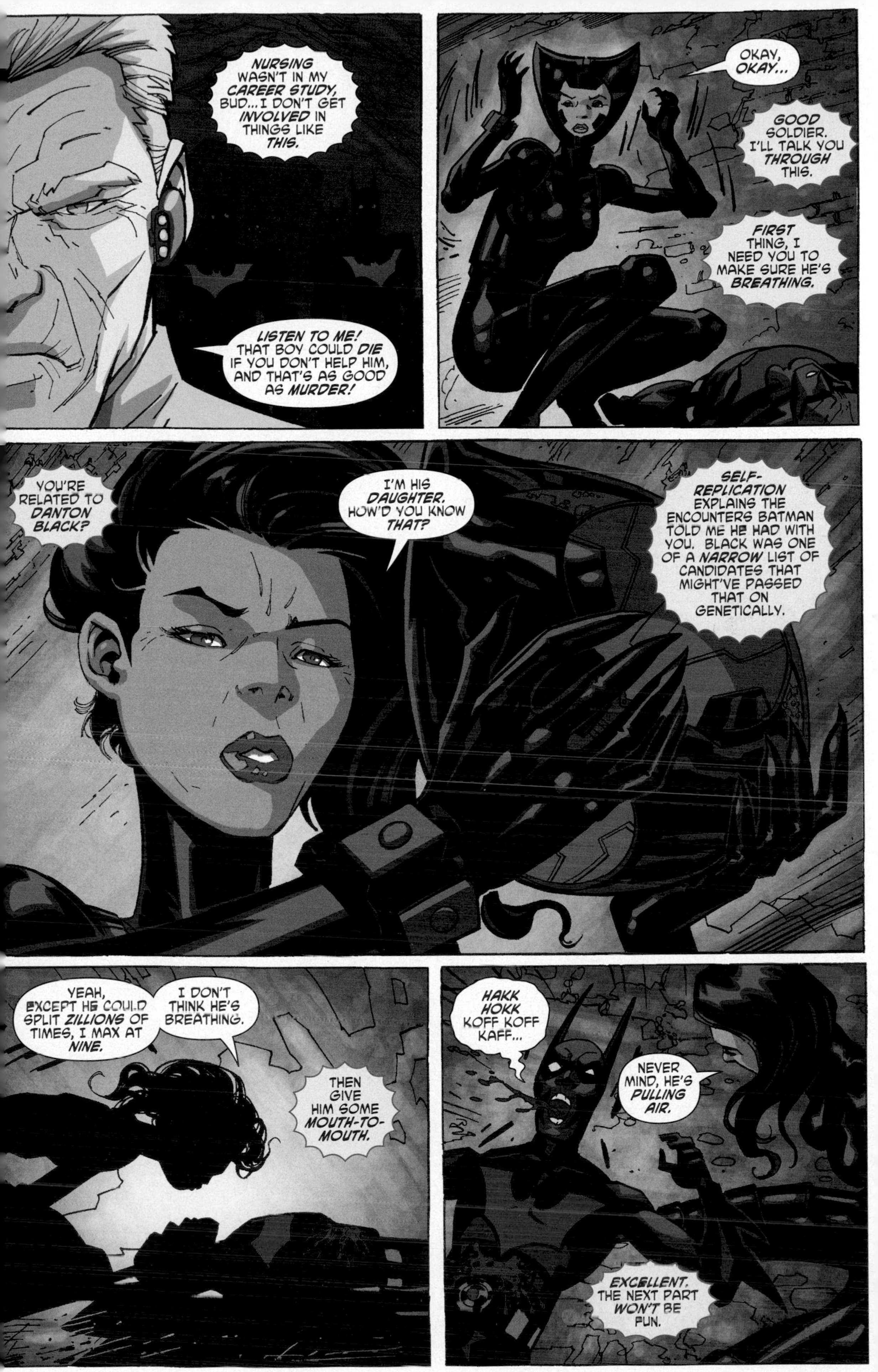
NURSING WASN'T IN MY CAREER STUDY, BUD... I DON'T GET INVOLVED IN THINGS LIKE THIS.
LISTEN TO ME! THAT BOY COULD DIE IF YOU DON'T HELP HIM, AND THAT'S AS GOOD AS MURDER!
OKAY, OKAY...
GOOD SOLDIER. I'LL TALK YOU THROUGH THIS.
FIRST THING, I NEED YOU TO MAKE SURE HE'S BREATHING.
YOU'RE RELATED TO DANTON BLACK?
I'M HIS DAUGHTER. HOW'D YOU KNOW THAT?
SELF-REPLICATION EXPLAINS THE ENCOUNTERS BATMAN TOLD ME HE HAD WITH YOU. BLACK WAS ONE OF A NARROW LIST OF CANDIDATES THAT MIGHT'VE PASSED THAT ON GENETICALLY.
YEAH, EXCEPT HE COULD SPLIT ZILLIONS OF TIMES, I MAX AT NINE.
I DON'T THINK HE'S BREATHING.
THEN GIVE HIM SOME MOUTH-TO-MOUTH.
HAKK HOKK KOFF KOFF KAFF...
NEVER MIND, HE'S PULLING AIR.
EXCELLENT. THE NEXT PART WON'T BE FUN.

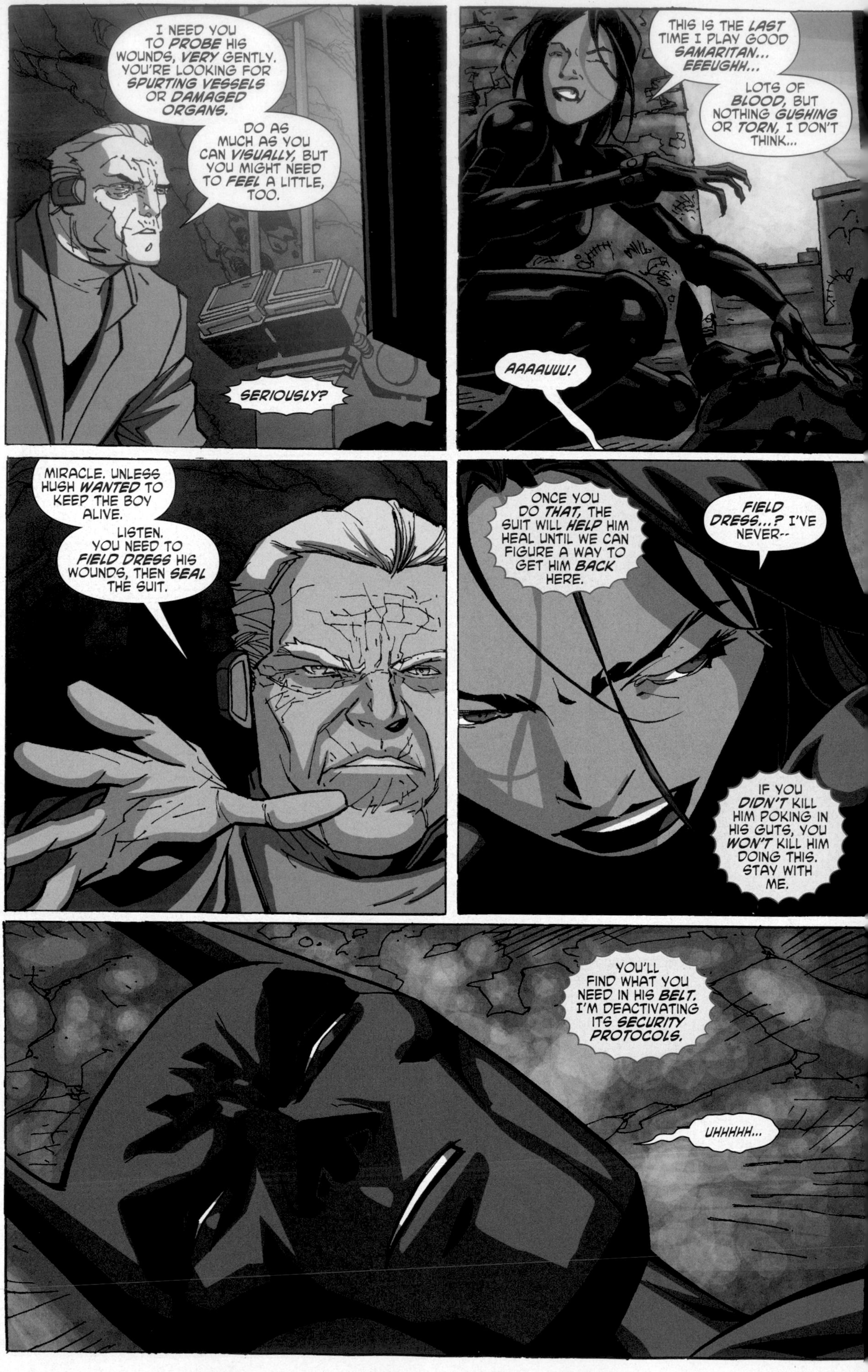
I NEED YOU TO PROBE HIS WOUNDS, VERY GENTLY. YOU'RE LOOKING FOR SPURTING VESSELS OR DAMAGED ORGANS.
DO AS MUCH AS YOU CAN VISUALLY, BUT YOU MIGHT NEED TO FEEL A LITTLE, TOO.
SERIOUSLY?
THIS IS THE LAST TIME I PLAY GOOD SAMARITAN... EEEUGHH...
LOTS OF BLOOD, BUT NOTHING GUSHING OR TORN, I DON'T THINK...
AAAAUUU!
MIRACLE. UNLESS HUSH WANTED TO KEEP THE BOY ALIVE.
LISTEN. YOU NEED TO FIELD DRESS HIS WOUNDS, THEN SEAL THE SUIT.
FIELD DRESS...? I'VE NEVER--
ONCE YOU DO THAT, THE SUIT WILL HELP HIM HEAL UNTIL WE CAN FIGURE A WAY TO GET HIM BACK HERE.
IF YOU DIDN'T KILL HIM POKING IN HIS GUTS, YOU WON'T KILL HIM DOING THIS. STAY WITH ME.
YOU'LL FIND WHAT YOU NEED IN HIS BELT. I'M DEACTIVATING ITS SECURITY PROTOCOLS.
UHHHHH...

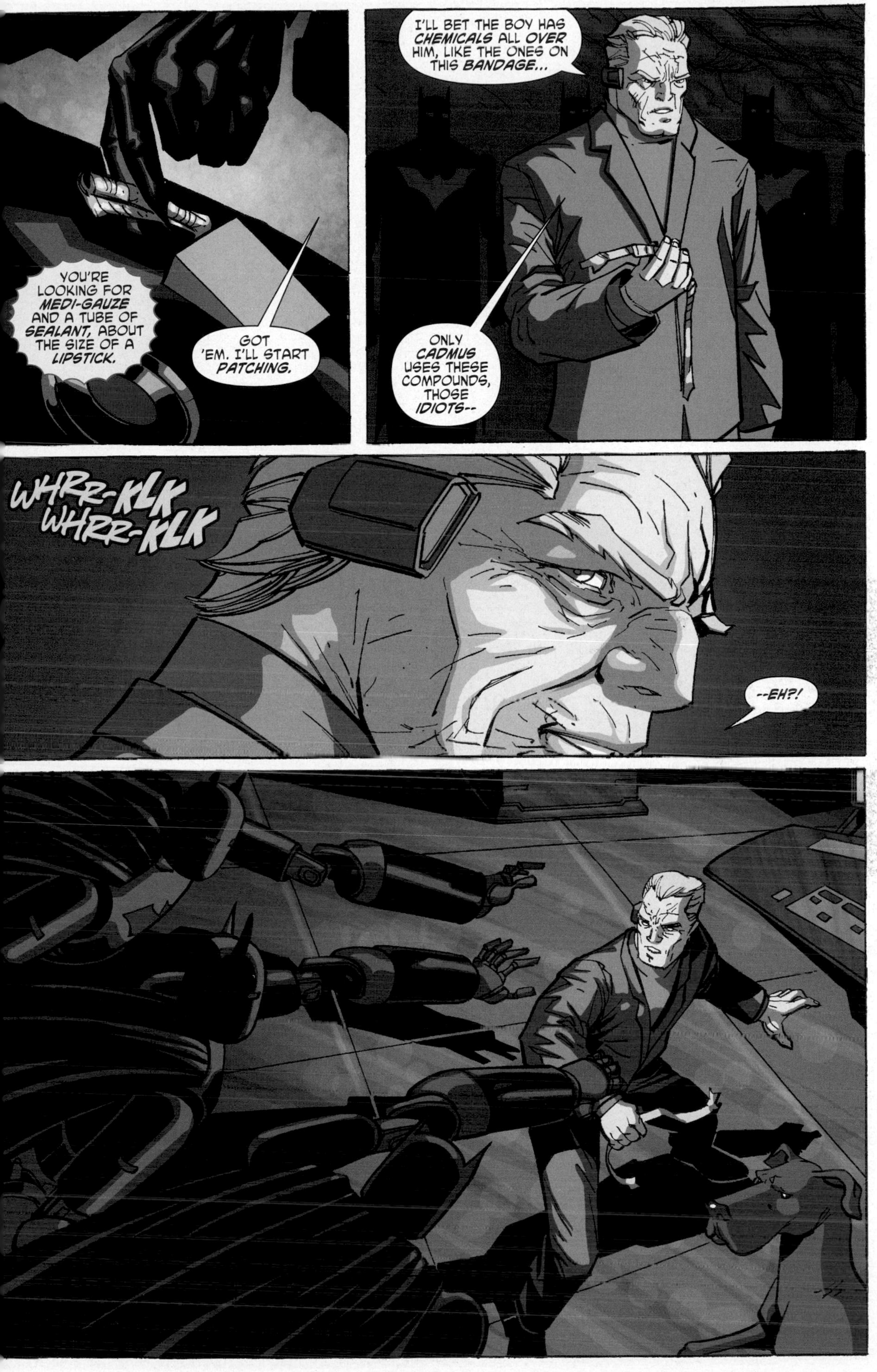
YOU'RE LOOKING FOR MEDI-GAUZE AND A TUBE OF SEALANT, ABOUT THE SIZE OF A LIPSTICK.
GOT 'EM. I'LL START PATCHING.
I'LL BET THE BOY HAS CHEMICALS ALL OVER HIM, LIKE THE ONES ON THIS BANDAGE...
ONLY CADMUS USES THESE COMPOUNDS, THOSE IDIOTS--
WHRR-KLK WHRR-KLK
--EH?!

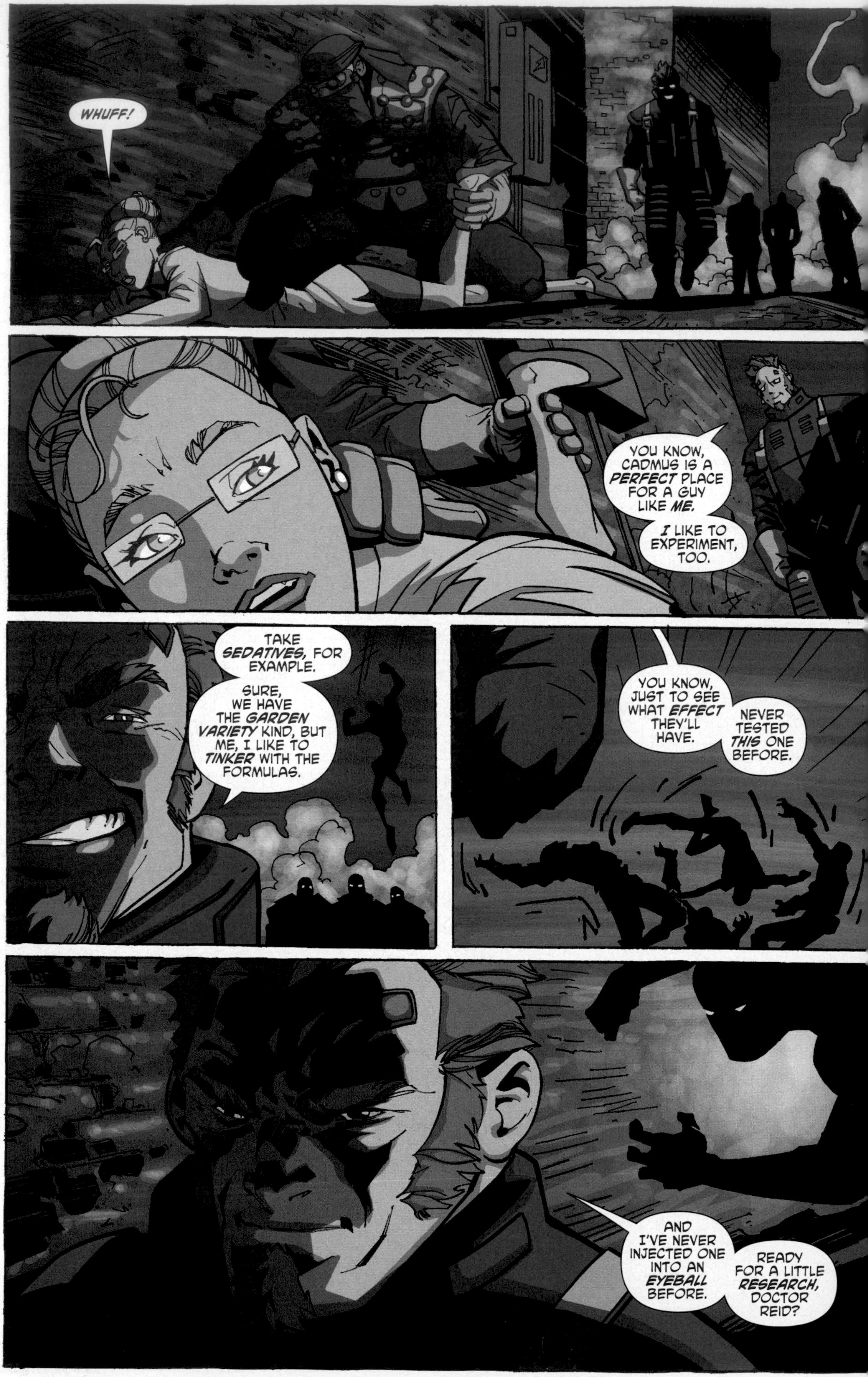
WHUFF!
YOU KNOW, CADMUS IS A PERFECT PLACE FOR A GUY LIKE ME.
I LIKE TO EXPERIMENT, TOO.
TAKE SEDATIVES, FOR EXAMPLE.
SURE, WE HAVE THE GARDEN VARIETY KIND, BUT ME, I LIKE TO TINKER WITH THE FORMULAS.
YOU KNOW, JUST TO SEE WHAT EFFECT THEY'LL HAVE.
NEVER TESTED THIS ONE BEFORE.
AND I'VE NEVER INJECTED ONE INTO AN EYEBALL BEFORE.
READY FOR A LITTLE RESEARCH, DOCTOR REID?

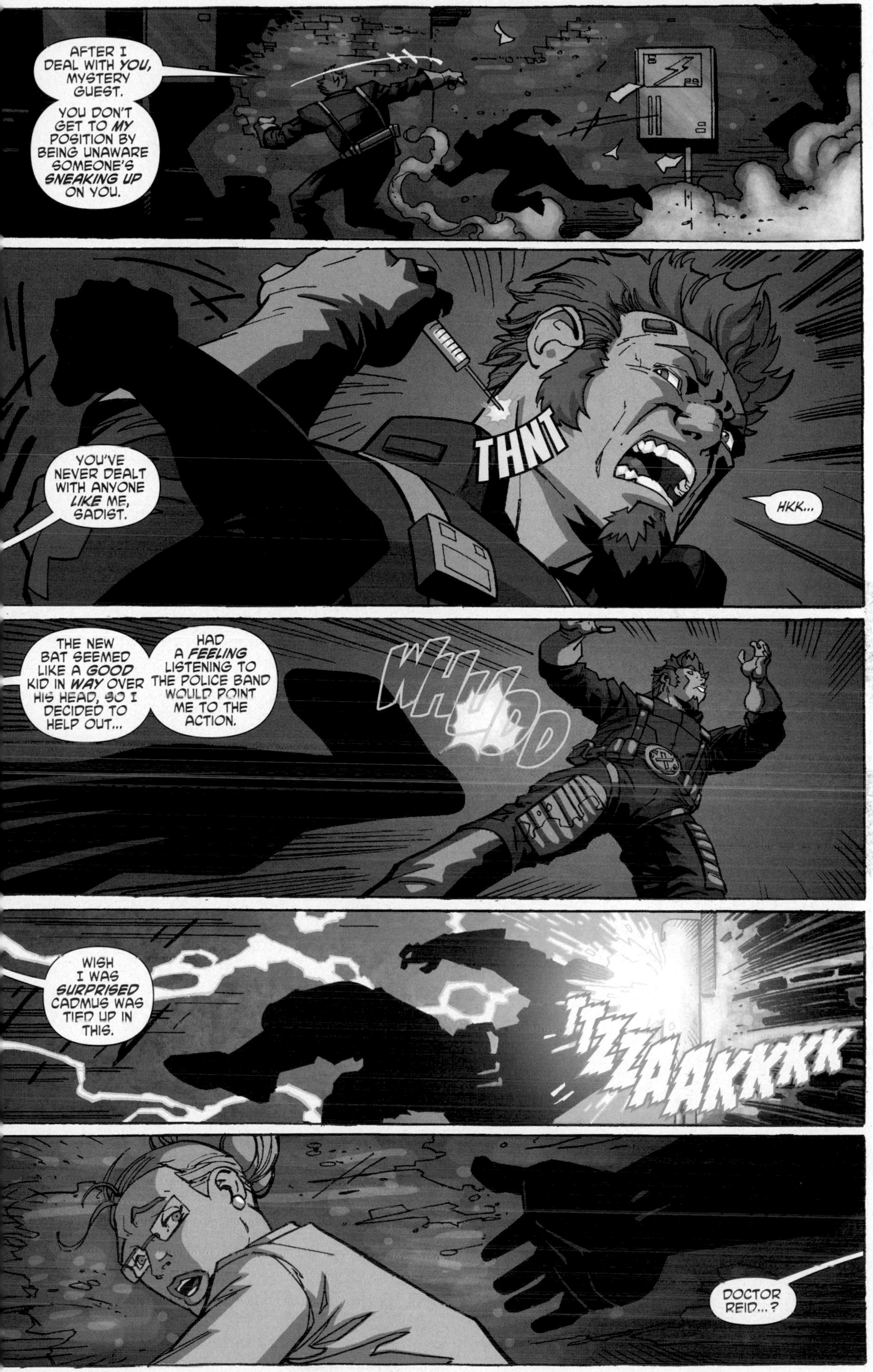
AFTER I DEAL WITH YOU, MYSTERY GUEST.
YOU DON'T GET TO MY POSITION BY BEING UNAWARE SOMEONE'S SNEAKING UP ON YOU.
THNT
YOU'VE NEVER DEALT WITH ANYONE LIKE ME, SADIST.
HKK...
THE NEW BAT SEEMED LIKE A GOOD KID IN WAY OVER HIS HEAD, SO I DECIDED TO HELP OUT...
HAD A FEELING LISTENING TO THE POLICE BAND WOULD POINT ME TO THE ACTION.
WHUDD
WISH I WAS SURPRISED CADMUS WAS TIED UP IN THIS.
TTZZAAKKKK
DOCTOR REID...?

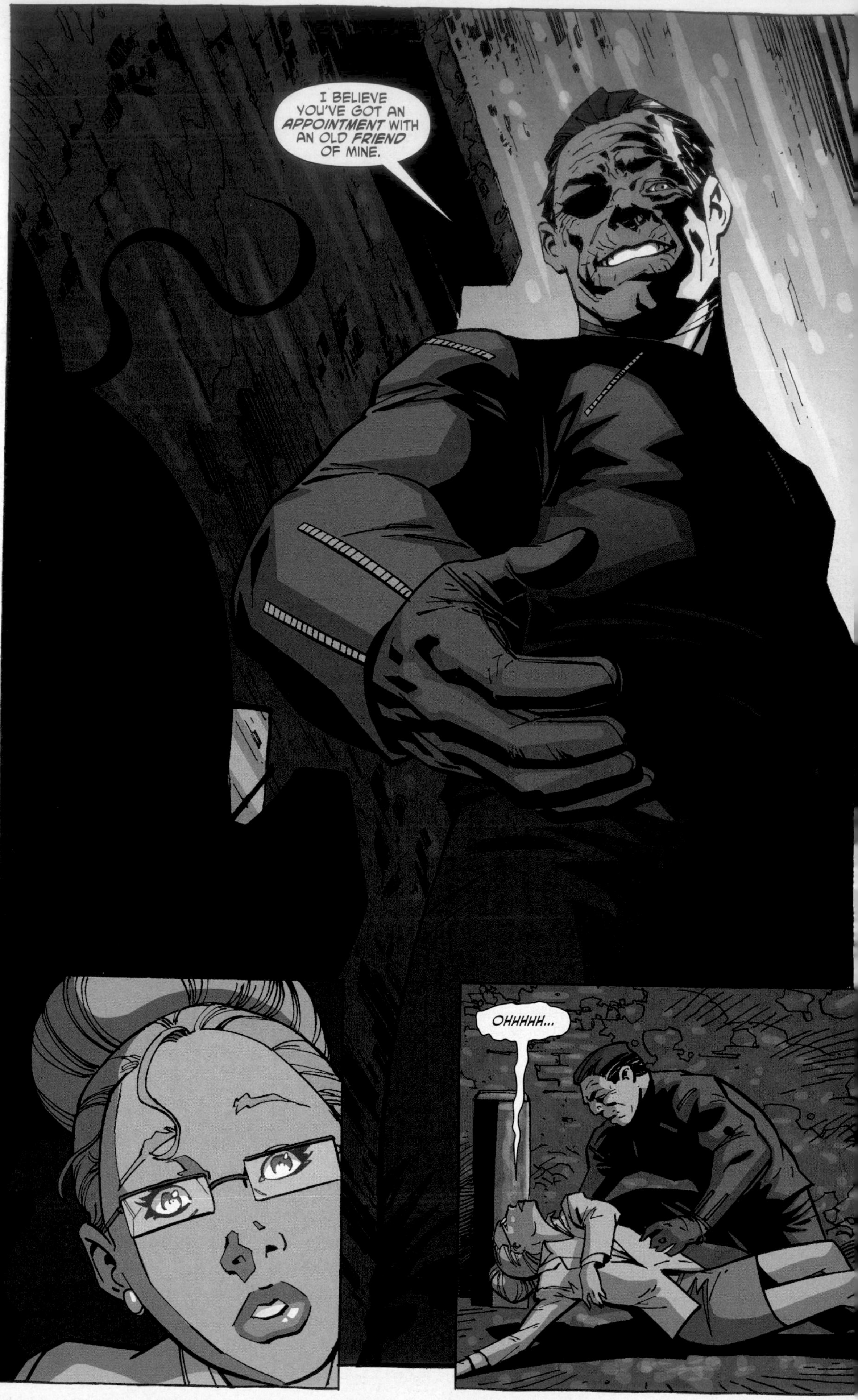
I BELIEVE YOU'VE GOT AN *APPOINTMENT* WITH AN OLD *FRIEND* OF MINE.
OHHHHH...

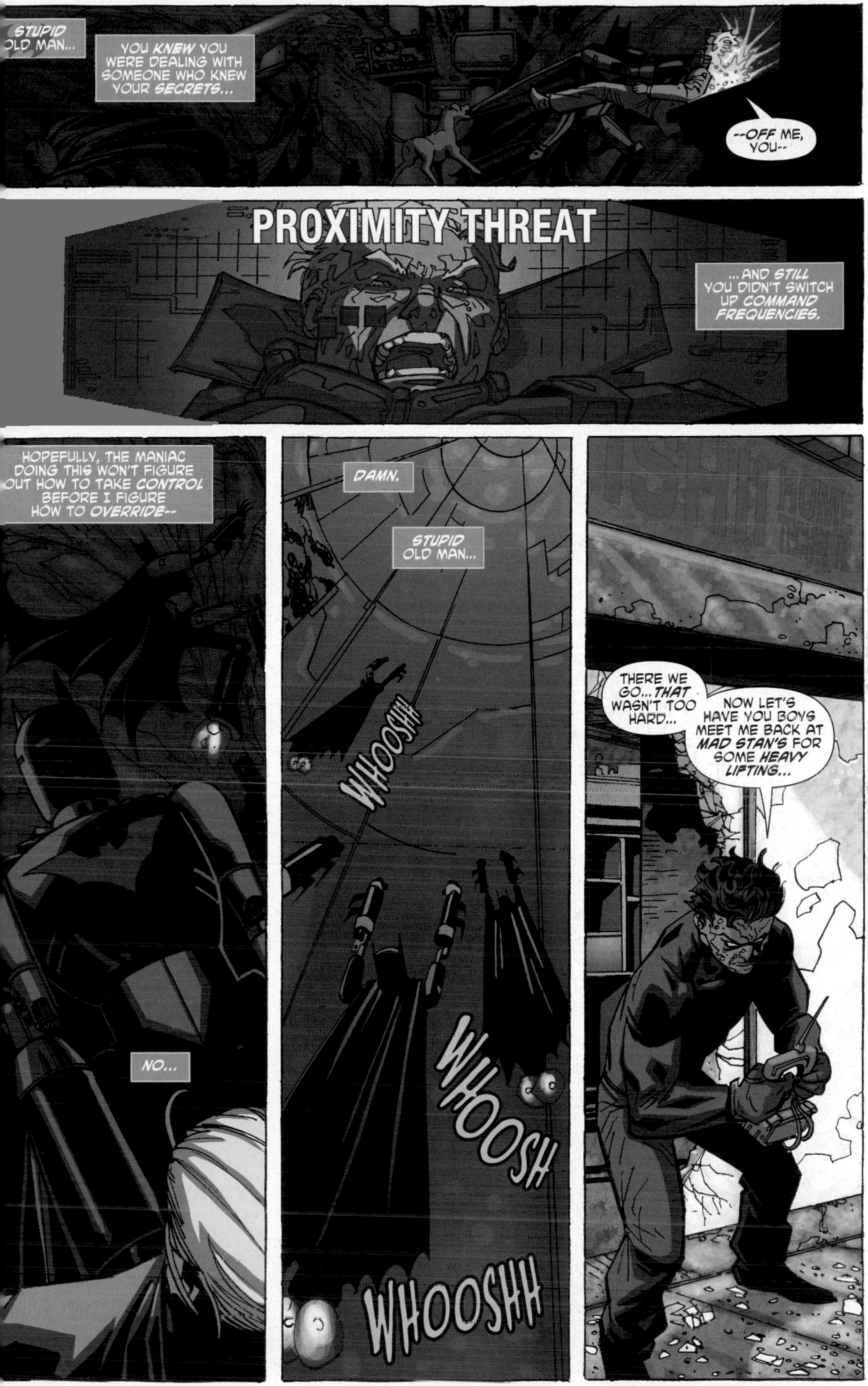
STUPID OLD MAN...
YOU KNEW YOU WERE DEALING WITH SOMEONE WHO KNEW YOUR SECRETS...
--OFF ME, YOU--
PROXIMITY THREAT
...AND STILL YOU DIDN'T SWITCH UP COMMAND FREQUENCIES.
HOPEFULLY, THE MANIAC DOING THIS WON'T FIGURE OUT HOW TO TAKE CONTROL BEFORE I FIGURE HOW TO OVERRIDE--
NO...
DAMN.
STUPID OLD MAN...
WHOOSHH
WHOOSH
WHOOSHH
THERE WE GO...THAT WASN'T TOO HARD...
NOW LET'S HAVE YOU BOYS MEET ME BACK AT MAD STAN'S FOR SOME HEAVY LIFTING...

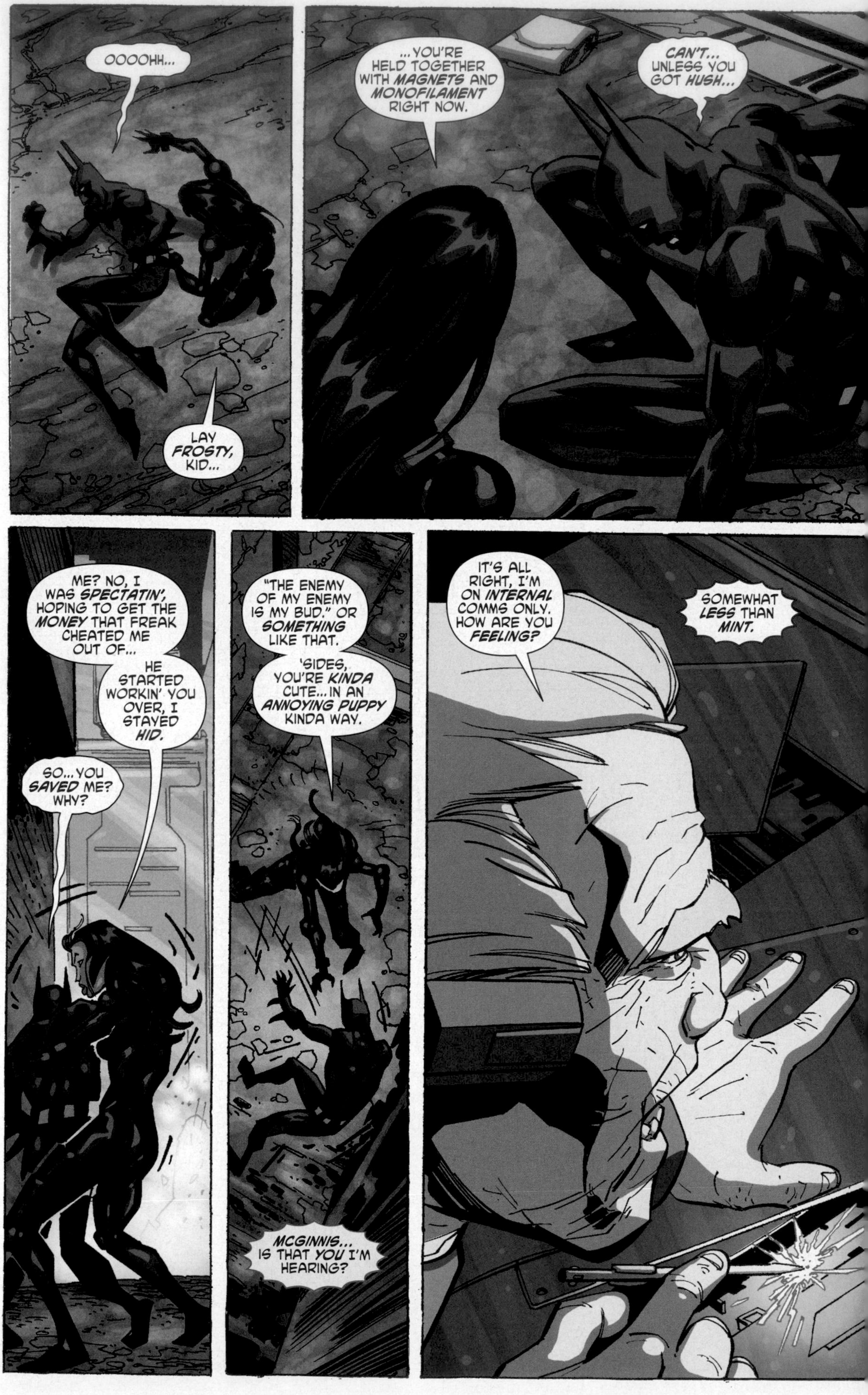
OOOOHH...
LAY FROSTY, KID...
...YOU'RE HELD TOGETHER WITH MAGNETS AND MONOFILAMENT RIGHT NOW.
CAN'T... UNLESS YOU GOT HUSH...
ME? NO, I WAS SPECTATIN', HOPING TO GET THE MONEY THAT FREAK CHEATED ME OUT OF...
HE STARTED WORKIN' YOU OVER, I STAYED HID.
SO...YOU SAVED ME? WHY?
"THE ENEMY OF MY ENEMY IS MY BUD." OR SOMETHING LIKE THAT.
'SIDES, YOU'RE KINDA CUTE...IN AN ANNOYING PUPPY KINDA WAY.
MCGINNIS... IS THAT YOU I'M HEARING?
IT'S ALL RIGHT, I'M ON INTERNAL COMMS ONLY. HOW ARE YOU FEELING?
SOMEWHAT LESS THAN MINT.

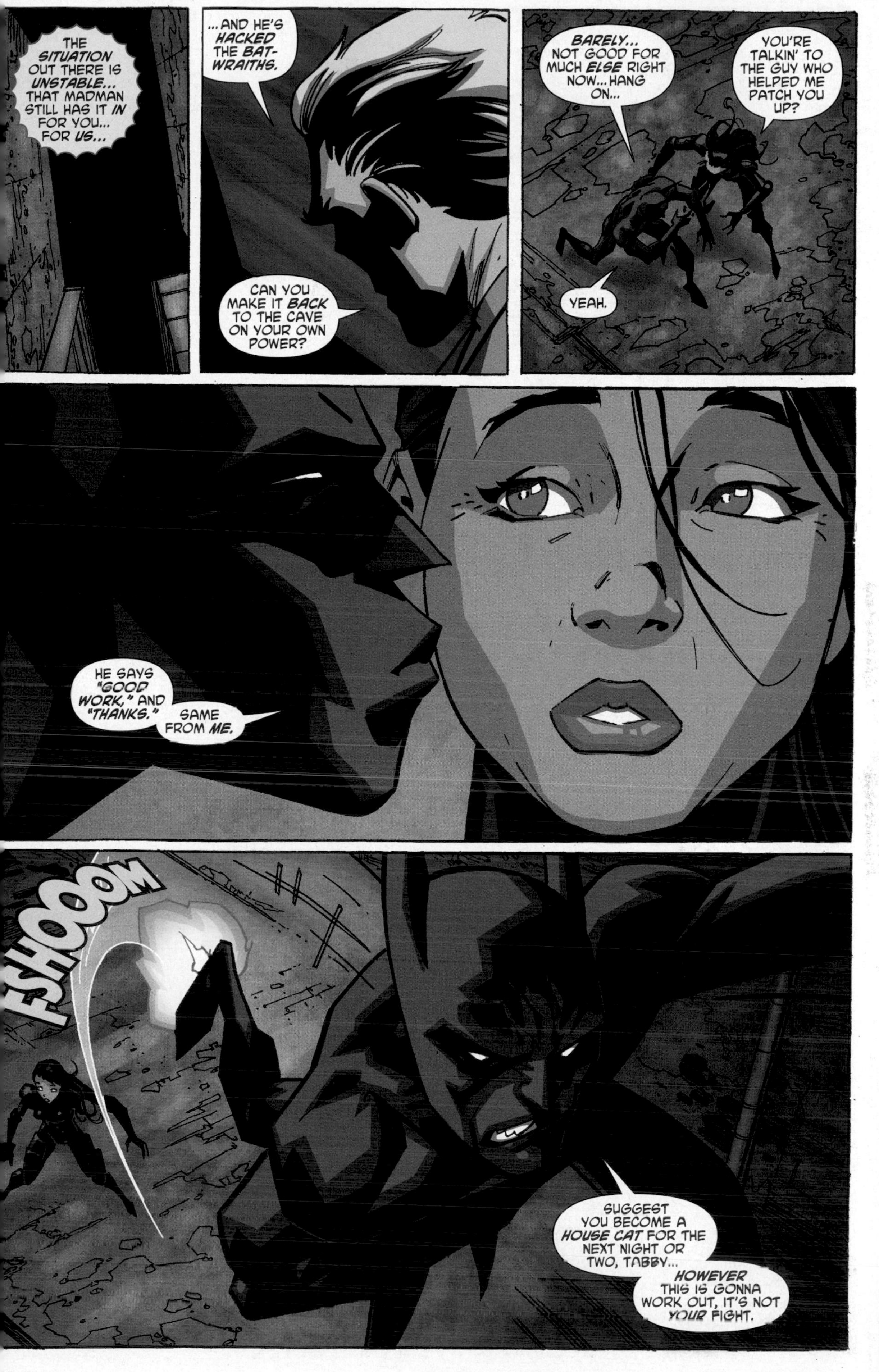
THE SITUATION OUT THERE IS UNSTABLE... THAT MADMAN STILL HAS IT IN FOR YOU... FOR US...
...AND HE'S HACKED THE BAT-WRAITHS.
CAN YOU MAKE IT BACK TO THE CAVE ON YOUR OWN POWER?
BARELY... NOT GOOD FOR MUCH ELSE RIGHT NOW... HANG ON...
YOU'RE TALKIN' TO THE GUY WHO HELPED ME PATCH YOU UP?
YEAH.
HE SAYS "GOOD WORK," AND "THANKS."
SAME FROM ME.
FSHOOOM
SUGGEST YOU BECOME A HOUSE CAT FOR THE NEXT NIGHT OR TWO, TABBY...
HOWEVER THIS IS GONNA WORK OUT, IT'S NOT YOUR FIGHT.

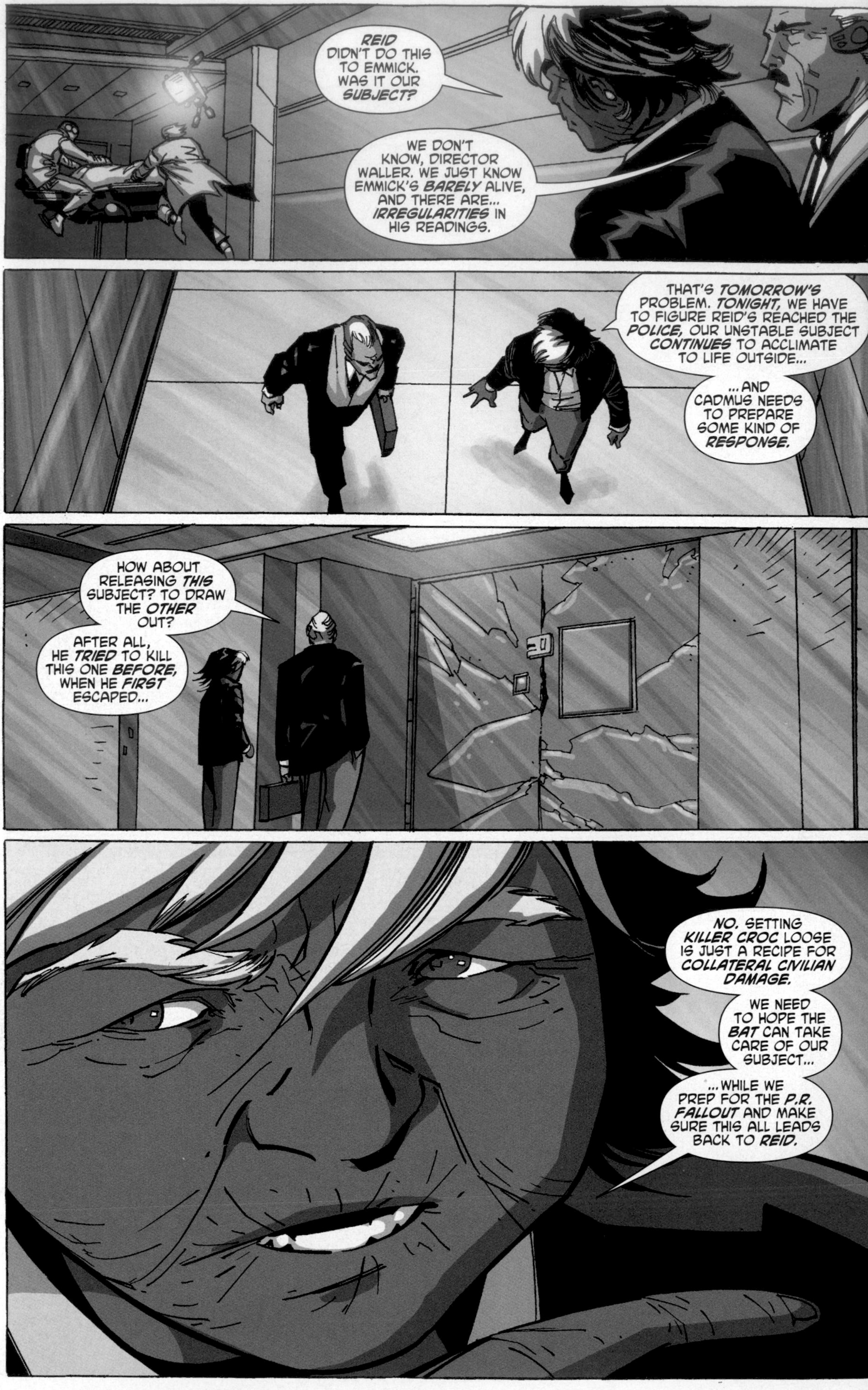
REID DIDN'T DO THIS TO EMMICK. WAS IT OUR SUBJECT?
WE DON'T KNOW, DIRECTOR WALLER. WE JUST KNOW EMMICK'S BARELY ALIVE, AND THERE ARE... IRREGULARITIES IN HIS READINGS.
THAT'S TOMORROW'S PROBLEM. TONIGHT, WE HAVE TO FIGURE REID'S REACHED THE POLICE, OUR UNSTABLE SUBJECT CONTINUES TO ACCLIMATE TO LIFE OUTSIDE...
...AND CADMUS NEEDS TO PREPARE SOME KIND OF RESPONSE.
HOW ABOUT RELEASING THIS SUBJECT? TO DRAW THE OTHER OUT?
AFTER ALL, HE TRIED TO KILL THIS ONE BEFORE, WHEN HE FIRST ESCAPED...
NO. SETTING KILLER CROC LOOSE IS JUST A RECIPE FOR COLLATERAL CIVILIAN DAMAGE.
WE NEED TO HOPE THE BAT CAN TAKE CARE OF OUR SUBJECT...
...WHILE WE PREP FOR THE P.R. FALLOUT AND MAKE SURE THIS ALL LEADS BACK TO REID.

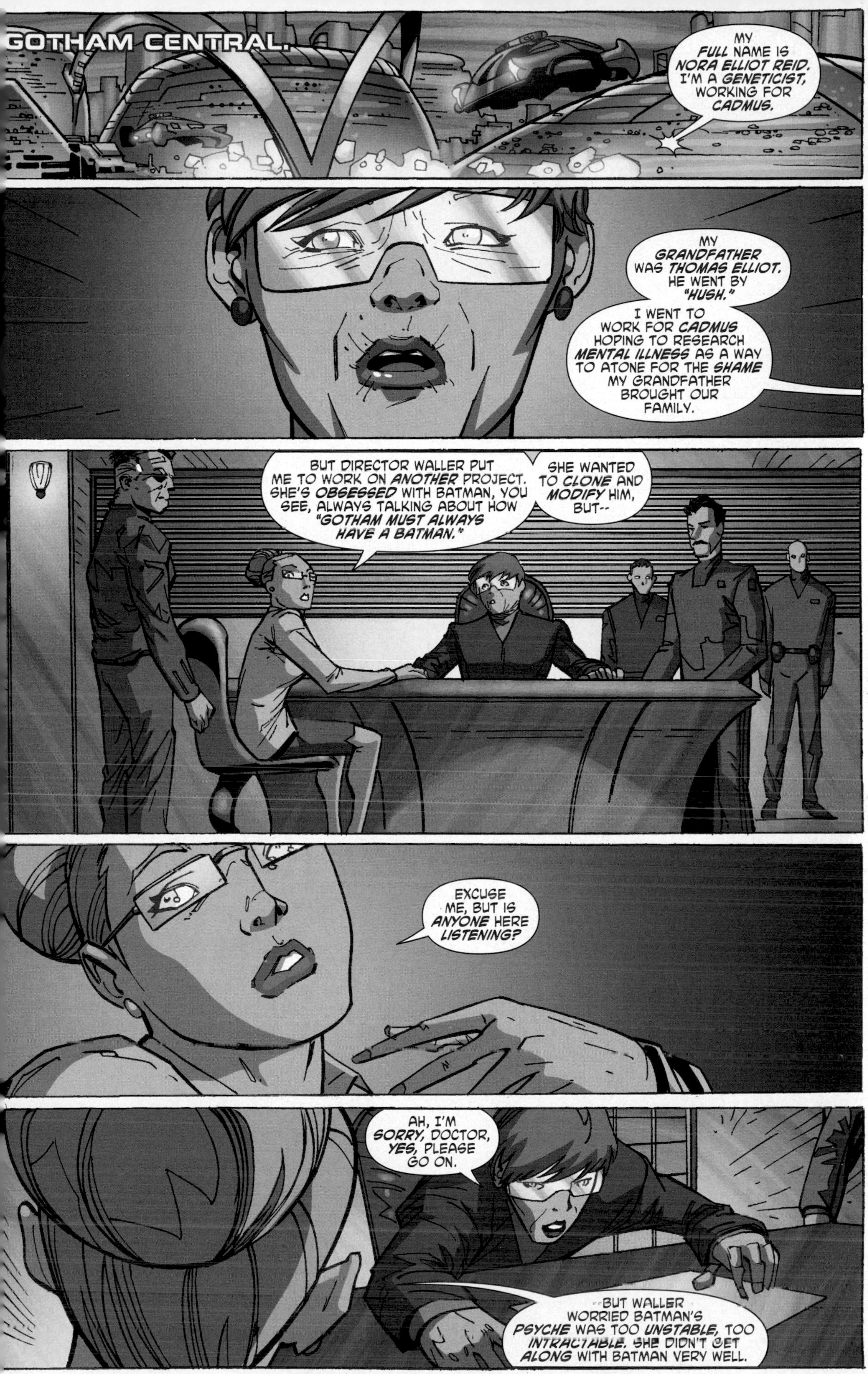
GOTHAM CENTRAL.
MY FULL NAME IS NORA ELLIOT REID. I'M A GENETICIST, WORKING FOR CADMUS.
MY GRANDFATHER WAS THOMAS ELLIOT. HE WENT BY "HUSH."
I WENT TO WORK FOR CADMUS HOPING TO RESEARCH MENTAL ILLNESS AS A WAY TO ATONE FOR THE SHAME MY GRANDFATHER BROUGHT OUR FAMILY.
BUT DIRECTOR WALLER PUT ME TO WORK ON ANOTHER PROJECT. SHE'S OBSESSED WITH BATMAN, YOU SEE, ALWAYS TALKING ABOUT HOW "GOTHAM MUST ALWAYS HAVE A BATMAN."
SHE WANTED TO CLONE AND MODIFY HIM, BUT--
EXCUSE ME, BUT IS ANYONE HERE LISTENING?
AH, I'M SORRY, DOCTOR, YES, PLEASE GO ON.
BUT WALLER WORRIED BATMAN'S PSYCHE WAS TOO UNSTABLE, TOO INTRACTABLE. SHE DIDN'T GET ALONG WITH BATMAN VERY WELL.

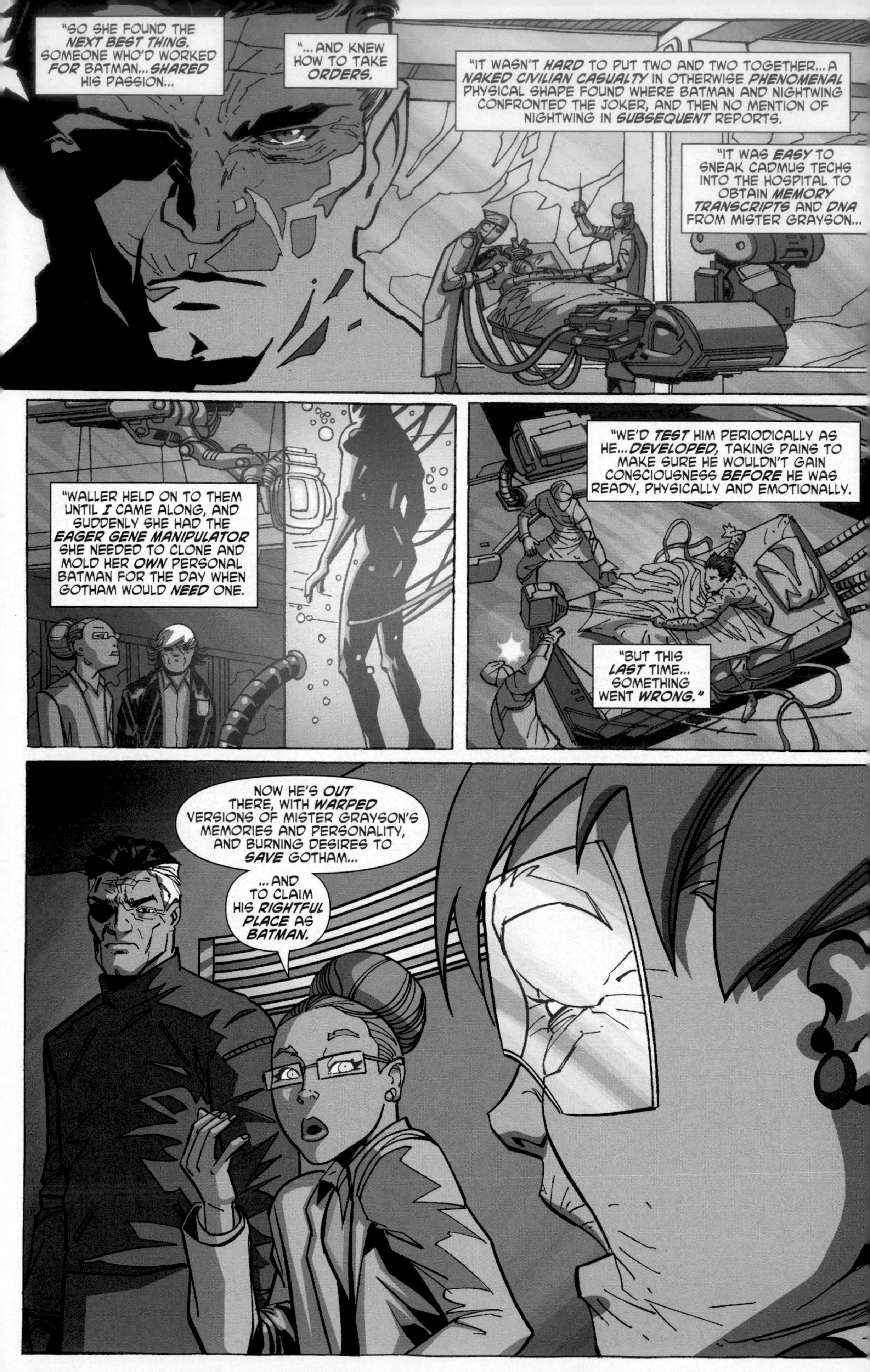
"SO SHE FOUND THE NEXT BEST THING. SOMEONE WHO'D WORKED FOR BATMAN...SHARED HIS PASSION...
"...AND KNEW HOW TO TAKE ORDERS.
"IT WASN'T HARD TO PUT TWO AND TWO TOGETHER... A NAKED CIVILIAN CASUALTY IN OTHERWISE PHENOMENAL PHYSICAL SHAPE FOUND WHERE BATMAN AND NIGHTWING CONFRONTED THE JOKER, AND THEN NO MENTION OF NIGHTWING IN SUBSEQUENT REPORTS.
"IT WAS EASY TO SNEAK CADMUS TECHS INTO THE HOSPITAL TO OBTAIN MEMORY TRANSCRIPTS AND DNA FROM MISTER GRAYSON...
"WALLER HELD ON TO THEM UNTIL I CAME ALONG, AND SUDDENLY SHE HAD THE EAGER GENE MANIPULATOR SHE NEEDED TO CLONE AND MOLD HER OWN PERSONAL BATMAN FOR THE DAY WHEN GOTHAM WOULD NEED ONE.
"WE'D TEST HIM PERIODICALLY AS HE...DEVELOPED, TAKING PAINS TO MAKE SURE HE WOULDN'T GAIN CONSCIOUSNESS BEFORE HE WAS READY, PHYSICALLY AND EMOTIONALLY.
"BUT THIS LAST TIME... SOMETHING WENT WRONG."
NOW HE'S OUT THERE, WITH WARPED VERSIONS OF MISTER GRAYSON'S MEMORIES AND PERSONALITY, AND BURNING DESIRES TO SAVE GOTHAM...
...AND TO CLAIM HIS RIGHTFUL PLACE AS BATMAN.

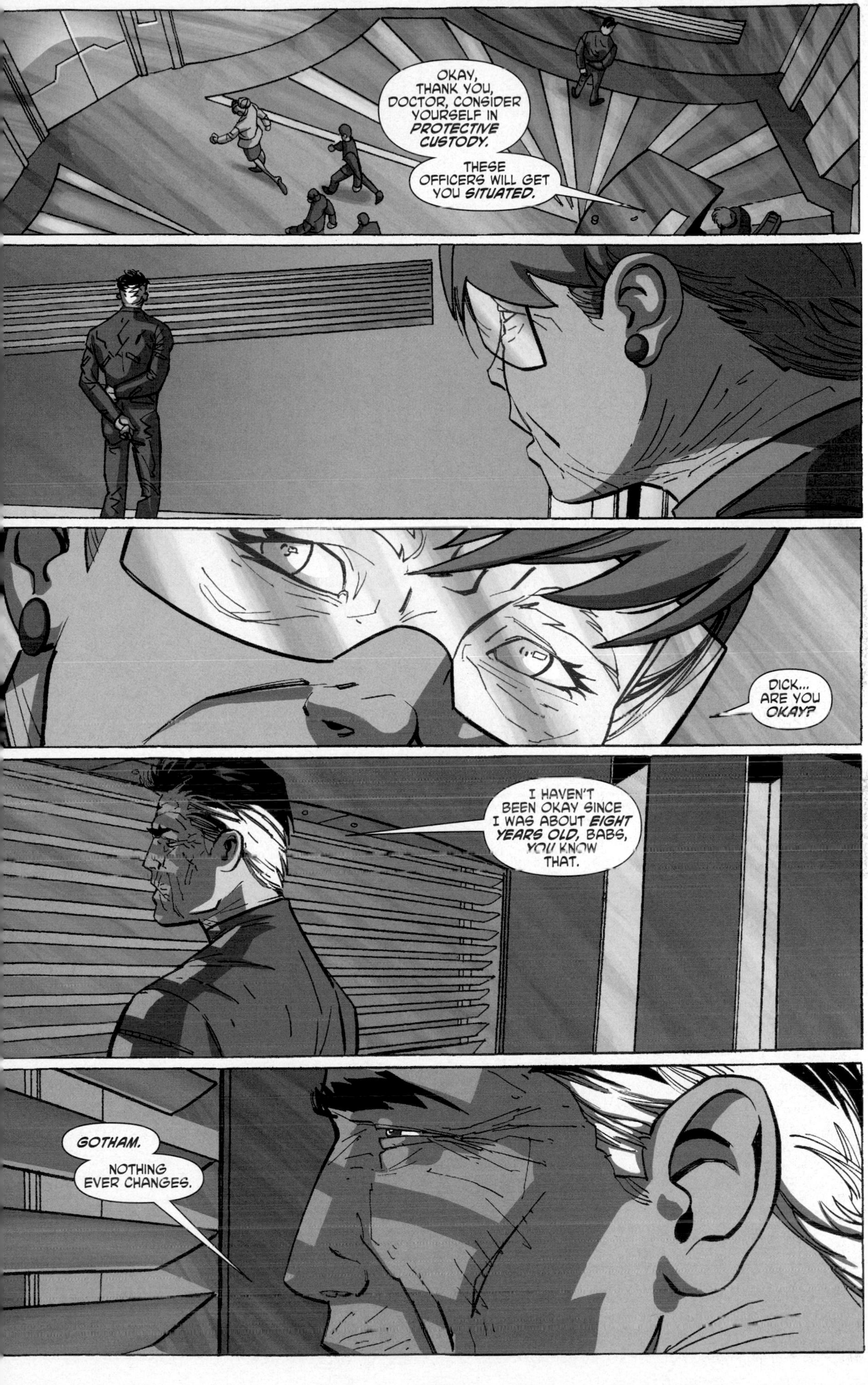
OKAY, THANK YOU, DOCTOR, CONSIDER YOURSELF IN PROTECTIVE CUSTODY.
THESE OFFICERS WILL GET YOU SITUATED.
DICK... ARE YOU OKAY?
I HAVEN'T BEEN OKAY SINCE I WAS ABOUT EIGHT YEARS OLD, BABS, YOU KNOW THAT.
GOTHAM.
NOTHING EVER CHANGES.

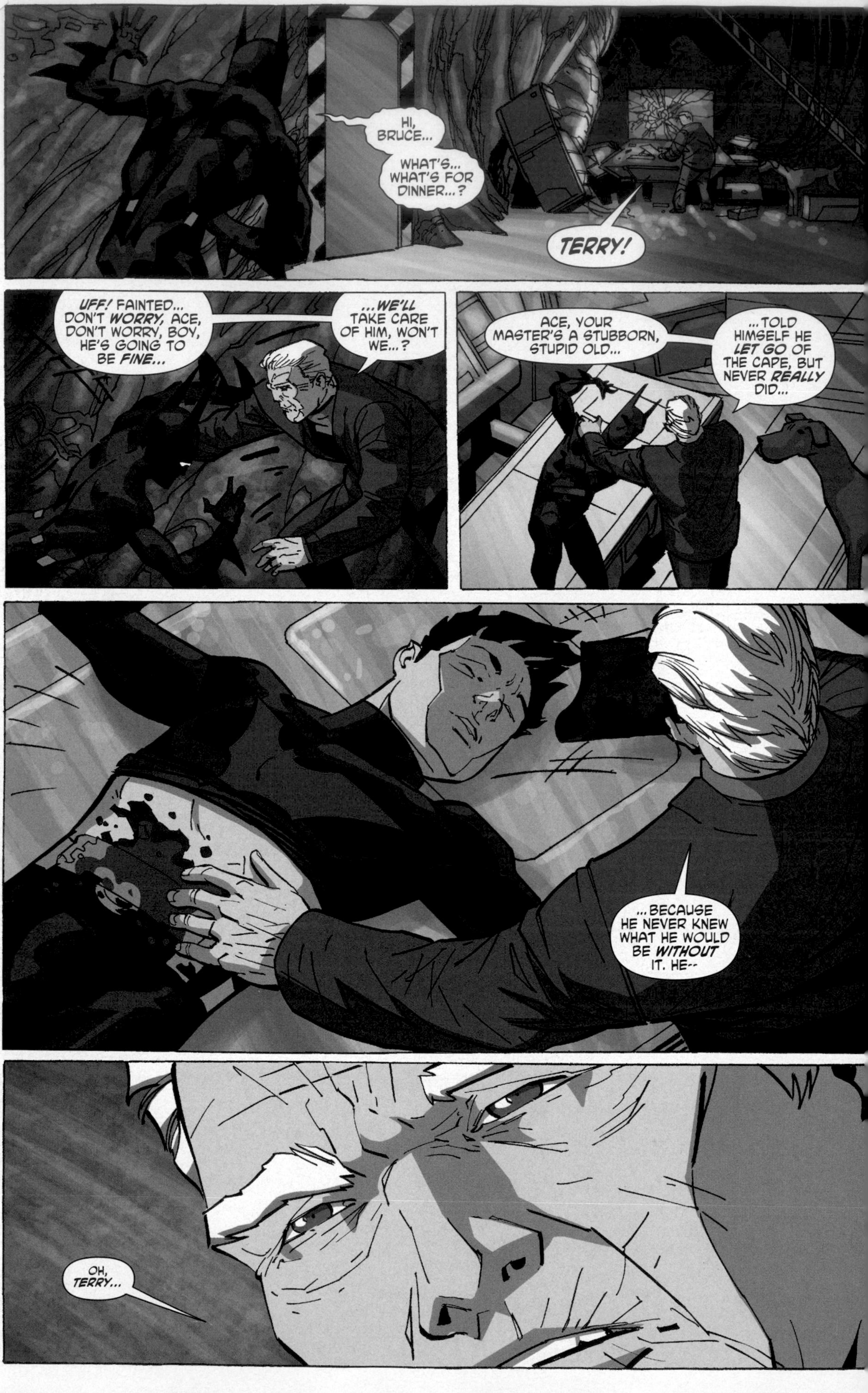
HI, BRUCE...
WHAT'S... WHAT'S FOR DINNER...?
TERRY!
UFF! FAINTED... DON'T WORRY, ACE, DON'T WORRY, BOY, HE'S GOING TO BE FINE...
...WE'LL TAKE CARE OF HIM, WON'T WE...?
ACE, YOUR MASTER'S A STUBBORN, STUPID OLD...
...TOLD HIMSELF HE LET GO OF THE CAPE, BUT NEVER REALLY DID...
...BECAUSE HE NEVER KNEW WHAT HE WOULD BE WITHOUT IT. HE--
OH, TERRY...

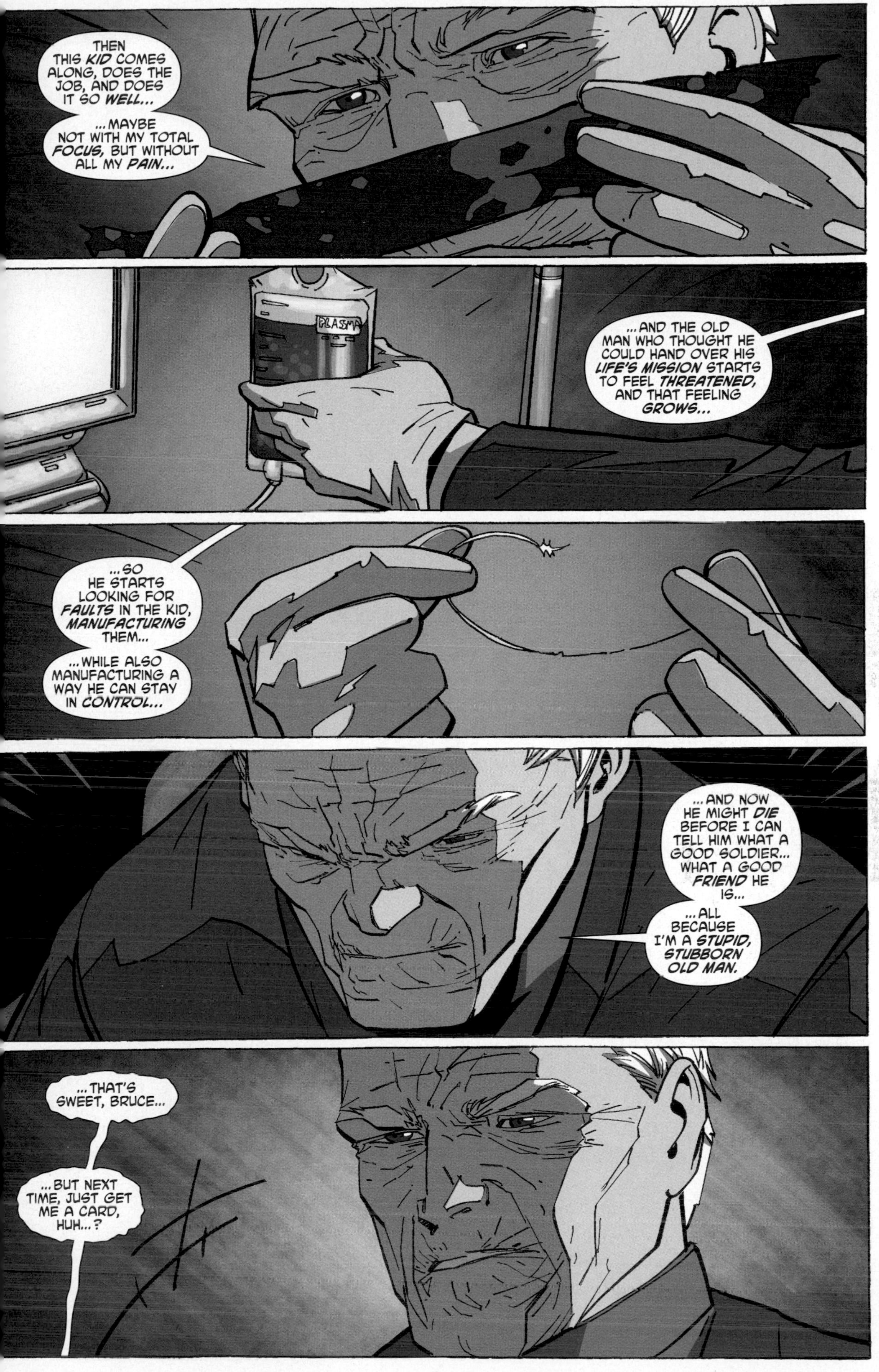
THEN THIS *KID* COMES ALONG, DOES THE JOB, AND DOES IT SO *WELL...*
...MAYBE NOT WITH MY TOTAL *FOCUS,* BUT WITHOUT ALL MY *PAIN...*
PLASMA
...AND THE OLD MAN WHO THOUGHT HE COULD HAND OVER HIS *LIFE'S MISSION* STARTS TO FEEL *THREATENED,* AND THAT FEELING *GROWS...*
...SO HE STARTS LOOKING FOR *FAULTS* IN THE KID, *MANUFACTURING* THEM...
...WHILE ALSO MANUFACTURING A WAY HE CAN STAY IN *CONTROL...*
...AND NOW HE MIGHT *DIE* BEFORE I CAN TELL HIM WHAT A GOOD SOLDIER... WHAT A GOOD *FRIEND* HE IS...
...ALL BECAUSE I'M A *STUPID, STUBBORN OLD MAN.*
...THAT'S SWEET, BRUCE...
...BUT NEXT TIME, JUST GET ME A CARD, HUH...?

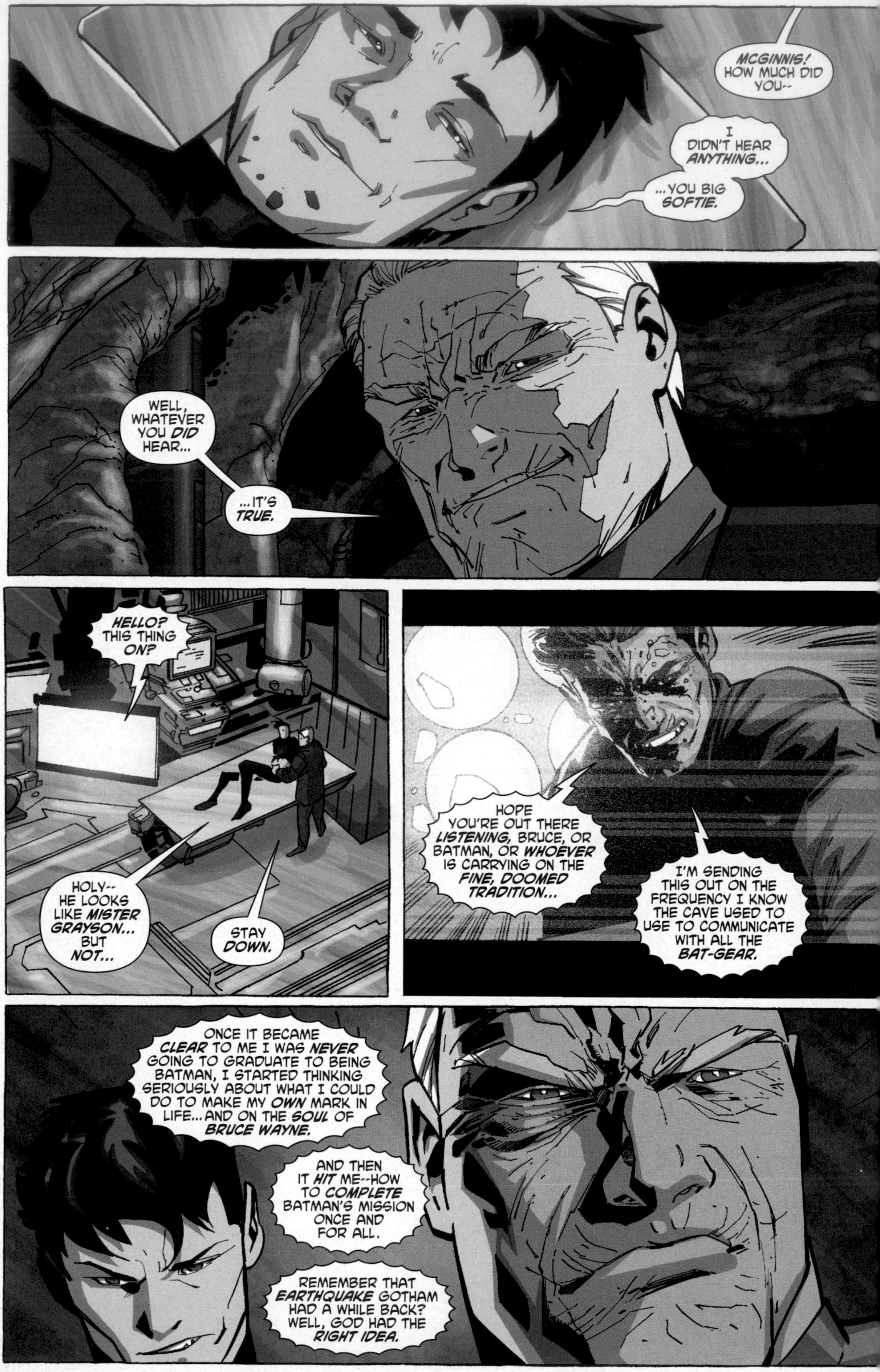
MCGINNIS! HOW MUCH DID YOU--
I DIDN'T HEAR ANYTHING...
...YOU BIG SOFTIE.
WELL, WHATEVER YOU DID HEAR...
...IT'S TRUE.
HELLO? THIS THING ON?
HOLY-- HE LOOKS LIKE MISTER GRAYSON... BUT NOT...
STAY DOWN.
HOPE YOU'RE OUT THERE LISTENING, BRUCE, OR BATMAN, OR WHOEVER IS CARRYING ON THE FINE, DOOMED TRADITION...
I'M SENDING THIS OUT ON THE FREQUENCY I KNOW THE CAVE USED TO USE TO COMMUNICATE WITH ALL THE BAT-GEAR.
ONCE IT BECAME CLEAR TO ME I WAS NEVER GOING TO GRADUATE TO BEING BATMAN, I STARTED THINKING SERIOUSLY ABOUT WHAT I COULD DO TO MAKE MY OWN MARK IN LIFE...AND ON THE SOUL OF BRUCE WAYNE.
AND THEN IT HIT ME--HOW TO COMPLETE BATMAN'S MISSION ONCE AND FOR ALL.
REMEMBER THAT EARTHQUAKE GOTHAM HAD A WHILE BACK? WELL, GOD HAD THE RIGHT IDEA.

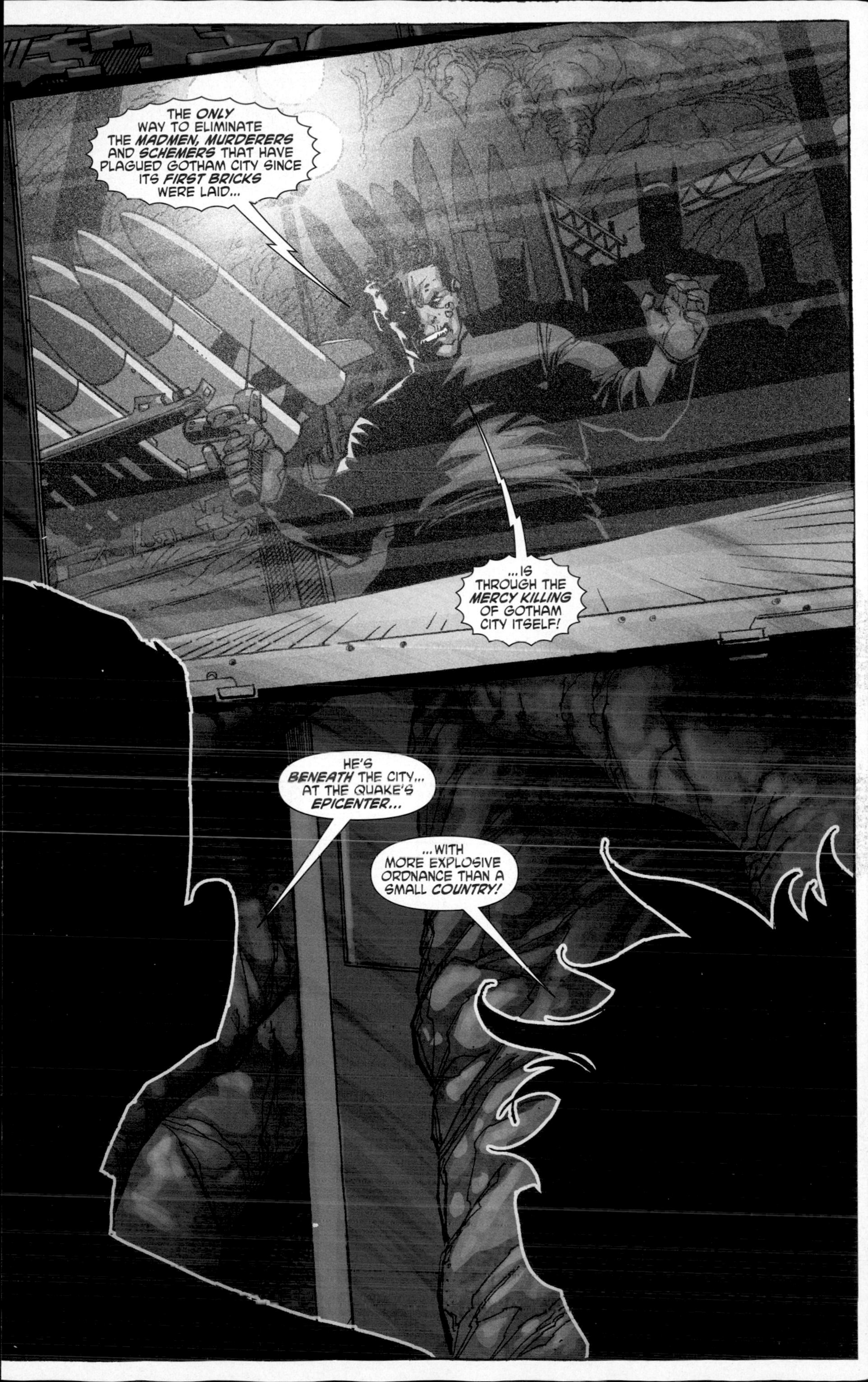
THE ONLY WAY TO ELIMINATE THE MADMEN, MURDERERS AND SCHEMERS THAT HAVE PLAGUED GOTHAM CITY SINCE ITS FIRST BRICKS WERE LAID...
...IS THROUGH THE MERCY KILLING OF GOTHAM CITY ITSELF!
HE'S BENEATH THE CITY... AT THE QUAKE'S EPICENTER...
...WITH MORE EXPLOSIVE ORDNANCE THAN A SMALL COUNTRY!

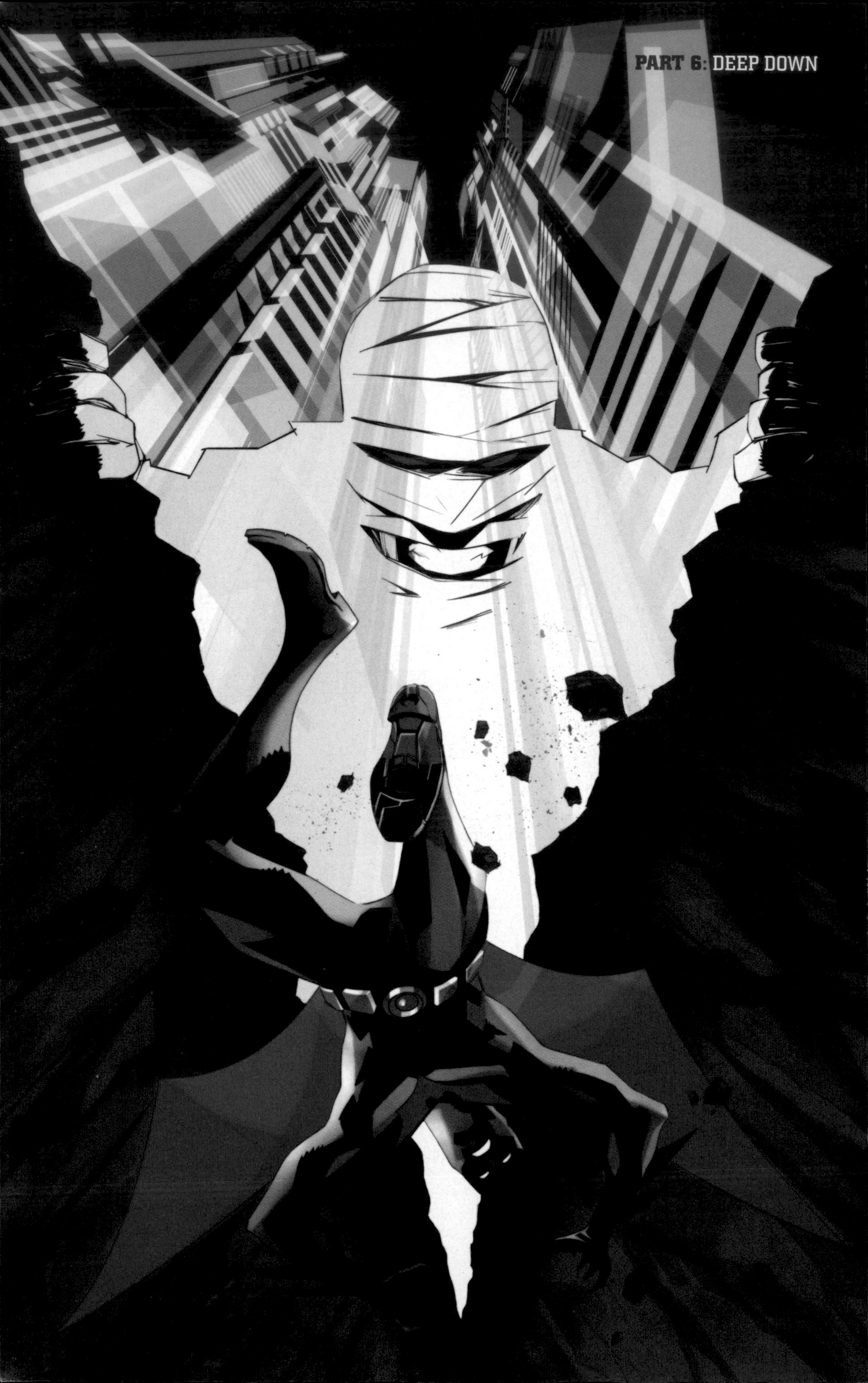
PART 6: DEEP DOWN

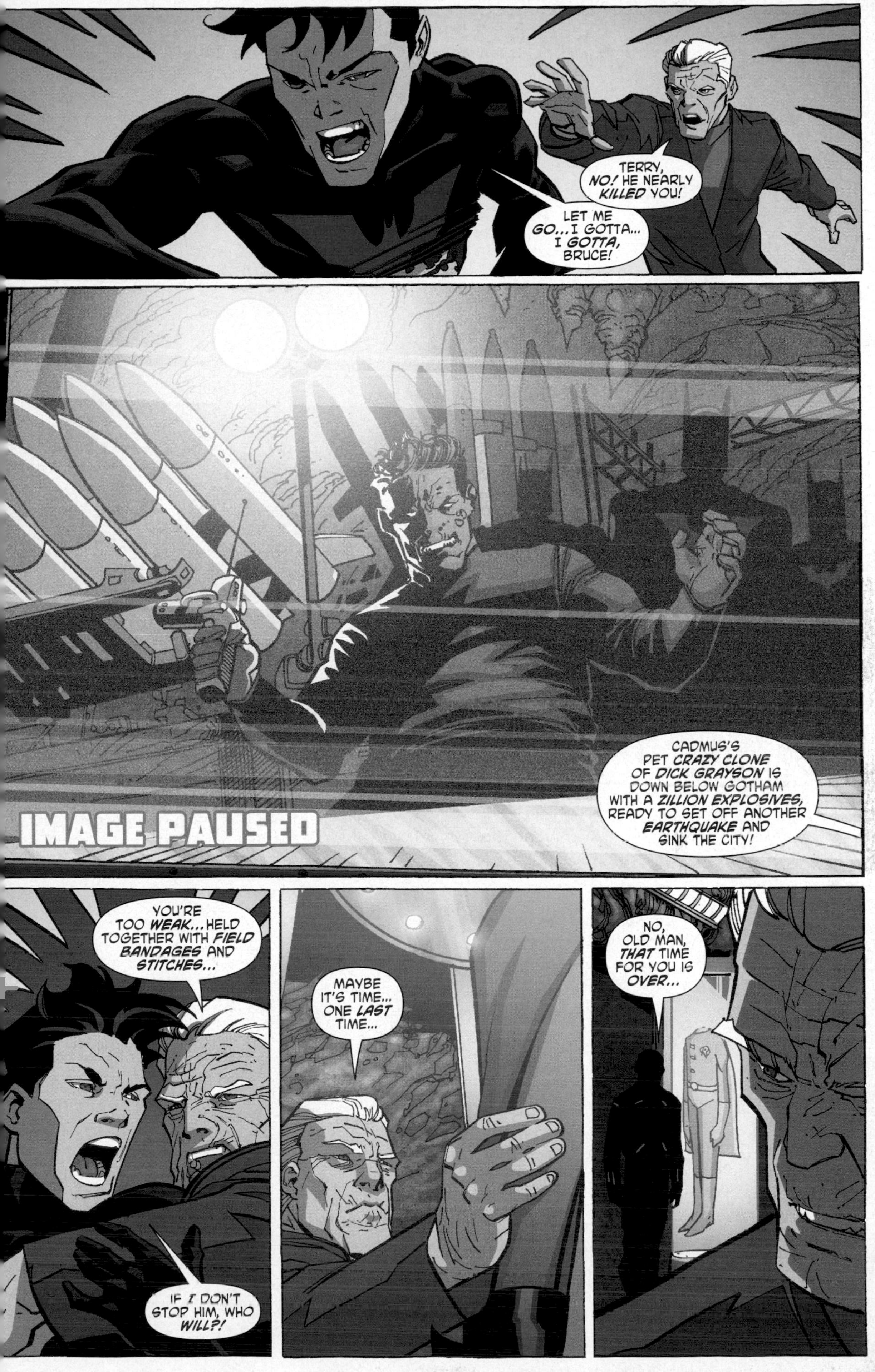

TERRY, NO! HE NEARLY KILLED YOU!
LET ME GO...I GOTTA... I GOTTA, BRUCE!
IMAGE PAUSED
CADMUS'S PET CRAZY CLONE OF DICK GRAYSON IS DOWN BELOW GOTHAM WITH A ZILLION EXPLOSIVES, READY TO SET OFF ANOTHER EARTHQUAKE AND SINK THE CITY!
YOU'RE TOO WEAK...HELD TOGETHER WITH FIELD BANDAGES AND STITCHES...
IF I DON'T STOP HIM, WHO WILL?!
MAYBE IT'S TIME... ONE LAST TIME...
NO, OLD MAN, THAT TIME FOR YOU IS OVER...

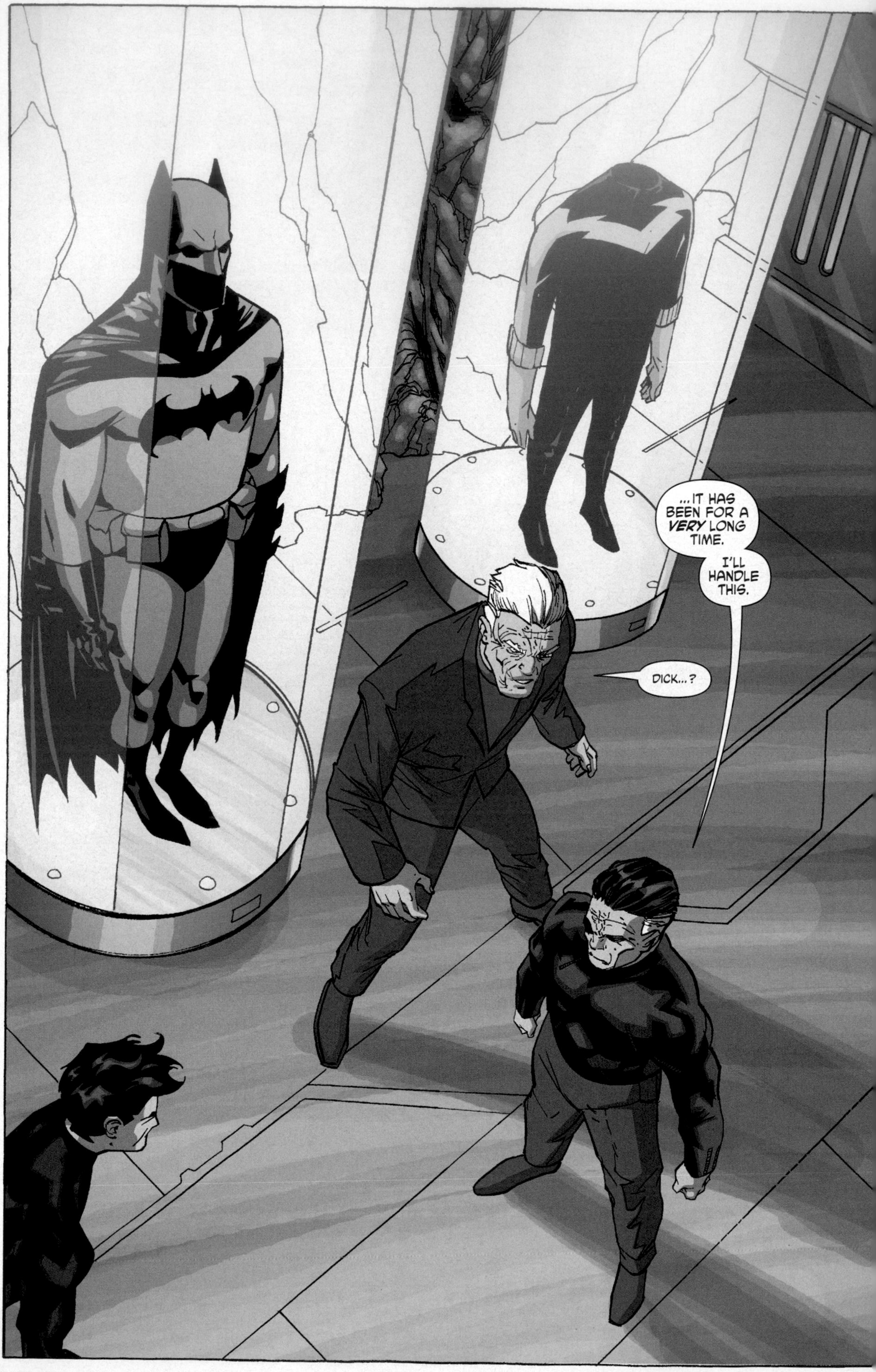
...IT HAS BEEN FOR A VERY LONG TIME.
I'LL HANDLE THIS.
DICK...?

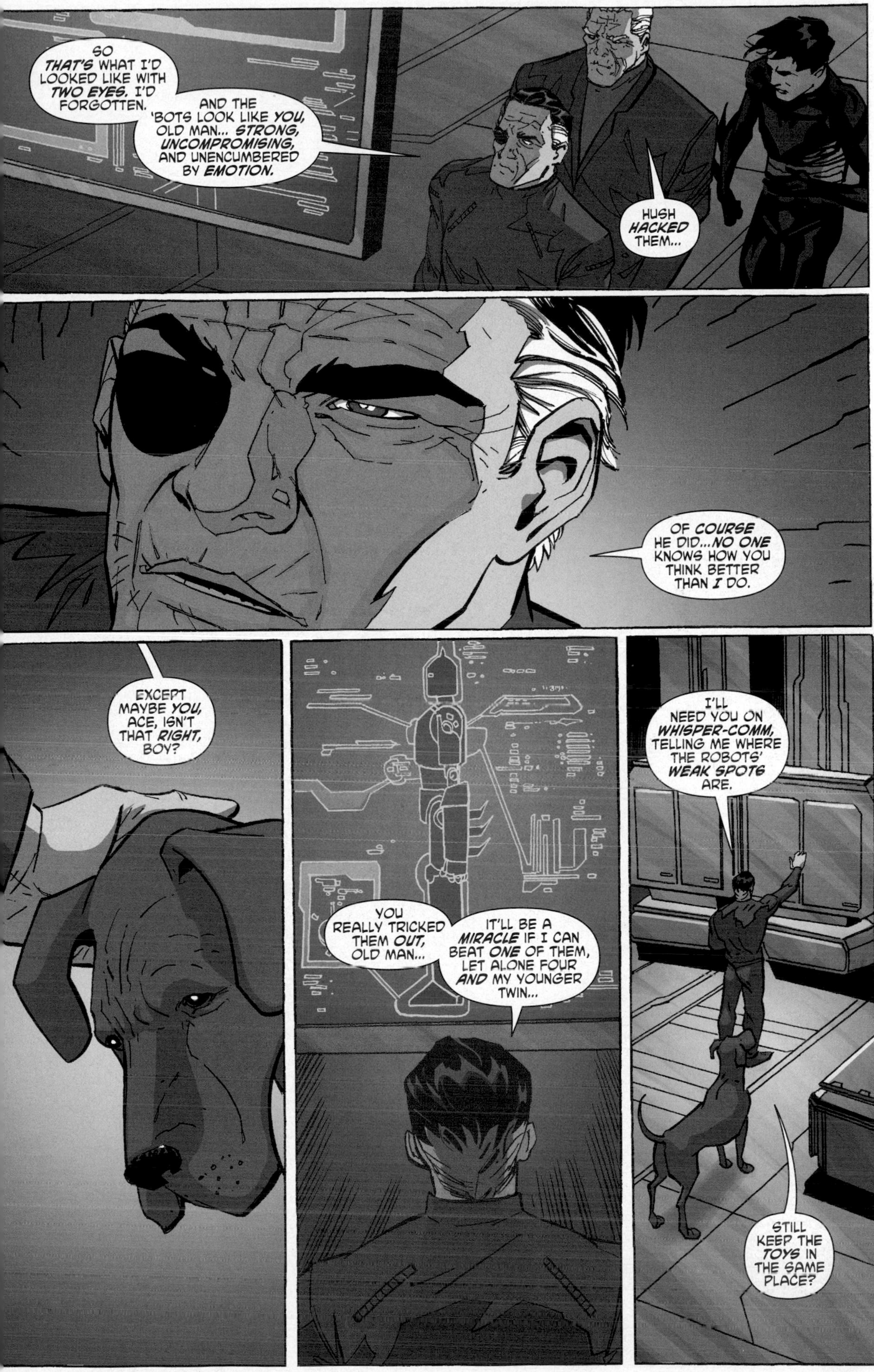
SO THAT'S WHAT I'D LOOKED LIKE WITH TWO EYES. I'D FORGOTTEN.
AND THE 'BOTS LOOK LIKE YOU, OLD MAN... STRONG, UNCOMPROMISING, AND UNENCUMBERED BY EMOTION.
HUSH HACKED THEM...
OF COURSE HE DID...NO ONE KNOWS HOW YOU THINK BETTER THAN I DO.
EXCEPT MAYBE YOU, ACE, ISN'T THAT RIGHT, BOY?
YOU REALLY TRICKED THEM OUT, OLD MAN...
IT'LL BE A MIRACLE IF I CAN BEAT ONE OF THEM, LET ALONE FOUR AND MY YOUNGER TWIN...
I'LL NEED YOU ON WHISPER-COMM, TELLING ME WHERE THE ROBOTS' WEAK SPOTS ARE.
STILL KEEP THE TOYS IN THE SAME PLACE?

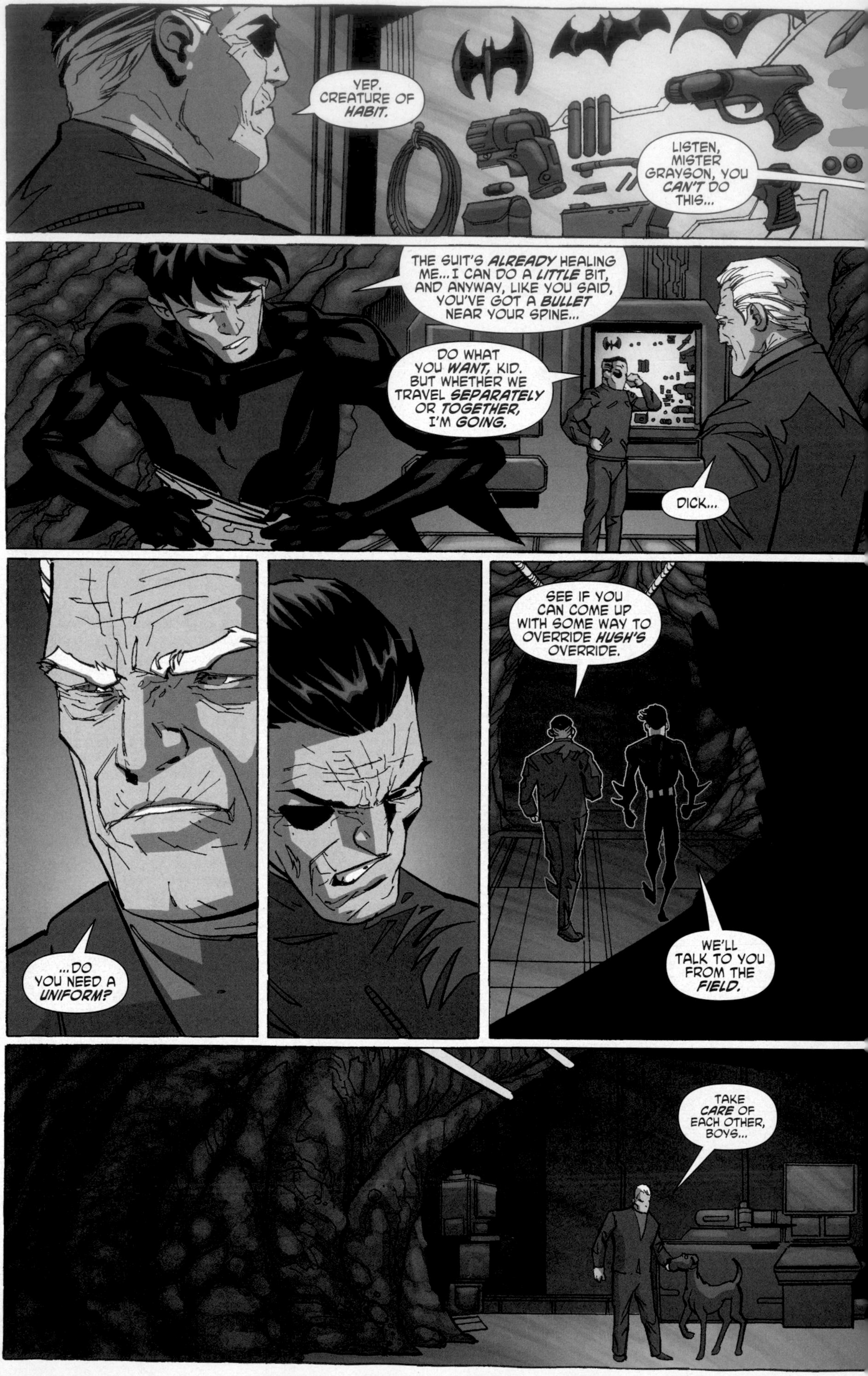

YEP. CREATURE OF HABIT.
LISTEN, MISTER GRAYSON, YOU CAN'T DO THIS...
THE SUIT'S ALREADY HEALING ME... I CAN DO A LITTLE BIT, AND ANYWAY, LIKE YOU SAID, YOU'VE GOT A BULLET NEAR YOUR SPINE...
DO WHAT YOU WANT, KID. BUT WHETHER WE TRAVEL SEPARATELY OR TOGETHER, I'M GOING.
DICK...
...DO YOU NEED A UNIFORM?
SEE IF YOU CAN COME UP WITH SOME WAY TO OVERRIDE HUSH'S OVERRIDE.
WE'LL TALK TO YOU FROM THE FIELD.
TAKE CARE OF EACH OTHER, BOYS...

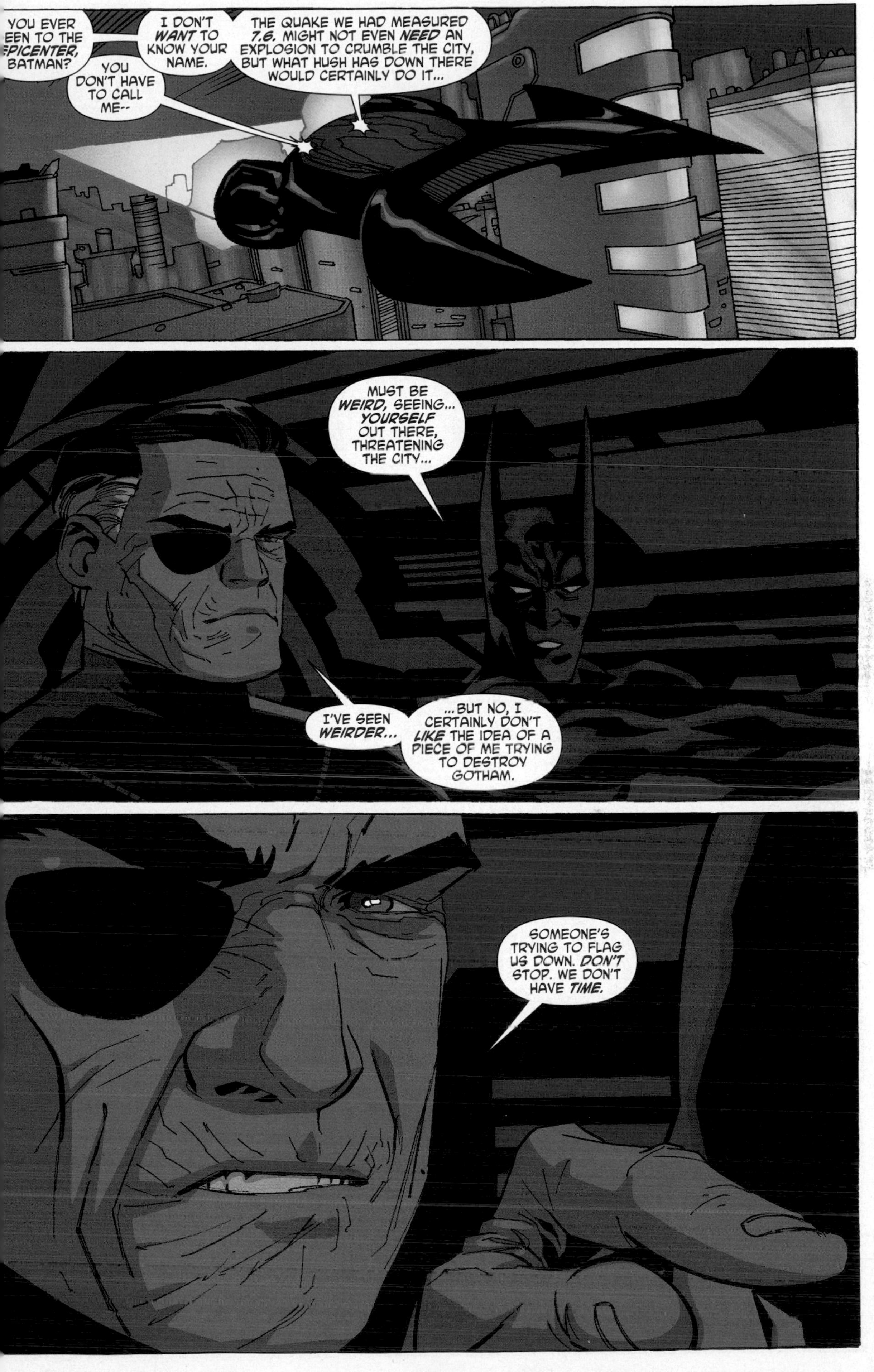
YOU EVER [B]EEN TO THE [E]PICENTER, BATMAN?
I DON'T WANT TO KNOW YOUR NAME.
YOU DON'T HAVE TO CALL ME--
THE QUAKE WE HAD MEASURED 7.6. MIGHT NOT EVEN NEED AN EXPLOSION TO CRUMBLE THE CITY, BUT WHAT HUSH HAS DOWN THERE WOULD CERTAINLY DO IT...
MUST BE WEIRD, SEEING... YOURSELF OUT THERE, THREATENING THE CITY...
I'VE SEEN WEIRDER...
...BUT NO, I CERTAINLY DON'T LIKE THE IDEA OF A PIECE OF ME TRYING TO DESTROY GOTHAM.
SOMEONE'S TRYING TO FLAG US DOWN. DON'T STOP. WE DON'T HAVE TIME.

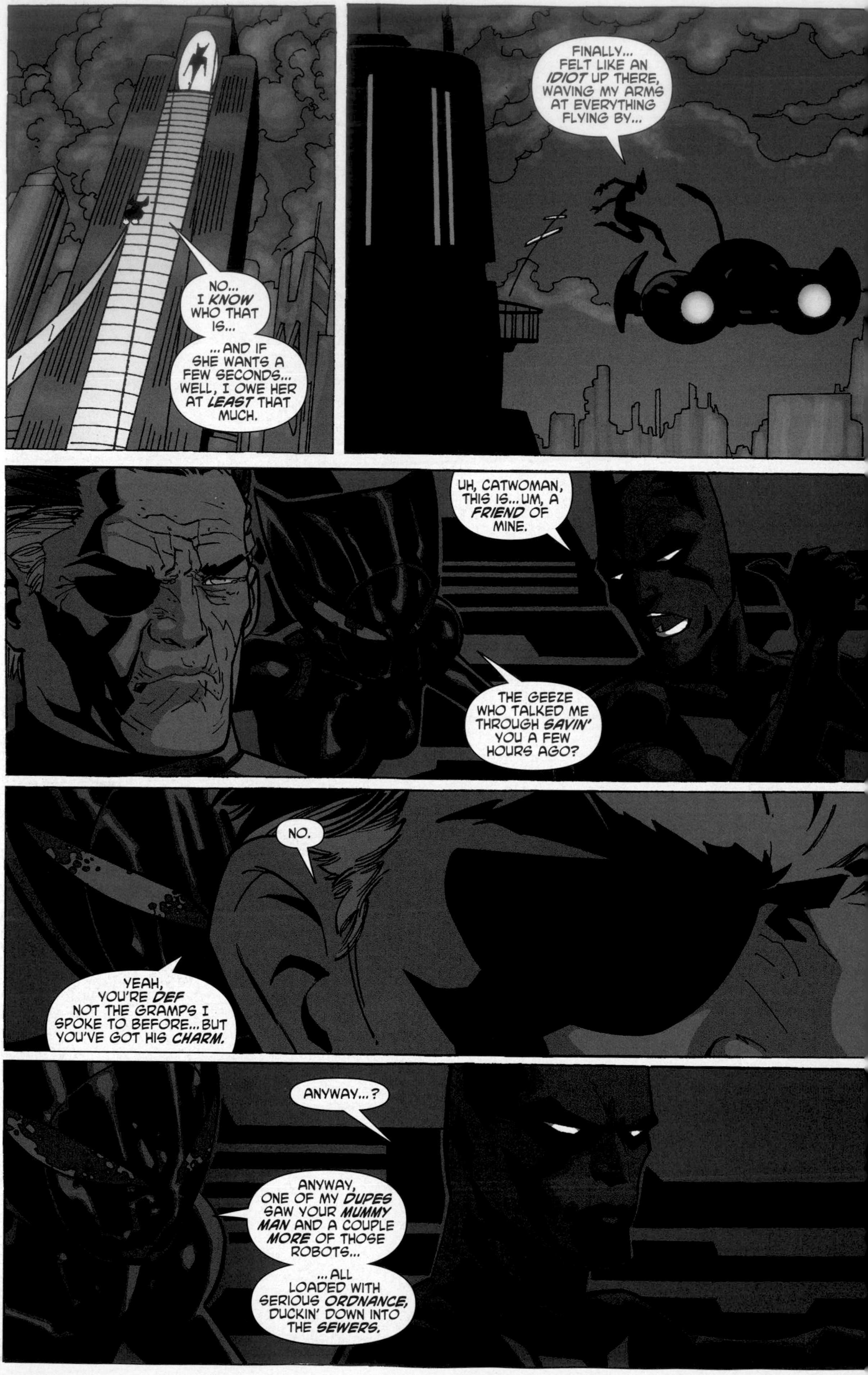
NO... I KNOW WHO THAT IS...
...AND IF SHE WANTS A FEW SECONDS... WELL, I OWE HER AT LEAST THAT MUCH.
FINALLY... FELT LIKE AN IDIOT UP THERE, WAVING MY ARMS AT EVERYTHING FLYING BY...
UH, CATWOMAN, THIS IS...UM, A FRIEND OF MINE.
THE GEEZE WHO TALKED ME THROUGH SAVIN' YOU A FEW HOURS AGO?
NO.
YEAH, YOU'RE DEF NOT THE GRAMPS I SPOKE TO BEFORE...BUT YOU'VE GOT HIS CHARM.
ANYWAY...?
ANYWAY, ONE OF MY DUPES SAW YOUR MUMMY MAN AND A COUPLE MORE OF THOSE ROBOTS...
...ALL LOADED WITH SERIOUS ORDNANCE, DUCKIN' DOWN INTO THE SEWERS.

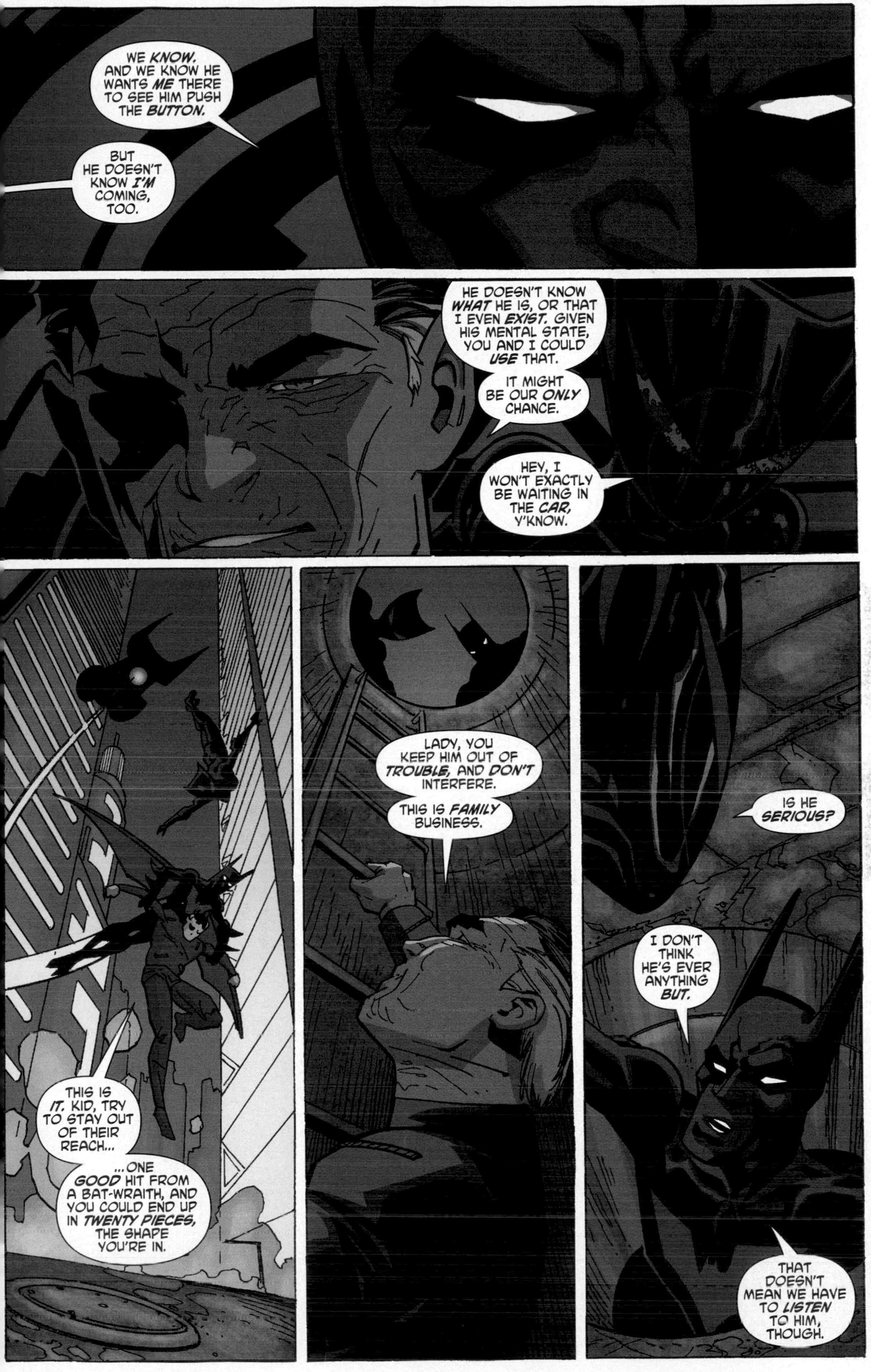
WE KNOW. AND WE KNOW HE WANTS ME THERE TO SEE HIM PUSH THE BUTTON.
BUT HE DOESN'T KNOW I'M COMING, TOO.
HE DOESN'T KNOW WHAT HE IS, OR THAT I EVEN EXIST. GIVEN HIS MENTAL STATE, YOU AND I COULD USE THAT.
IT MIGHT BE OUR ONLY CHANCE.
HEY, I WON'T EXACTLY BE WAITING IN THE CAR, Y'KNOW.
THIS IS IT, KID, TRY TO STAY OUT OF THEIR REACH...
...ONE GOOD HIT FROM A BAT-WRAITH, AND YOU COULD END UP IN TWENTY PIECES, THE SHAPE YOU'RE IN.
LADY, YOU KEEP HIM OUT OF TROUBLE, AND DON'T INTERFERE.
THIS IS FAMILY BUSINESS.
IS HE SERIOUS?
I DON'T THINK HE'S EVER ANYTHING BUT.
THAT DOESN'T MEAN WE HAVE TO LISTEN TO HIM, THOUGH.

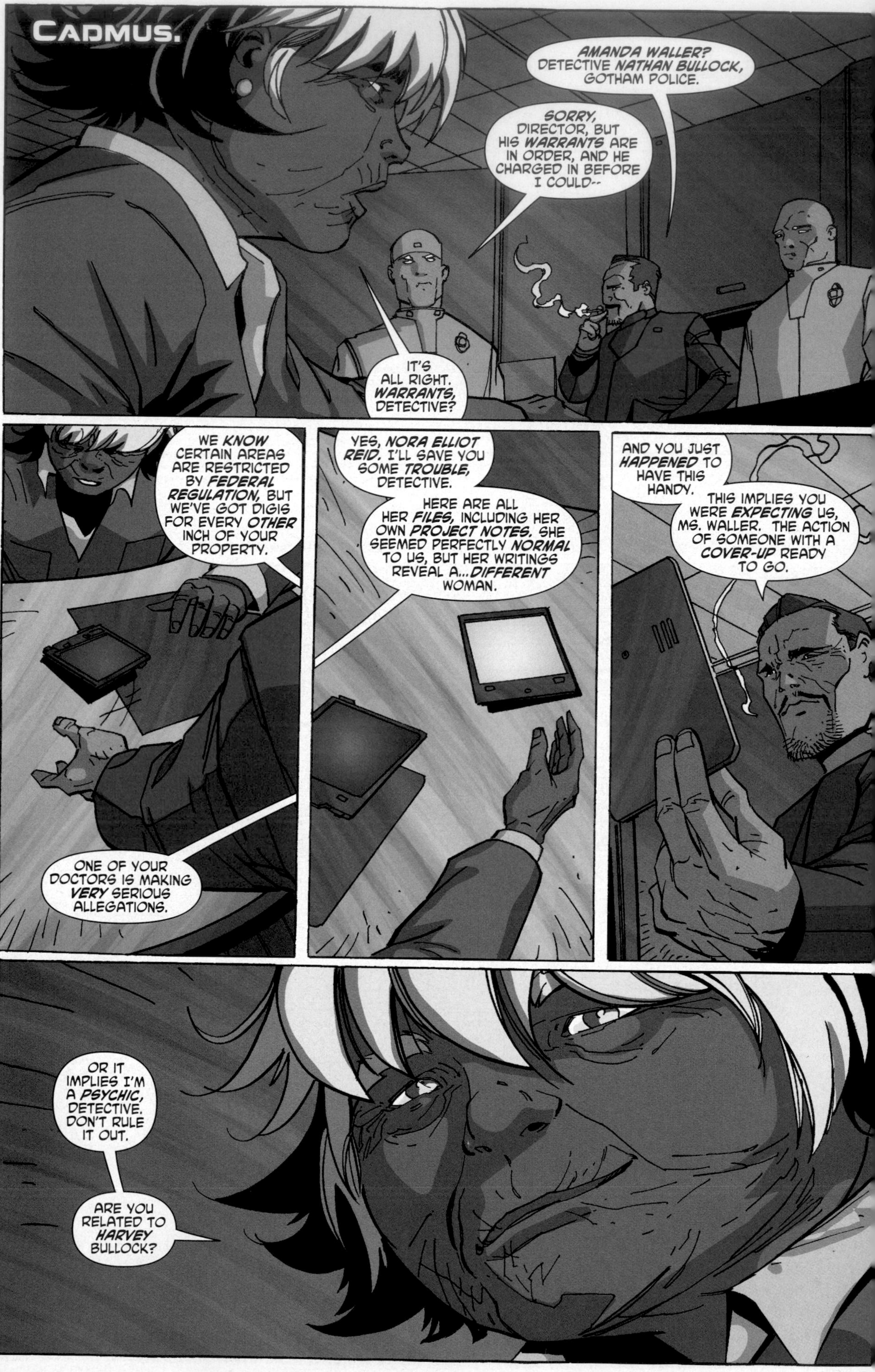
CADMUS.
AMANDA WALLER? DETECTIVE NATHAN BULLOCK, GOTHAM POLICE.
SORRY, DIRECTOR, BUT HIS WARRANTS ARE IN ORDER, AND HE CHARGED IN BEFORE I COULD--
IT'S ALL RIGHT. WARRANTS, DETECTIVE?
WE KNOW CERTAIN AREAS ARE RESTRICTED BY FEDERAL REGULATION, BUT WE'VE GOT DIGIS FOR EVERY OTHER INCH OF YOUR PROPERTY.
ONE OF YOUR DOCTORS IS MAKING VERY SERIOUS ALLEGATIONS.
YES, NORA ELLIOT REID. I'LL SAVE YOU SOME TROUBLE, DETECTIVE.
HERE ARE ALL HER FILES, INCLUDING HER OWN PROJECT NOTES. SHE SEEMED PERFECTLY NORMAL TO US, BUT HER WRITINGS REVEAL A...DIFFERENT WOMAN.
AND YOU JUST HAPPENED TO HAVE THIS HANDY.
THIS IMPLIES YOU WERE EXPECTING US, MS. WALLER. THE ACTION OF SOMEONE WITH A COVER-UP READY TO GO.
OR IT IMPLIES I'M A PSYCHIC, DETECTIVE. DON'T RULE IT OUT.
ARE YOU RELATED TO HARVEY BULLOCK?

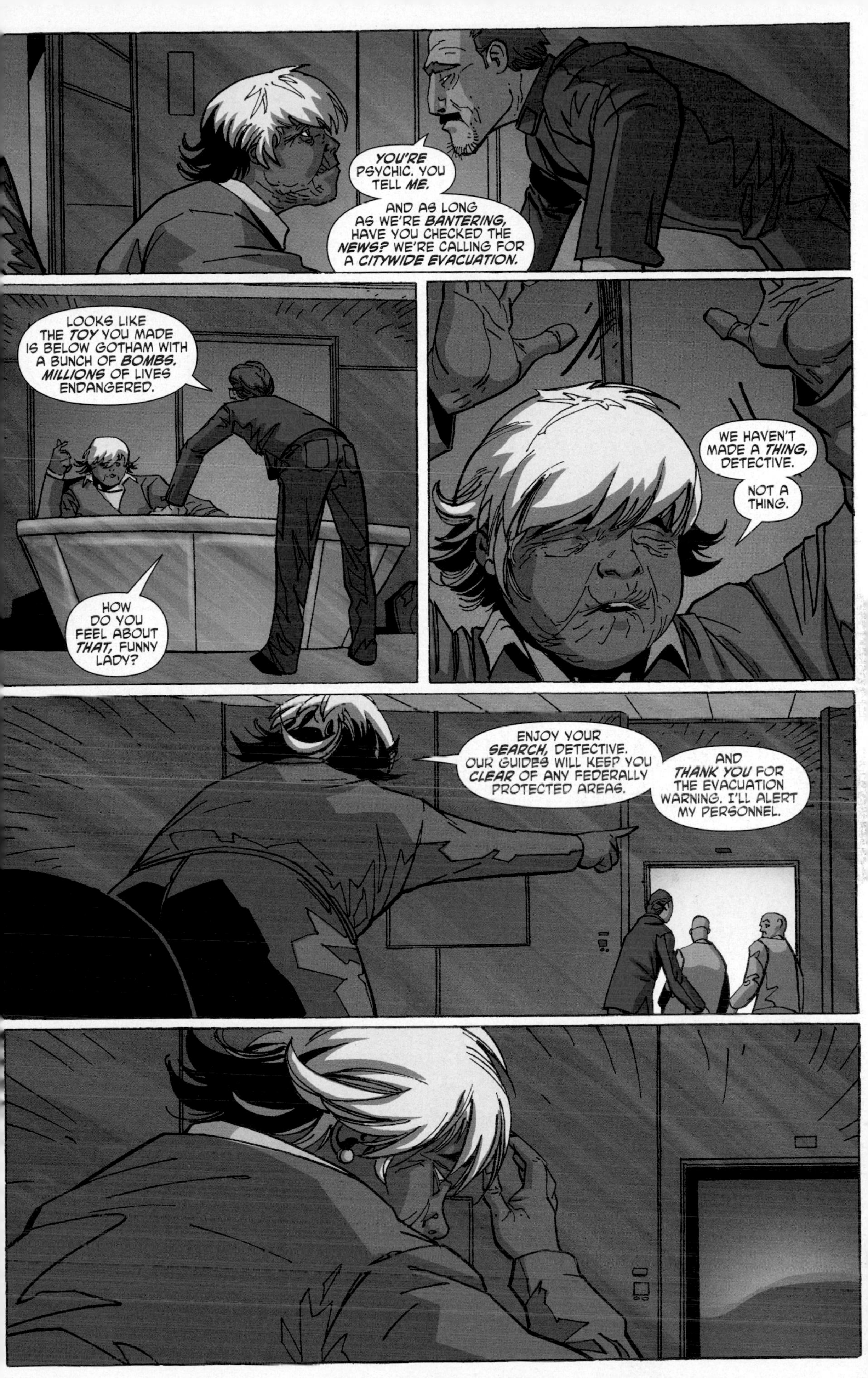
YOU'RE PSYCHIC. YOU TELL ME.
AND AS LONG AS WE'RE BANTERING, HAVE YOU CHECKED THE NEWS? WE'RE CALLING FOR A CITYWIDE EVACUATION.
LOOKS LIKE THE TOY YOU MADE IS BELOW GOTHAM WITH A BUNCH OF BOMBS. MILLIONS OF LIVES ENDANGERED.
HOW DO YOU FEEL ABOUT THAT, FUNNY LADY?
WE HAVEN'T MADE A THING, DETECTIVE.
NOT A THING.
ENJOY YOUR SEARCH, DETECTIVE. OUR GUIDES WILL KEEP YOU CLEAR OF ANY FEDERALLY PROTECTED AREAS.
AND THANK YOU FOR THE EVACUATION WARNING. I'LL ALERT MY PERSONNEL.

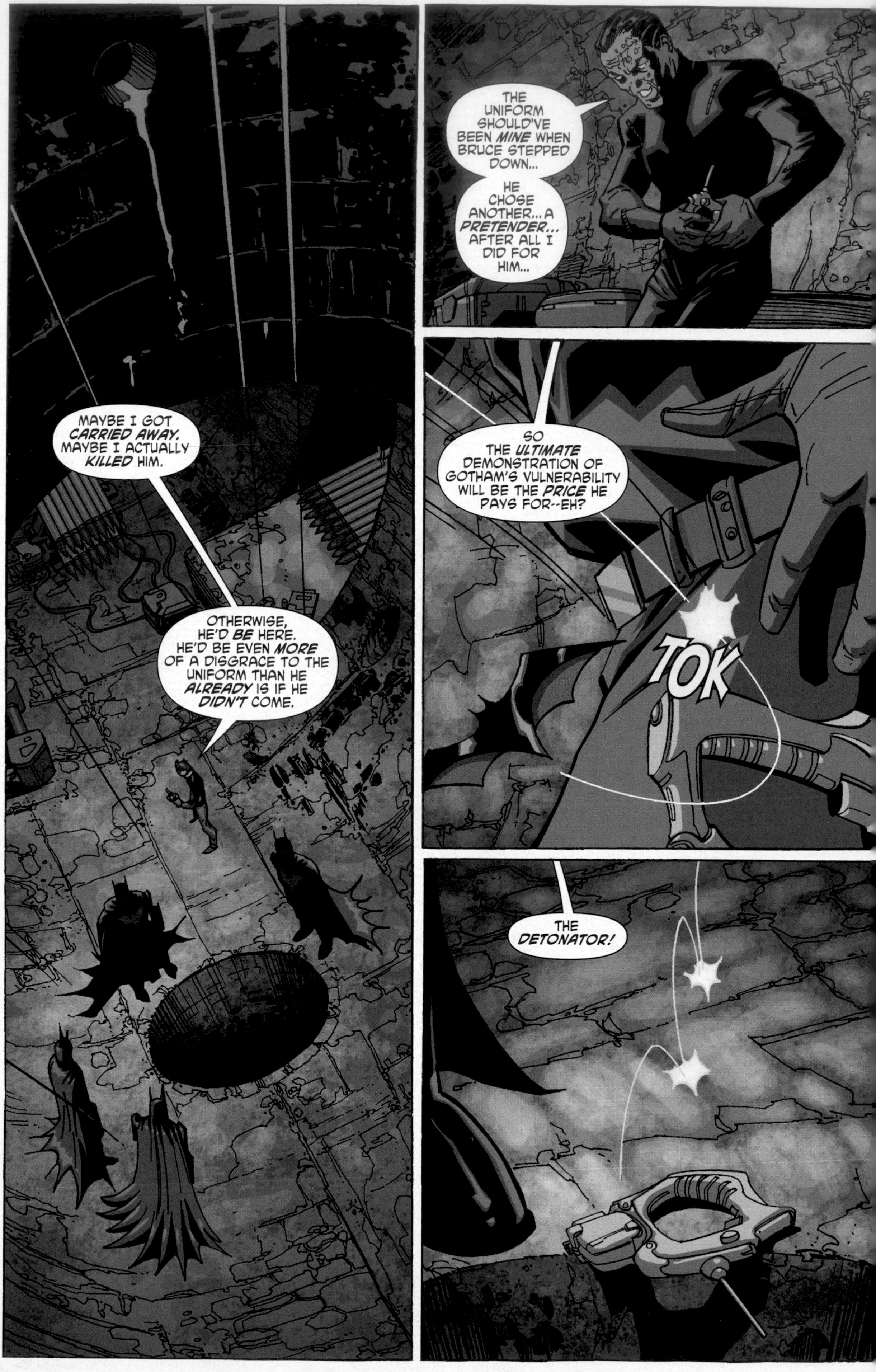
MAYBE I GOT CARRIED AWAY. MAYBE I ACTUALLY KILLED HIM.
OTHERWISE, HE'D BE HERE. HE'D BE EVEN MORE OF A DISGRACE TO THE UNIFORM THAN HE ALREADY IS IF HE DIDN'T COME.
THE UNIFORM SHOULD'VE BEEN MINE WHEN BRUCE STEPPED DOWN...
HE CHOSE ANOTHER... A PRETENDER... AFTER ALL I DID FOR HIM...
SO THE ULTIMATE DEMONSTRATION OF GOTHAM'S VULNERABILITY WILL BE THE PRICE HE PAYS FOR--EH?
TOK
THE DETONATOR!

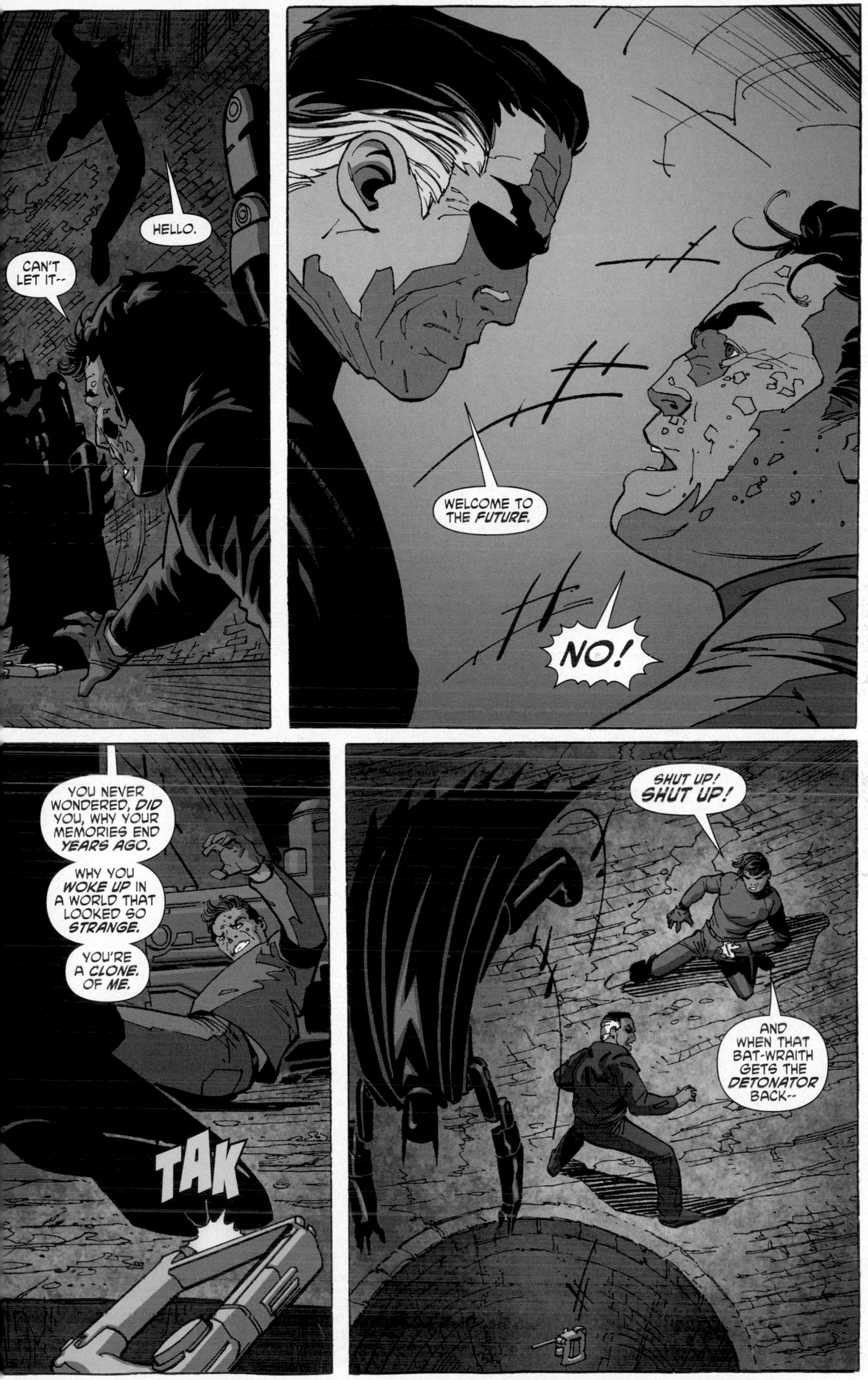
HELLO.
CAN'T LET IT--
WELCOME TO THE FUTURE.
NO!
YOU NEVER WONDERED, DID YOU, WHY YOUR MEMORIES END YEARS AGO.
WHY YOU WOKE UP IN A WORLD THAT LOOKED SO STRANGE.
YOU'RE A CLONE. OF ME.
TAK
SHUT UP! SHUT UP!
AND WHEN THAT BAT-WRAITH GETS THE DETONATOR BACK--

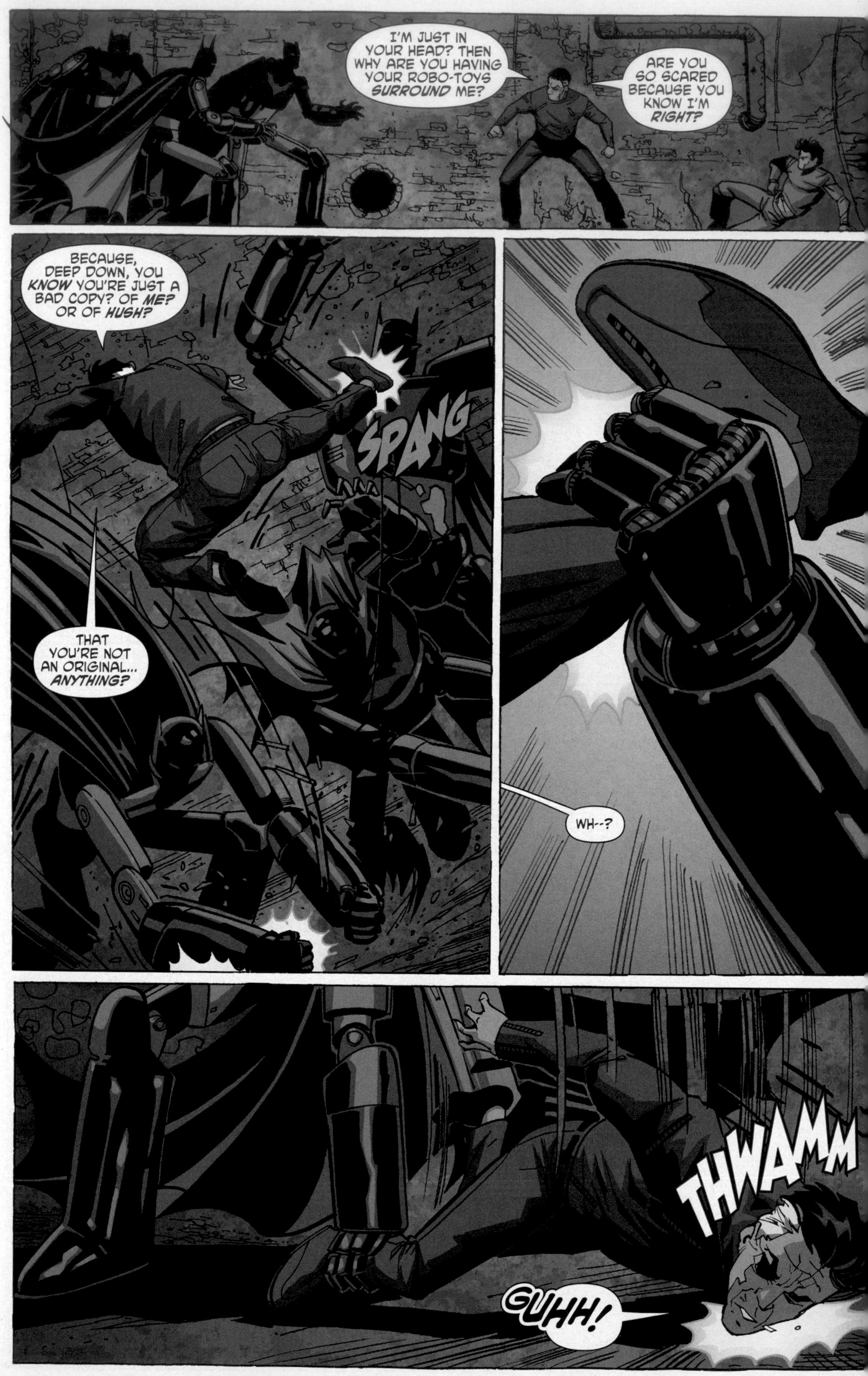
I'M JUST IN YOUR HEAD? THEN WHY ARE YOU HAVING YOUR ROBO-TOYS SURROUND ME?
ARE YOU SO SCARED BECAUSE YOU KNOW I'M RIGHT?
BECAUSE, DEEP DOWN, YOU KNOW YOU'RE JUST A BAD COPY? OF ME? OR OF HUSH?
SPANG
THAT YOU'RE NOT AN ORIGINAL... ANYTHING?
WH--?
THWAMM
GUHH!

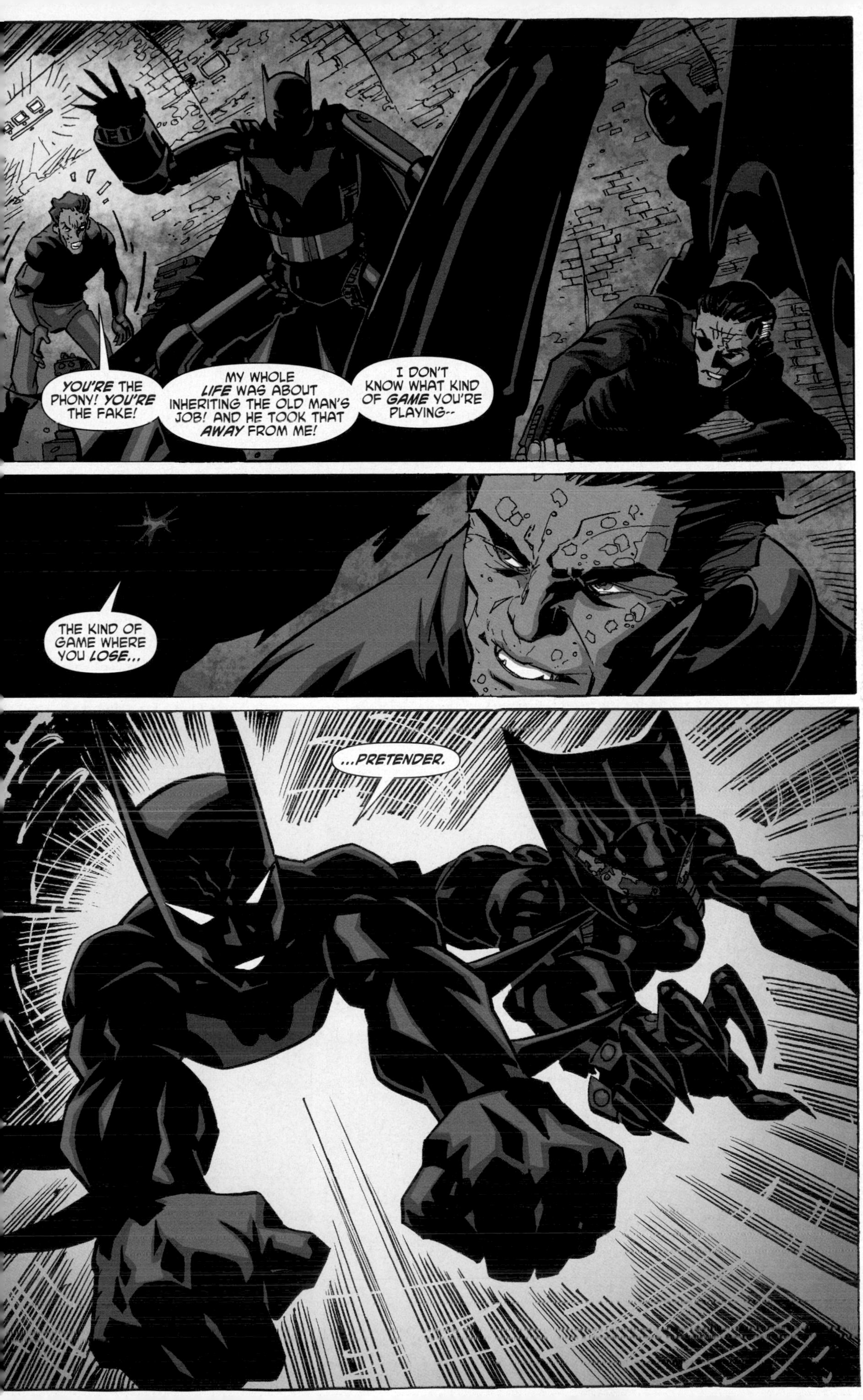
YOU'RE THE PHONY! YOU'RE THE FAKE!
MY WHOLE LIFE WAS ABOUT INHERITING THE OLD MAN'S JOB! AND HE TOOK THAT AWAY FROM ME!
I DON'T KNOW WHAT KIND OF GAME YOU'RE PLAYING--
THE KIND OF GAME WHERE YOU LOSE...
...PRETENDER.

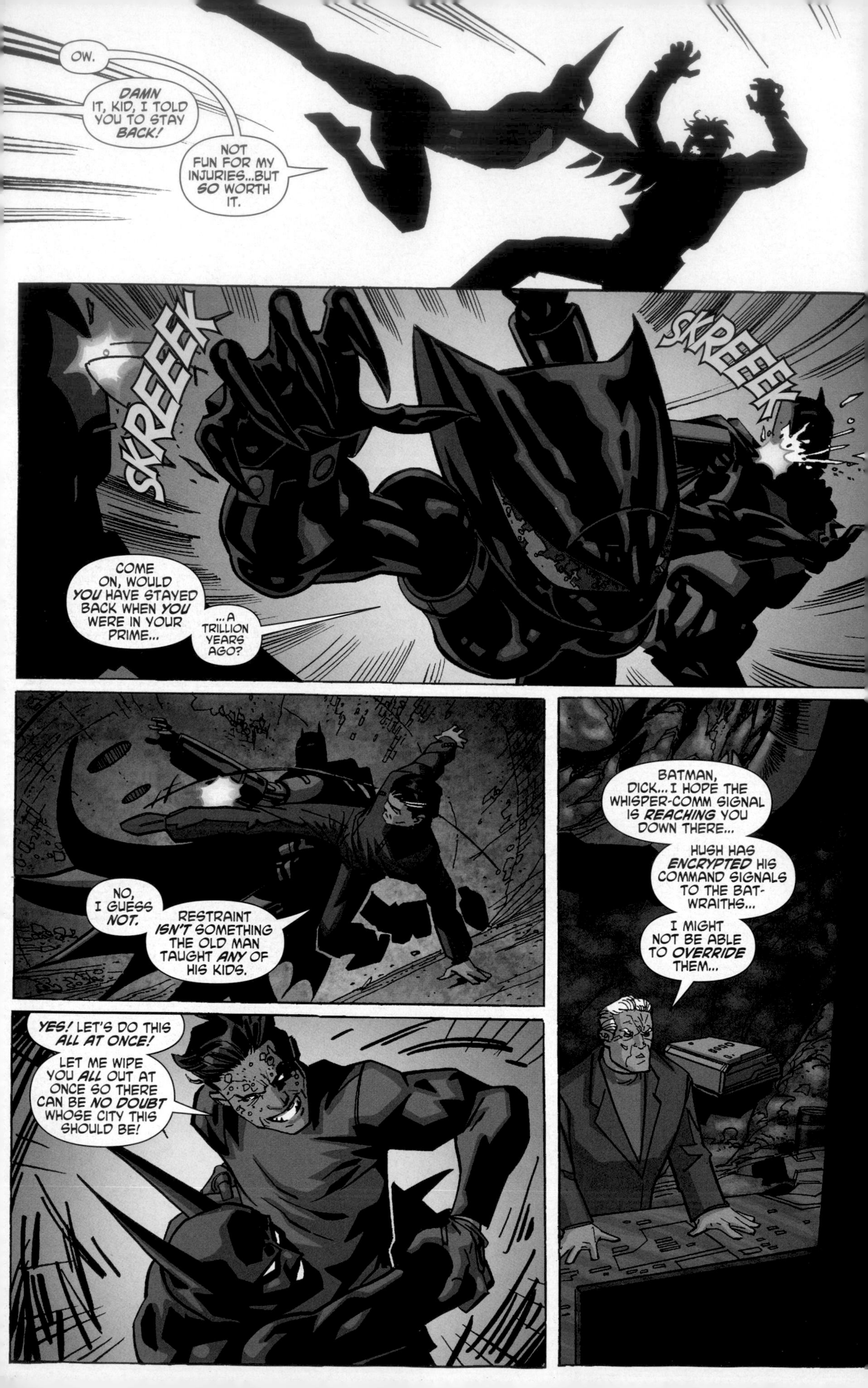
OW.
DAMN IT, KID, I TOLD YOU TO STAY BACK!
NOT FUN FOR MY INJURIES...BUT SO WORTH IT.
SKREEEK
SKREEEK
COME ON, WOULD YOU HAVE STAYED BACK WHEN YOU WERE IN YOUR PRIME...
...A TRILLION YEARS AGO?
NO, I GUESS NOT.
RESTRAINT ISN'T SOMETHING THE OLD MAN TAUGHT ANY OF HIS KIDS.
BATMAN, DICK...I HOPE THE WHISPER-COMM SIGNAL IS REACHING YOU DOWN THERE...
HUSH HAS ENCRYPTED HIS COMMAND SIGNALS TO THE BAT-WRAITHS...
I MIGHT NOT BE ABLE TO OVERRIDE THEM...
YES! LET'S DO THIS ALL AT ONCE!
LET ME WIPE YOU ALL OUT AT ONCE SO THERE CAN BE NO DOUBT WHOSE CITY THIS SHOULD BE!

...BUT I'M LOOKING FOR A WAY TO *INTERRUPT* THEM.

HURRY, PLEASE...

MEANTIME, HE'S CONTROLLING THEM FROM HIS *BELT*... SEE IF YOU CAN GET TO *THAT* SOMEHOW...

WHUMP

AGH!

DIE!

WISH THERE WAS *ROOM* IN HERE FOR ME TO GO MY FULL *NINE*...

WISH THERE WAS *ROOM* IN HERE FOR ME TO GO MY FULL *NINE*...

WISH THERE WAS *ROOM* IN HERE FOR ME TO GO MY FULL *NINE*...

...BUT I'M *NOT* SURE EVEN *THAT* WOULD MAKE A DIFFERENCE!

...BUT I'M *NOT* SURE EVEN *THAT* WOULD MAKE A DIFFERENCE!

SKANGG

BATMAN... STAY *WITH* HIM, KID!

SOON AS I TAKE THESE THINGS APART--

KLIK

I WOULDN'T WRITE ANY *APPOINTMENTS* IN MY *CALENDAR*, IF I WERE YOU...

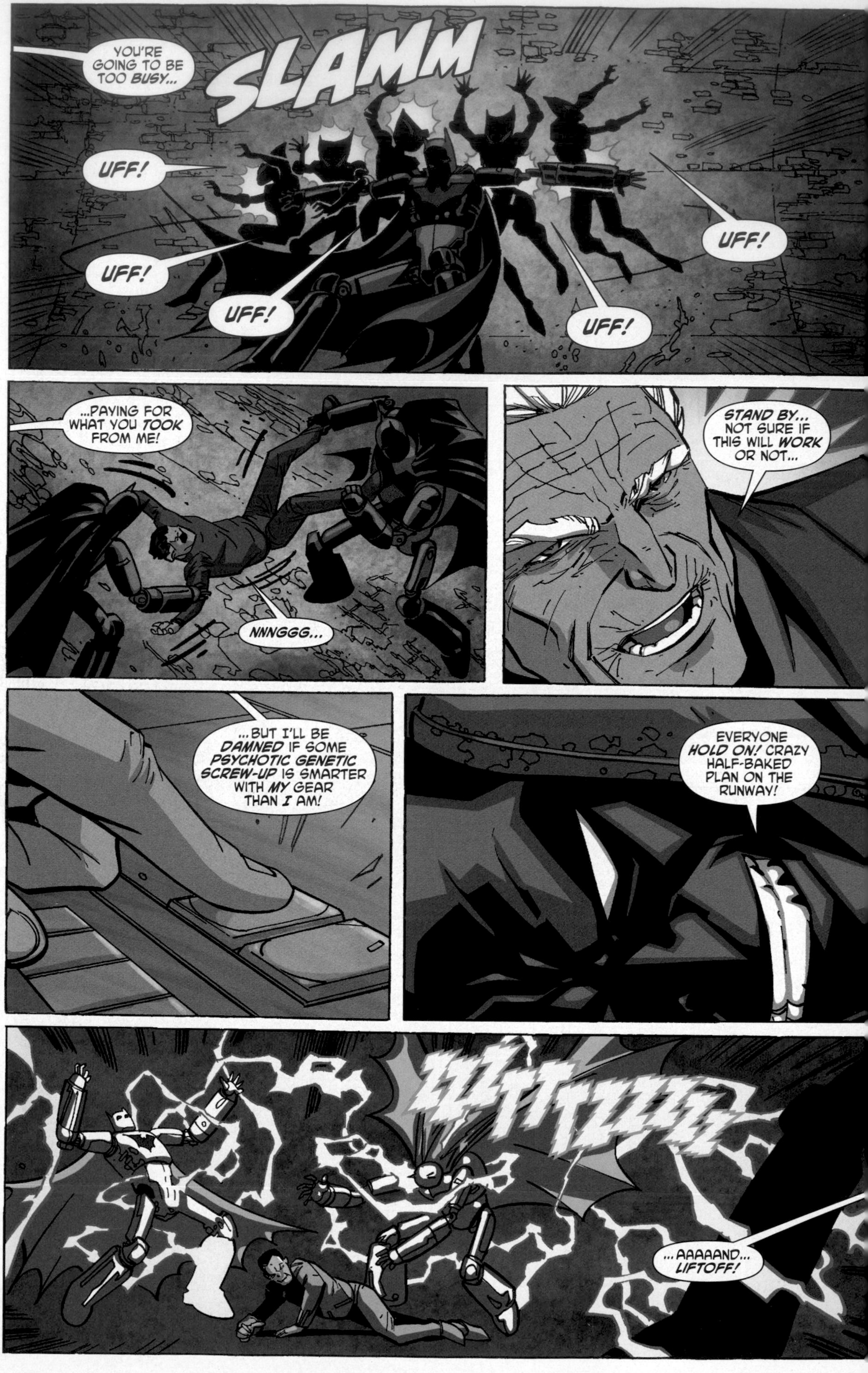
YOU'RE GOING TO BE TOO BUSY...
SLAMM
UFF!
UFF!
UFF!
UFF!
UFF!
...PAYING FOR WHAT YOU TOOK FROM ME!
NNNGGG...
STAND BY... NOT SURE IF THIS WILL WORK OR NOT...
...BUT I'LL BE DAMNED IF SOME PSYCHOTIC GENETIC SCREW-UP IS SMARTER WITH MY GEAR THAN I AM!
EVERYONE HOLD ON! CRAZY HALF-BAKED PLAN ON THE RUNWAY!
ZZZTTTZZZZZ
...AAAAAND... LIFTOFF!

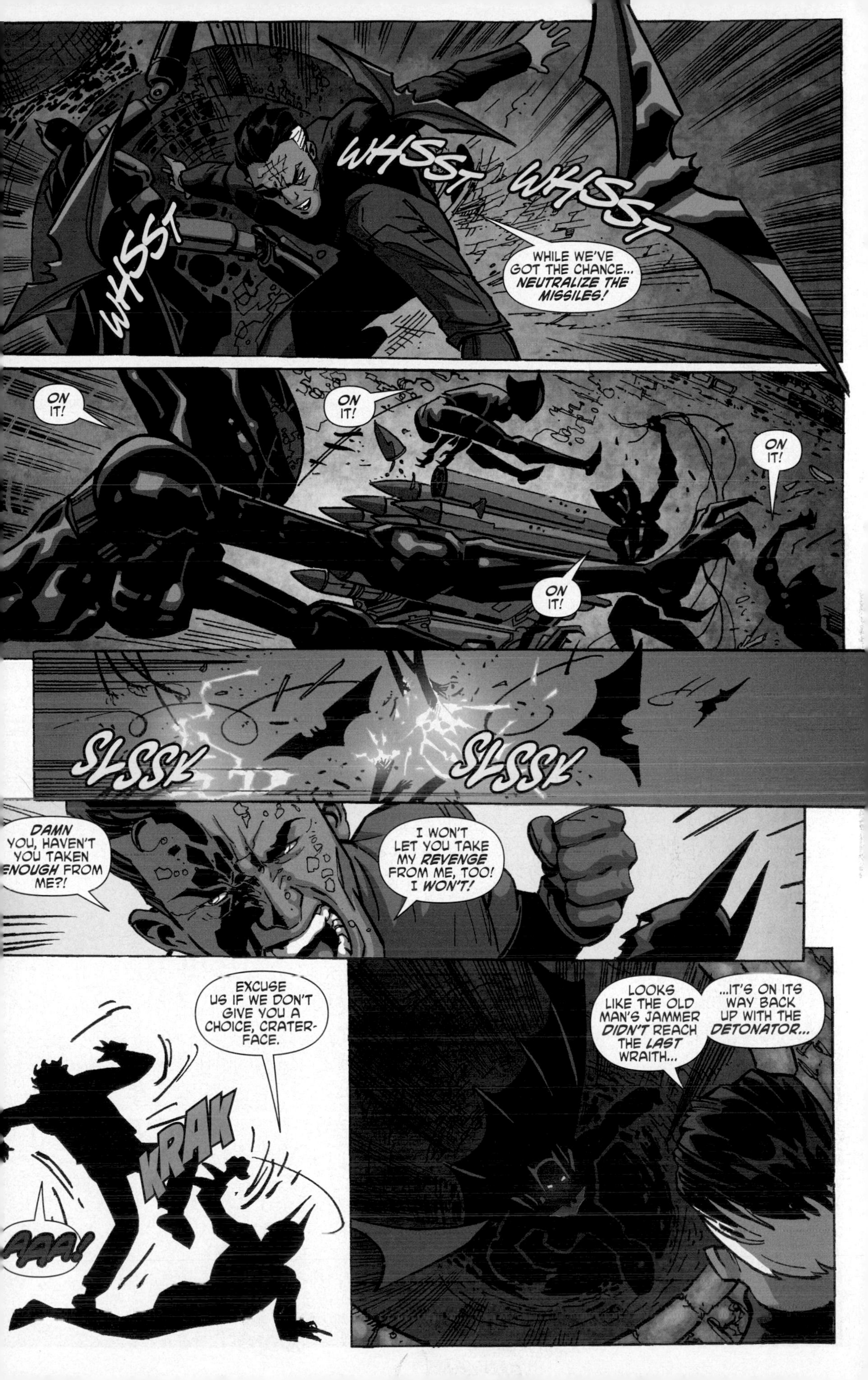

WHSST
WHSST
WHSST
WHSST
WHILE WE'VE GOT THE CHANCE... NEUTRALIZE THE MISSILES!
ON IT!
ON IT!
ON IT!
ON IT!
SLSSK
SLSSK
DAMN YOU, HAVEN'T YOU TAKEN ENOUGH FROM ME?!
I WON'T LET YOU TAKE MY REVENGE FROM ME, TOO! I WON'T!
EXCUSE US IF WE DON'T GIVE YOU A CHOICE, CRATER-FACE.
KRAK
AAA!
LOOKS LIKE THE OLD MAN'S JAMMER DIDN'T REACH THE LAST WRAITH...
...IT'S ON ITS WAY BACK UP WITH THE DETONATOR...

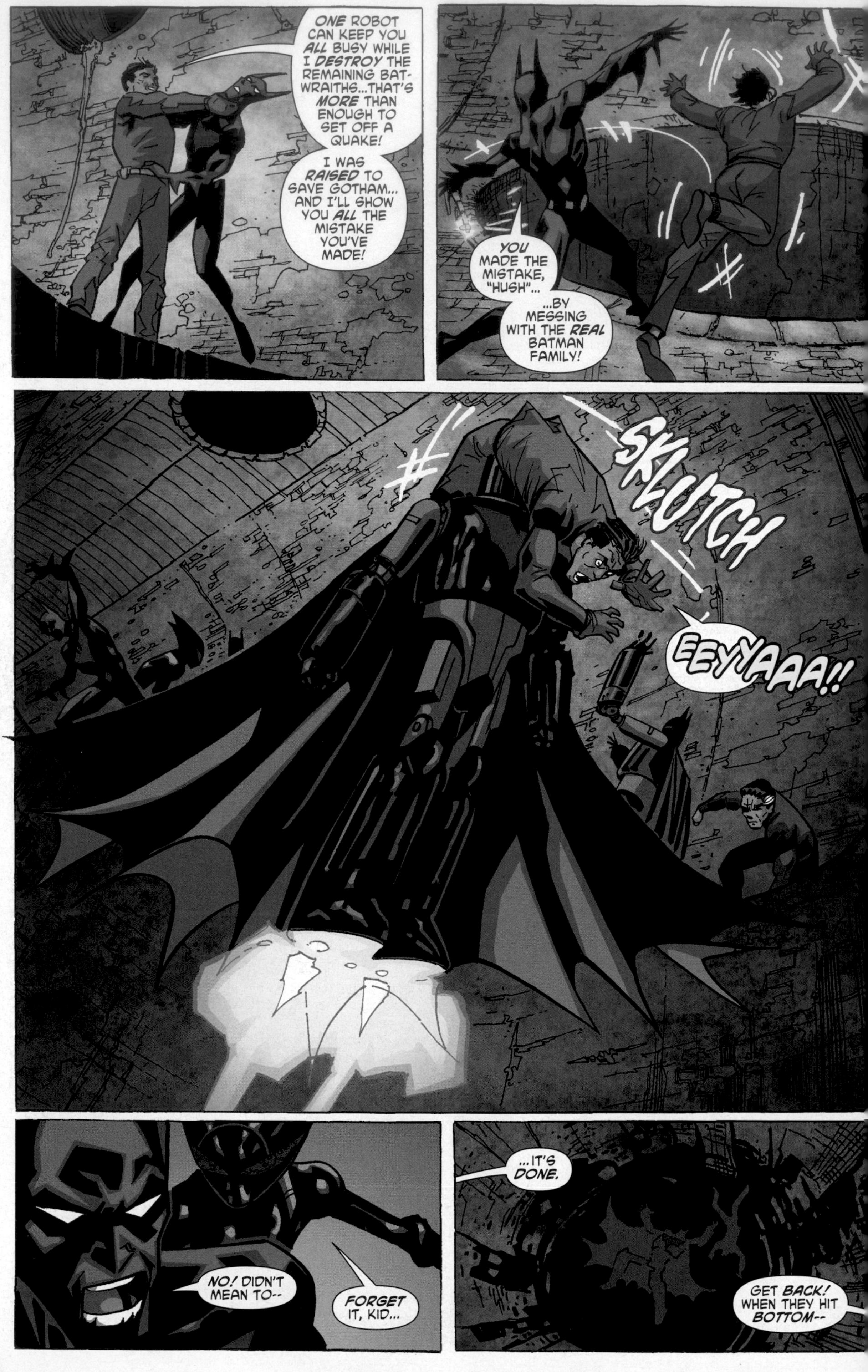
ONE ROBOT CAN KEEP YOU ALL BUSY WHILE I DESTROY THE REMAINING BAT-WRAITHS...THAT'S MORE THAN ENOUGH TO SET OFF A QUAKE!
I WAS RAISED TO SAVE GOTHAM... AND I'LL SHOW YOU ALL THE MISTAKE YOU'VE MADE!
YOU MADE THE MISTAKE, "HUSH"...
...BY MESSING WITH THE REAL BATMAN FAMILY!
SKLUTCH
EEYYAAA!!
NO! DIDN'T MEAN TO--
FORGET IT, KID...
...IT'S DONE.
GET BACK! WHEN THEY HIT BOTTOM--

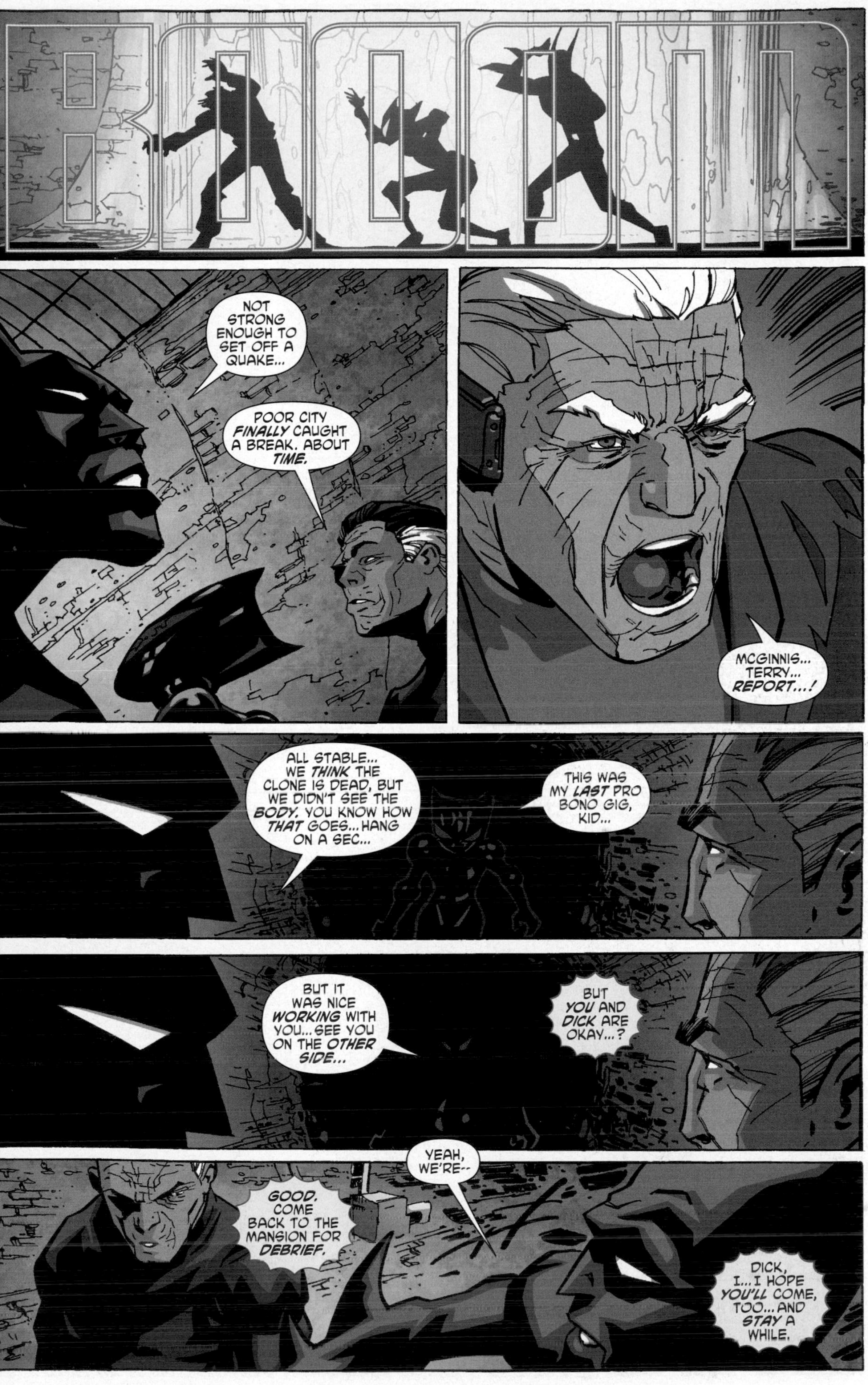
BOOOM
NOT STRONG ENOUGH TO SET OFF A QUAKE...
POOR CITY *FINALLY* CAUGHT A BREAK. ABOUT *TIME.*
MCGINNIS... TERRY... *REPORT...!*
ALL STABLE... WE *THINK* THE CLONE IS DEAD, BUT WE DIDN'T SEE THE *BODY.* YOU KNOW HOW *THAT* GOES... HANG ON A SEC...
THIS WAS MY *LAST* PRO BONO GIG, KID...
BUT IT WAS NICE *WORKING* WITH YOU... SEE YOU ON THE *OTHER SIDE...*
BUT *YOU* AND *DICK* ARE OKAY...?
YEAH, WE'RE--
GOOD. COME BACK TO THE MANSION FOR *DEBRIEF.*
DICK, I... I HOPE *YOU'LL* COME, TOO... AND *STAY* A WHILE.

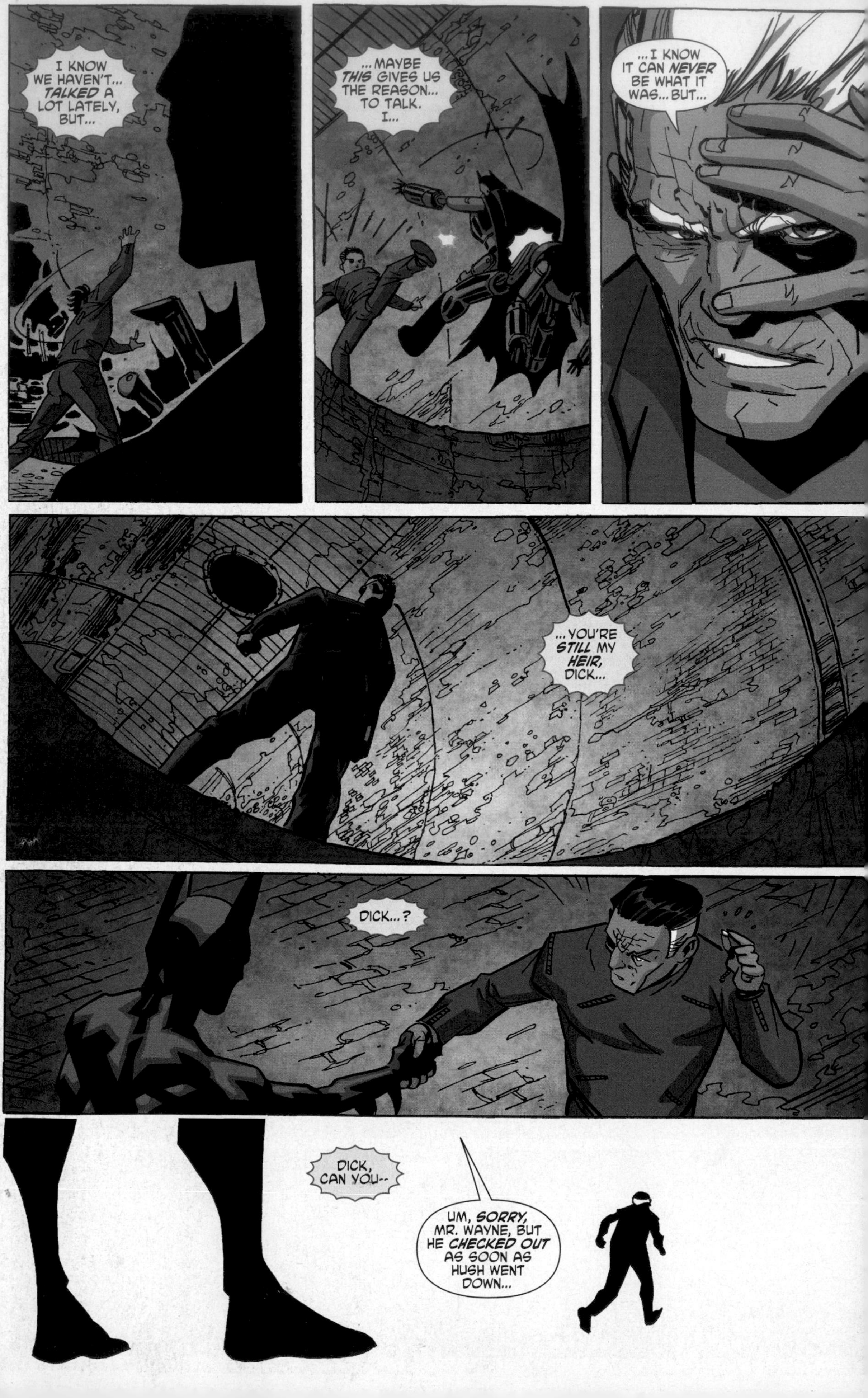
I KNOW WE HAVEN'T... TALKED A LOT LATELY, BUT...
...MAYBE THIS GIVES US THE REASON... TO TALK. I...
...I KNOW IT CAN NEVER BE WHAT IT WAS... BUT...
...YOU'RE STILL MY HEIR, DICK...
DICK...?
DICK, CAN YOU--
UM, SORRY, MR. WAYNE, BUT HE CHECKED OUT AS SOON AS HUSH WENT DOWN...

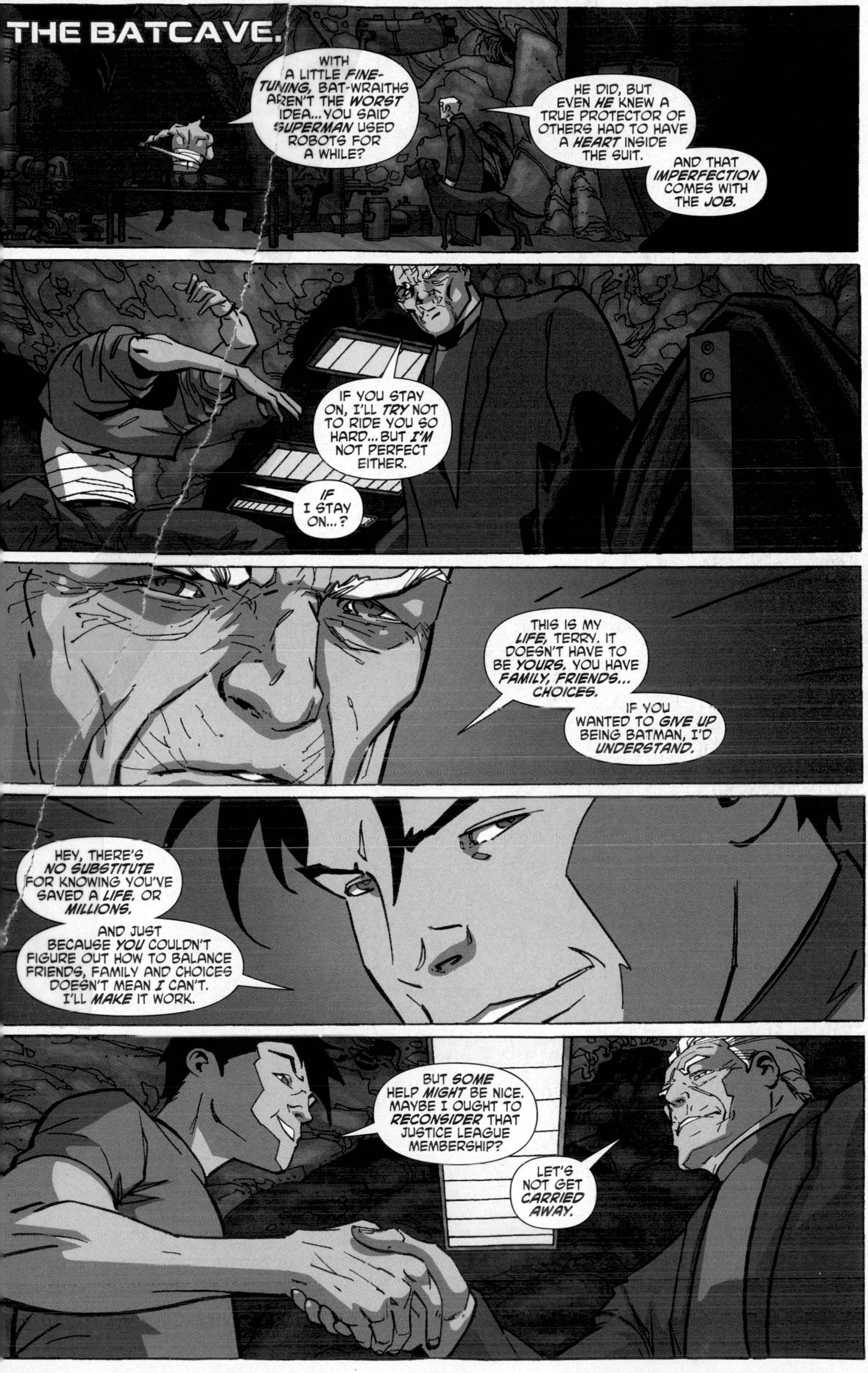
THE BATCAVE.
WITH A LITTLE FINE-TUNING, BAT-WRAITHS AREN'T THE WORST IDEA...YOU SAID SUPERMAN USED ROBOTS FOR A WHILE?
HE DID, BUT EVEN HE KNEW A TRUE PROTECTOR OF OTHERS HAD TO HAVE A HEART INSIDE THE SUIT.
AND THAT IMPERFECTION COMES WITH THE JOB.
IF YOU STAY ON, I'LL TRY NOT TO RIDE YOU SO HARD...BUT I'M NOT PERFECT EITHER.
IF I STAY ON...?
THIS IS MY LIFE, TERRY. IT DOESN'T HAVE TO BE YOURS. YOU HAVE FAMILY, FRIENDS... CHOICES.
IF YOU WANTED TO GIVE UP BEING BATMAN, I'D UNDERSTAND.
HEY, THERE'S NO SUBSTITUTE FOR KNOWING YOU'VE SAVED A LIFE. OR MILLIONS.
AND JUST BECAUSE YOU COULDN'T FIGURE OUT HOW TO BALANCE FRIENDS, FAMILY AND CHOICES DOESN'T MEAN I CAN'T. I'LL MAKE IT WORK.
BUT SOME HELP MIGHT BE NICE. MAYBE I OUGHT TO RECONSIDER THAT JUSTICE LEAGUE MEMBERSHIP?
LET'S NOT GET CARRIED AWAY.

EPILOGUE

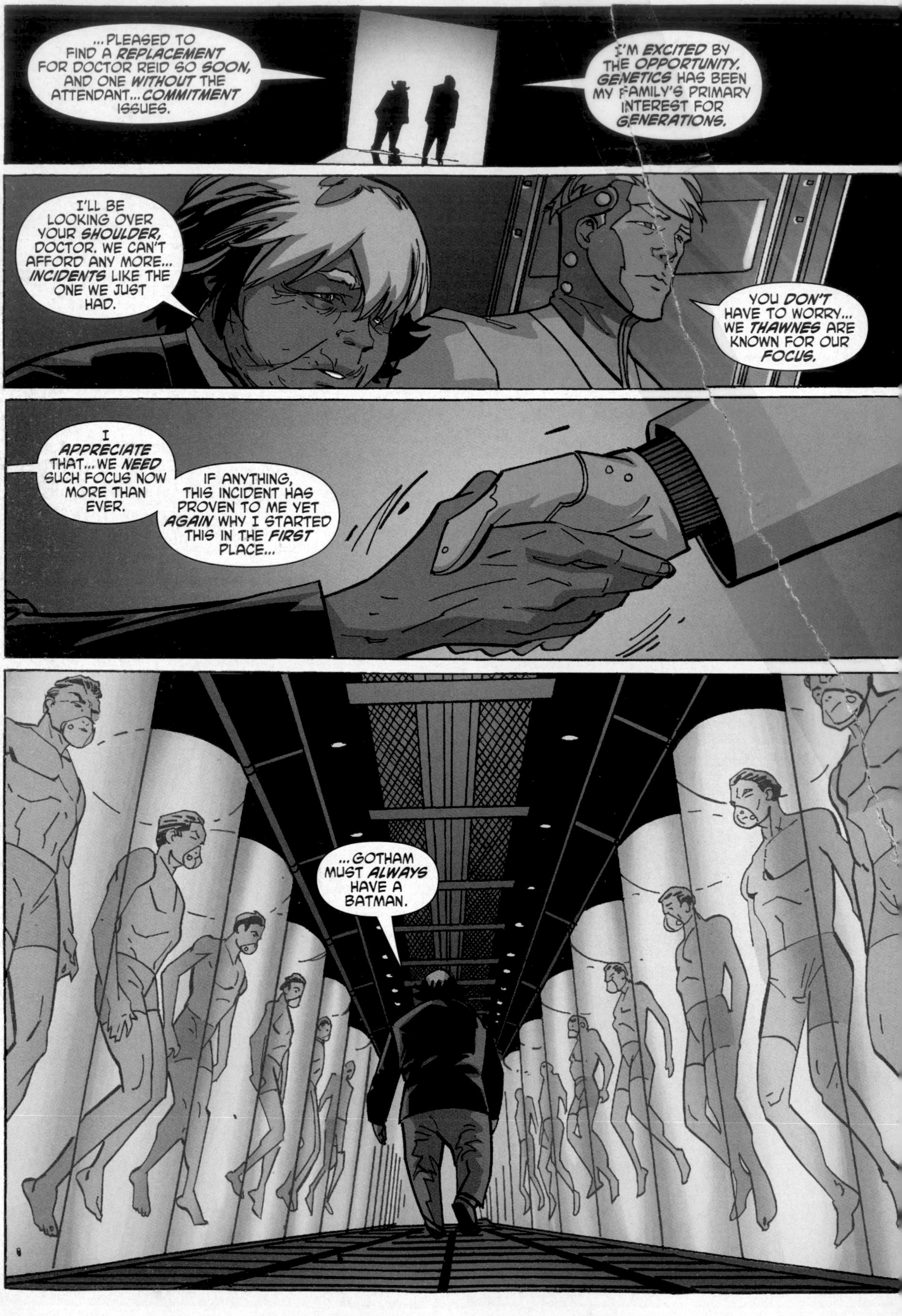
...PLEASED TO FIND A REPLACEMENT FOR DOCTOR REID SO SOON, AND ONE WITHOUT THE ATTENDANT... COMMITMENT ISSUES.
I'M EXCITED BY THE OPPORTUNITY. GENETICS HAS BEEN MY FAMILY'S PRIMARY INTEREST FOR GENERATIONS.
I'LL BE LOOKING OVER YOUR SHOULDER, DOCTOR. WE CAN'T AFFORD ANY MORE... INCIDENTS LIKE THE ONE WE JUST HAD.
YOU DON'T HAVE TO WORRY... WE THAWNES ARE KNOWN FOR OUR FOCUS.
I APPRECIATE THAT... WE NEED SUCH FOCUS NOW MORE THAN EVER.
IF ANYTHING, THIS INCIDENT HAS PROVEN TO ME YET AGAIN WHY I STARTED THIS IN THE FIRST PLACE...
...GOTHAM MUST ALWAYS HAVE A BATMAN.